COPARENTING WITH A NARCISSIST

EFFECTIVE TECHNIQUES TO RAISE RESILIENT CHILDREN AND PROTECT THEM FROM EMOTIONAL ABUSE IN YOUR TOXIC RELATIONSHIP WITH A NARCISSISTIC PARENT AND EX

TABLE OF CONTENTS

HOW TO BUILD RESILIENCE IN YOUR CHILD 371

HOW TO BECOME A COMMONSENSE PARENT 376

VALUES TO PASS ON TO YOUR SON/DAUGHTER 382

WHAT TO SAY AND WHAT NOT TO SAY TO YOUR SON/DAUGHTER ABOUT THE NARCISSISTIC PARENT

HOW TO PROTECT YOUR CHILD FROM ALIENATION AND LOYALTY CONFLICTS

WHEN IT IS APPROPRIATE TO STEP AWAY FROM THE RELATIONSHIP

BOOK1
CO-PARENTING WITH A
NARCISSISTIC EX

How to Protect Your Child
from a Toxic Parent & Start Healing
from Emotional Abuse in Your
Relationship
Tips & Tricks For Co-Parenting With A
Narcissist

INTRODUCTION

If you have a narcissistic partner in your life, you know how painful this can be. Not only are you dealing with an emotionally deficient individual who refuses to acknowledge his shortcomings or apologize for past mistakes, but also you're co-parenting now.

You might be wondering how someone can achieve this in today's world, especially when his ex has never been trustworthy throughout his entire life. The best way is to have a calm and rational discussion about the future.

You're in no position to dictate what your children should or shouldn't do, but you can determine whether you want to be around your ex or not, and you can decide which parent they should spend time with.

If you're the narcissistic father or mother, you need to think about your role in this, seriously. You must sit down with your ex and discuss how to proceed with the children. You don't have to be in love or anything close to it, but you do have to collaborate on whatever plan is agreed upon for the kids' benefits.

The process of co-parenting with a narcissistic ex can be challenging. It's hard for both parents to rebuild trust; it's easy for the children to question your motivations; therefore, the situation is costly, not only from lack of money going into a giant pot but also from all the therapy that needs to be done.

Yet, despite the money, time and energy to invest, it's still worth doing.

For starters, even if one parent is more than happy to be done with the other, they have a responsibility to act in the children's best interest and, therefore, must co-parent in some capacity. It's also essential for the children's emotional well-being to get to know both parents and not grow up feeling like one of you doesn't exist.

And let's face it, their well-being is intrinsically linked to yours. They will always be in your life, and you want to make sure they're healthy and happy adults.

Even if you hate your ex and are happier without him or her, have an adult conversation with yourself and determine how many hours a week you're going to spend communicating with or thinking about your ex outside, scheduled time with the kids.

And then, do it. It will not be easy to do, but it will be well worth your time.

With that commitment, you can focus on your recovery and co-parenting with a narcissist instead of being consumed by anger and resentment.

The hardest part of co-parenting is trusting back the relationship. If both parents do not entirely agree about the course of action, they will have to communicate and talk through decisions that affect them both.

If one or both of you still believe the problem is the mother, you'll never be able to work together. If you don't believe in your ex's ability to parent, you will never feel truly comfortable with them as a co-parent.

You'll always be worried that your ex will make a mistake and take it out on the children, but if you're willing to put those fears aside and let go of the past, then you have a chance to rebuild and trust.

It's not always a smooth ride, but it is possible.

PROFILE OF THE NARCISSIST

Narcissism is a character trait in which someone displays heightened overconfidence due to his self-admiration; they can do no wrong. This is an exaggerated behavior that breathes and exudes arrogance, pretentiousness, and a deep-rooted ideology of false superiority. "I am special. Everyone else in the world is inferior than me because they are not me."

A person who exhibits narcissistic characteristics is often described as cocky, self-centered, self-absorbed, and rude. They view life as a playground for manipulating emotions, as an untapped market to exploit and bend the truth at will. They can be viewed as "winners," but they are crude people to be involved with, due to their self-described perfection. Also, they are liars.

Their success—in most cases—relies on their total and complete disregard for others and their feelings. Or rather, narcissists will push past people no matter what those people are feeling. They view other individuals as obstacles or hurdles to get over. They would most likely push us off the edge of a top-floor balcony if it meant that they would get just a little more ahead of everyone else.

Narcissists are the perennial interrupters of conversation. They constantly crave the limelight; they feel they deserve everyone's attention at every single turn. They want to be seen. They want to be heard. They want to be the leading individual in any small gathering, working groups, friendship circles, and among the large crowds. They are the people who ooze confidence in every moment.

They are very charming, and more often than not, quite funny, very sarcastic. They are good company in public, but once at home and in their respective comfort zones, they shed their charming skins for the emotionally deprived, ostentatious colors that they don't have when returned to their private and intimate places. They use manipulation and excessive, yet believable, lies as a tool, to such an extent, that narcissists are almost fanatical individuals regarding their use of such methods.

Narcissists have such a deep self-belief burning within them. But behind all those attitudes we have a person who has been deeply affected by life. Their past traumas and experiences have crafted them into a person with such anxiety that the line between nervousness and abandonment has morphed and blurred into an individualistic focus. In that context, the admiration they are constantly seeking is due to Their inner mental conflicts rooted in a possible lonely and unloved childhood.

This has made them develop what we could call external spotlighted arrogance. The definition of this is a spotlight. Some form of an inner spotlight externalizes itself—or switches on when it feels like it needs to be seen. It burns so bright that it forces people to shift and focus all undivided attention on the narcissist. If looked at from a psychological perspective, this trait or behavioral characteristic is most common in children below the age of 10. It is that need to stand out from the rest, to get attention, whether that is from your parents, family, friends; it's a phase our brains go through during early childhood development that can be best linked to the behavior of being boastful or to brag about something. In a narcissist's case, what they are essentially bragging about is themselves.

We all know a narcissist. They could be our mother or our father; they could have been this way for as long as we can remember and have left us, now in adulthood, shattered, confused, exhausted. They could be our brother or our sister; they were always showered with praise and told that they were the star. They were serial winners and developed selfishness that has made our lives difficult and still affects us. They could be a work colleague or an employee. But what are the roots of narcissism?

Narcissists tend to view themselves quite differently when compared to others, and they often make those around them feel inadequate and devalued. Here's the kicker—a narcissist always wants everything to be about themselves. You might not mind showering a one-year-old infant with all your attention, but you will start to mind when a 35-year-old demands the same level of attention and achieves it at your expense.

Narcissists easily victimize others by just being themselves, and it is unlikely they will ever change. This might seem rather severe, but you will not realize how toxic such individuals can be until you deal with one of them.

Where Does Narcissism Come From

Narcissism usually develops in early childhood. People say many times that narcissistic behavior reminds them of a toddler throwing a tantrum.

It seems the emotional trauma responsible for narcissism occurs around the age of a toddler. Hence the narcissist's ability to handle emotions gets stuck at that level of mental development. That explains his dangerous emotional immaturity.

We all get exposed to trauma during the early stages of our development. It's simply inevitable. Trauma results from something as simple as not being picked up by our parents as a baby or being fed against our will. It could also result from something more severe like our mother leaving us at the kindergarten for the first time, which can cause a long-lasting fear of separation. Our parents fighting and screaming at each other in our presence can leave its imprints on our subconscious mind, too. So, what kind of trauma produces a narcissist?

Growing up with an overbearing or completely neglectful parent can warp a child's mind and cause them to be narcissistic adults later in life. A parent can be overbearing when it comes to a child's performance in school and neglectful when it comes to the child's emotional needs.

The trauma of a narcissist is the perceived lack of control. The inability to acknowledge his own emotions makes a narcissist extremely uncomfortable. Admitting one "wrong" thing about themselves would make him feel as though everything is wrong. Every abusive and manipulative action he takes only serves one purpose: to feel in control.

The root of their toxic behavior towards you has nothing to do with you, and it has everything to do with them. If you pay close attention to their accusations, you will see that they project their behavior, fears, and doubts on you. A narcissist may often lie yet accuse you of lying all the time, no matter the proofs you show to know he is wrong. He may feel as if everyone is out to get him and they always get the short end of the stick, so he projects his subconscious beliefs on you by accusing you of plotting schemes against him every time there is a simple misunderstanding.

You must keep in mind that narcissists never truly learned how to express and process their emotions. Their parents may have been overly protective and proud of them—but only when they fulfilled their parents' expectations. One could try to do some research about the past of the narcissist in question. However, it is usually difficult to get a clear picture. It's not easy to find the truth about a narcissist, especially when his parents admit to not handling his child.

In many cases, one or both of his parents may display some egotistic traits, too. However, that does not mean that the children of a narcissist are bound to become narcissistic as well.

It's not up to you to determine why the person that treated you so badly has become who he is today, and it is also not necessary for your recovery process. However, you must understand that it's not your fault in any way that he is a narcissist. With that, you are not responsible for his chronic toxicity.

This can be an environmental cause that can lead to a forced image of perfection later in life. Another aspect is early childhood abuse. One best way to deal with abuse is to see yourself above it, too clean for it. Taking an abusive history into account, narcissism acts as a wall to prevent being hurt further in the future. Despite the several ways the disorder can be environmental, some believe that the trait can be hereditary. With genetics, though, seeing a specific behavioral trait can be difficult. Often, though it may seem genetic, it is moreover the way that the parent or grandparent was raised that gives them the condition. This brings up the question of actual genetics. Science has yet to come to a clear conclusion on that, though. Studies have not been able to come to a solid decision, and with many different conditions, it is hard to see which is environmental and which is genetic.

HOW TO UNDERSTAND AND RECOGNIZE THE LANGUAGE OF THE NARCISSIST

Y ou can tell if the person you are in a relationship with is a narcissist based on his behavior. Ideally, you can figure out if your boyfriend, girlfriend, or even an acquaintance has narcissistic tendencies so that you can sever ties with them before you are too invested in that relationship. Here are ten points that a narcissist will always do in a relationship.

He Will Try to Charm You

Narcissists can be quite charismatic and charming when they want something from you. If you are in a relationship with one, he will go out of his way to make you feel special in the beginning so that you trust him enough to let your guard down. As long as you are serving the purpose, he wants you to serve. The narcissist will give you a lot of attention and make you feel like the center of his world. If someone puts you on a pedestal during the early stages of your relationship, you should pay more attention to the way they act to see if they are faking it.

He Will Make You Feel Worthless

After hanging out with a narcissist for a while, you will notice that when you have any disagreement or argument, his first instinct is to dismiss you in a way that makes you feel worthless. He will criticize you in the sort of contemptuous tone that will make you feel dehumanized. When you disagree with ordinary people, you always feel that your opinion matters to them, but with a narcissist, that is not the case. All the things about you that the narcissist claimed to like when he was charming you will somehow turn into negative attributes, and the narcissist will portray himself as a "saint" for putting up with those attributes.

He Will Hog Your Conversations

Narcissists are in love with the way people perceive them, so they will take every chance to talk about themselves. Whenever you try to have a conversation, the topic will always change, and it will suddenly be about them. It's never a 2-way conversation with a narcissist unless he is trying to manipulate you into thinking he cares about you. You will struggle to hear your views or get him to acknowledge your feelings. When you start telling a story about something that happened to you at work, you will never get to the end of it because he will start his own story before you are done with yours. If you make comments on certain topics of conversation, your comments will be ignored, dismissed, or even corrected unnecessarily.

He Will Violate Your Boundaries

From very early in the relationship, the narcissist will start showing disregard for your boundaries. You will notice that he violates your personal space, and he has no qualms about asking you to do him favors that he has by no means earned. He will borrow your items or even money and fail to return it. When you ask, he will say that he didn't know it was such a big deal to you—the point is to make you seem petty for insisting on boundaries that most decent people would consider reasonable.

He Will Break the Rules

The narcissist will break the rules you set for your relationship, and other social rules, without any compunction. The problem is that sometimes, we are initially attracted to rule-breakers because they seem to be "bad boys" or "rebels," but those traits are tell-tale signs of narcissism. A person who breaks social norms is going to break relationship rules because relationships are essentially social contracts. If someone is trying to charm you, but in your first few interactions, you observe that he cuts lines, tips poorly, disregards traffic rules, etc., you can be certain that you are dealing with a narcissist.

He Will Try to Change You

When you are in a relationship with someone, they will change you in a few minor ways (often unintentionally). However, when you are in a relationship with a narcissist, he will make a deliberate and perceptible effort to change you, and more often than not, it won't be for the better. He will try to break you and make you more subservient to him.

You will find yourself giving concession until, in the end, any objective observer can tell you that you are under his thumb. He will cause you to lose your sense of identity so that you end up being a mere extension of him. When you get out of that relationship, you will find it difficult to figure out who you are as an individual because he would have spent the entire relationship defining and redefining you.

He Will Exhibit a Sense of Entitlement

The narcissist will demonstrate a sense of entitlement for most of your relationship. At first, he may seem generous and considerate to draw you in, but after that, you will see his entitlement rear its ugly head. He will be expecting preferential treatment all the time, and he will expect you to make him a priority in your life (even ahead of your career or your family). There will be a clear disconnect between what he offers and what he expects, and he will want to be the center of your universe.

He Will Try to Isolate You

Any narcissist who wants to control you and make you subservient to him understands that you have friends and family as a support system who won't stand by and let him harm you. So, one of the things he will do once he has faked affection and earned some of your trust is, he is going to try and isolate you. He will insist that every time you hang out, you shouldn't bring anyone along. He will make up lies to drive a wedge between you and your friends. He will play into the conflicts between you and your family members to make you lean on them a lot less. If you let him get rid of your support system, he will have free reign, and you won't stand a chance against his manipulation.

He Will Express a Lot of Negative Emotions

Narcissists trade on negative emotions because they want to be the center of attention. When you are in a relationship with one of them, he will be upset when you don't do what he wants, when you are slightly critical of him, or when you don't give him the attention he is looking for. He will use anger, insincere sadness, and other negative emotions to make you insecure, get your attention, or gain a sense of control over you. If someone you are dating throws a tantrum over minor disagreements or when you can't give him attention, it means that he has a fragile ego, which is a clear sign that he could be a narcissist.

He Will Play the Blame Game

This is perhaps the most common indicator that you are in a relationship with a narcissist. He will never acknowledge any wrongdoing, and he will always find a way of turning everything into your fault. When anything doesn't go according to plan, he will always point out your part in it, even if he too could have done something to change the event's outcome. He will never take responsibility for anything, and when he takes action to solve a mutual problem that you have, he will always make it clear that you owe him.

THE REAL PROBLEMS ASSOCIATED WITH DEALING WITH A MENTALLY UNSTABLE EX

Mental illness is a scary thing for many people, not just those who suffer from it. It's hard to understand how to approach someone mentally unstable, leading to feelings of fear, anxiety, and helplessness.

It's not easy to recognize how to handle a mentally unstable ex-partner. Many people will tell you to walk away, but sometimes it's not that easy. There may be legal obligations or shared children and all sorts of family and community ties that make it challenging to leave him or her. If you've experienced abuse, there is the added complication that the abusive partner will often rely on you for emotional support—as well as material support—even after they have mistreated you.

Even if you're not living with your ex-partner, they may still be a significant part of your daily life. If that's the case, you need to look at what is best for all parties concerned. You need to decide what is best for the children or anyone else who is close to someone mentally unstable.

Look at your own needs as well as those of your ex-partner. The bottom line is that it's best to be in a situation where no one is being hurt. If you can't do this, then break contact. Break all links with your ex-partner completely if at all possible. You can call the police if you are physically threatened or if your ex-partner breaches any court orders or injunctions.

However, sometimes it's not possible to be completely disconnected because the children are involved and occasionally other family or friends are too. Whatever the case, it's essential to establish a good relationship with anyone who might be affected by your ex-partner's mental instability. It can help to create a plan for action that can address any concerns that might arise.

Everyone will deal with a mentally unstable ex-partner in his way and at a pace that suits him. You need to think about some points before making any decisions. Some of these things are about practicalities, including medical and legal issues. However, some of the considerations are no less important but are about your emotional well-being and that of your ex-partner and other people who might be affected by what you do.

The legal matters can be complicated. If the mental illness has been formally diagnosed, then you will have some legal rights in this respect, but these will vary depending on things like where you live and any court orders that have been issued.

In terms of practicalities, it is important to consider where your ex-partner is living. You will need to decide whether they're in a position to look after themselves, not just financially, but also with things like food and shelter. If you can't take care of them yourself, it is best to try and get someone else to do so. It may be that the person with mental illness can make his own decisions or arrange somewhere suitable for themselves. If that's the case, then you don't have any responsibilities in this respect.

If you have the right to see the children without your ex-partner present, it may help to arrange something like this well in advance. This way, you can give yourself time to think about how you will deal with the situation before you get there.

It's very important to consider your feelings and how you might react when you come into contact with a mentally unstable ex-partner. You may be frightened or angry, or even sad. Be aware that you will be dealing with a 'raw' situation, and so it's important to keep your own emotions as stable as possible. You can write down any questions you have before seeing your ex-partner so that you can think things through beforehand.

PERSONALITY TRAITS OF A NARCISSIST AND BORDERLINE NARCISSISTIC DISORDER

People with narcissistic personality disorder are relatively unique. Their behaviors lead them to improved social skills and public standing; in the short term, they may appear well-integrated and adapted. However, in a long time, the majority of the following symptoms will become apparent:

Sense of Self Importance

Most driven people in the world have achieved great things because they believe in themselves and their capabilities. However, once this becomes at the point that this self-importance is exaggerated, and they feel that no one else could be worthy enough to challenge them, their sole aim is for the gratification of self.

Superiority

No human should feel superior to another; everyone has different skills, and people should be accepted for what they are and for what they are capable of. Differences must be embraced as this is essential to the normal functioning of society.

44

However, someone with NPD will feel superior to all those around them, even if they have not achieved anything to back up this feeling.

This attitude will become so integral to their personality that they will find it impossible to connect on a deeper level. They think that only a few people are gifted enough to understand and associate with them.

Abilities

An extension of this feeling of superiority is the ability to exaggerate skill levels and achievements. This is partly to ensure that others understand they are superior and partly because they feel more important than anyone else and believe no one would dare to challenge their view of themselves and the world around them. Their conviction and self-belief are often powerful enough for people to follow them without ever witnessing their actual abilities.

Fantasy

Someone with NPD will spend much of his time dreaming about himself being rich, famous, or overwhelmingly beautiful. His fantasies will revolve around others worshipping them for their amazing abilities and achievements and ways in which they will rise to a position of power. They may also create an image of the perfect partner; this can often set the bar too high for any real person to achieve, making it impossible to meet the perfect mate.

Admiration

A classic trait of someone with a narcissistic personality is vanity. They are generally self-obsessed and believe they are beautiful and, as such, should be constantly praised and admired. This can get to the point where they will quickly feel entitled to this praise and will get enraged easily if they are not receiving it.

Entitlement

Alongside expecting to be admired, someone with an NPD will feel entitled to success or recognition of his talents and abilities. Failure is simply someone else interfering in his work; they are entitled to success in every field of life and will react extremely badly if this does not happen.

Someone with NPD will expect to be the center of attention at all times; they believe they deserve this response from others because they are superior.

Favors

Someone with NPD can't conceive the fact that they are not entitled to whatever they need. They will ask for special favors from anyone they encounter and expect others to follow their rules and expectations, which are linked to the belief that they are superior and can get whatever they want or need.

Using Others

As other people are seen as inferior, it is difficult, if not impossible, for someone suffering from NPD to see them as individuals in their own right, with dreams and goals of their own. They are more likely to perceive them as a tool that can be used and discarded as required to assist in reaching their aims and goals.

Needs and Emotions

Someone with NPD does not recognize the needs or emotions of others. This is generally through a physical inability to feel or understand these needs unless their desires are linked with his aims. As they feel superior to everyone else, they do not need to take other people's emotions into account. They generally do not even realize these people have emotions and needs!

Envy

Surprisingly, someone with a narcissistic personality is highly likely to be envious of those around them and anything they have but the sufferer does not. They are also very likely to believe that others envy their achievements, lifestyle, and abilities. They believe this is fitting considering their own highly inflated opinion of themselves.

Envy is often difficult to see; it is most commonly displayed through malicious actions to ensure someone else does not have something that the sufferer has not yet got. This can also be recognized as jealousy toward others and what they have; this is often shown by their hugely exaggerated stories; emphasizing how much better their achievement is compared to one particular person.

Arrogance

If you genuinely believe that you are better than others and capable of anything you want to do, you are likely to become arrogant. This will then become evident in the way you talk to people and your expectations of their behavior. People with NPD may even come across as haughty as well as arrogant.

Criticism

Anyone with NPD will not respond well to criticism; the most likely response is to become very angry and defensive; they will attack your argument and your personal beliefs or morals to ensure others devalue your argument and agree with them. The idea that anyone they believe is inferior could be right is impossible to grasp for a narcissist.

Occasionally, the reaction may be to socially withdraw as they are humiliated and ashamed of their inability to override the criticism. This can often lead to a targeted campaign to destroy the credibility of the attacker.

Many of the above features can be attributed to a high level of self-confidence. However, there is a difference between being confident and having a narcissistic personality. Someone suffering from NPD will cross the line regarding what is considered a healthy level of confidence. They are likely to put themselves on a pedestal and genuinely believe their life has more value than the lives of other people.

Borderline Personality Disorder

People with borderline personality disorder are like narcissists in that they are self-centered, emotionally unstable, and unpredictable. Living with someone who has a borderline personality disorder (BPD) can be like trying to stop a full, boiling pot of water from overflowing. Eventually, it will bubble over, and there is no way of avoiding it.

Most people with BPD, like narcissists, seek attention and admiration from their spouse as a constant source of supply, and it is only a matter of time when they decide it isn't enough. When this happens, they will most likely seek this same attention outside the marriage or relationship. For histrionics, their most common tactic is using seduction as a means to gain favor with others.

While narcissists and people with BPD may practice the same pattern, they might use a new co-worker, neighbor, or someone unfamiliar with their tactics to "win" them over and use them for their bidding and prop up Their sense of entitlement. For many new friends and acquaintances, a person who appears kind and well-intentioned will encourage them to show gratitude and praise, which the narcissist wants in return.

How can you cope with living with someone who has a borderline personality disorder? It's not an easy task, and most people will eventually leave due to the erratic nature of this person. Learning about the signs to identify BPD is just one step and deciding whether you can continue a relationship is the next stage. It's important to understand how the signs of BPD are incorporated into the context of a relationship, as some symptoms may be minor and others more obvious.

- A person with BPD will avoid living alone and often uses his relationships with others to fill a gap in his life. When he first begins dating, he may be ecstatic to fall in love and strive towards pleasing you as much as possible. He may also seek validation and return compliments at every chance, which may seem harmless at first until it becomes repetitive and exhausting. You'll notice his emotional reactions become unstable at times, and the slightest hesitation of validating him can result in feelings of rejection.

- A borderline personality disorder often causes a lot of disruption in life because of people's unpredictable behavior; they are unable to keep a job or progress towards meaningful goals in their life. They may put a great deal of confidence in you to help them and expect that love can solve all problems. A person with BPD may start a new job, believing it is the perfect place to work with the ideal employer, only to become angry and disappointed at the slight deviation from their idea of perfection. For example, a supervisor may be reminded to perform a certain task at work and internalize it as criticism. This can propel an emotional outburst and sudden action, such as quitting the job or reacting uncontrollably. As a consequence, they are relieved of their duties or reprimanded further.

- Since they fear being alienated and alone, they may rely on you more than necessary. Even when someone with BPD is financially secure, their emotional and psychological needs are always in a deficit, and they will never feel completely accepted. There is a good chance that family and close friends may now avoid them due to their unpredictable actions.

- If you date someone with BPD or histrionic personality disorder, they will likely engage in seeking attention outside the relationship. You may notice risky tendencies initially, such as dressing in provocative clothing that doesn't fit a specific occasion, such as a formal dinner or meeting your family. They may even flirt or act in a similar matter around your friends, which should be a warning sign.

It's important to evaluate your situation from various perspectives. Ask a trusted friend or family member if they notice anything odd or unusual about someone new you are dating, or a partner, once you secure a relationship. While it's important to discover the signs of anti-social behavior early, it's not always possible. For this reason, always make sure you remain in close contact with someone you trust, who can help you later.

WHY YOU SHOULDN'T GO BACK TO YOUR NARCISSISTIC EX AND WHY YOU NEED TO MOVE ON

Once you leave the narcissist, you may feel like a huge weight has been lifted from your chest. You feel like you can breathe again for the first time. You feel like you have made the right choice for yourself. However, in a short period, you find that the narcissist is knocking at your door and asking you to come back or take him back. If he is not trying to get you to go back to him, you may find that you begin to miss him too.

This is only natural and is nothing to be ashamed of—when you have spent a part of your life with someone that you have loved, you are going to naturally miss him. However, you can miss him without going back, and when you can recognize that, you can truly stay away. Remember, staying away is what is in your own best interest. You must be able to stay far from the narcissist to protect yourself. Make sure of that and allow yourself to heal into the person that you know you can be.

You can take key actions to help yourself stay away. It is only natural that you may yearn for that connection, especially the connection you had initially. However, you must resist it to help yourself. These steps will help you keep busy and keep yourself reminded that the abuse did happen, and it is precisely because it occurred that you cannot afford to go back to the narcissist.

Resist the Temptation to Judge and Blame Yourself

As you begin to heal away from the narcissist, it can become easy to allow the blame to shift back to yourself. You may find that you are unhappy with the way things turned out once you have nothing to think about. You may feel guilty, asking how you could get caught up in a relationship like that in the first place. You may find that you are angry with yourself, wondering how you could not see the red flags when they were right in front of your face. You may feel like you made a royal mistake and that you should have done better. This can lead to you judging and blaming yourself, which will hurt your self-esteem even more.

The narcissist wants you to feel like you were to blame. You may question why you would deserve to escape in the first place. Even if you may not be aware of it as it happens, you may begin to feel like you do not deserve better, and this will lead to your unconscious self-sabotage.

You do not deserve to blame yourself. You were hurt enough by the narcissist—there is no reason to add to it in this manner. Turn your attention to something else that could be productive. Instead of dwelling further, you can find something else that you can do with your time.

Improve Yourself

When you keep yourself from dwelling, the best you can do is invest time in yourself. Once you do it, you can get productive instead. You get to learn something new. You take your bad situation and turn it into something good.

What you do with your life is up to you. No matter what it is, it is symbolic. Your escape from the abusive situation is affording you a chance to better yourself in some way, shape, or form. The narcissist may have intentionally kept you held back, holding you down to make sure that you felt like you could never actually do anything. He may have laughed at your desire to go to school for a new career. He may have told you that you are terrible at cooking when you said you wanted to learn how to bake cakes. He may have told you that you were a failure when you told him that you wanted to start a small business. He had no interest in you bettering yourself because if you had managed to pull it off, your success would have been a direct threat to him. He would have felt like your success was a challenge, a threat that he was not as good as he claimed. He wanted you to avoid bettering yourself for this very reason — he would be able to keep his position of power over you.

This means that when you succeed in bettering yourself somehow, you can acknowledge that you did work hard. You can acknowledge that you did it in the face of adversity, despite the narcissist's negative assumptions. You recognize that you did do something worthy, and you will hopefully have something to show for it, whether that is a degree, a new skill, a business, or anything else. Bettering yourself is never a waste of your time.

Focus on Self-Care

When you have been in a narcissistic relationship, you grow accustomed to dumping excessive amounts of your time into someone else. You were dedicated to trying to placate the narcissist, who was never satisfied, leaving you endlessly working to do so. When you finally break free, however, you have plenty of time that will keep you thinking about whether you made the right choice in the first place. After all, the narcissist spent the entire relationship making you doubt yourself—of course, and you would continue to do so at this point.

When you shift that free time that you would usually use to deliberate over your decision, you can begin to spend time caring for yourself. This is probably foreign to you after a long relationship—you got used to attending to someone else's needs before meeting your own needs when you were in a relationship with the narcissist. You spent your time making sure that he was satisfied, and you did not take care of yourself because he was never satisfied in the first place.

Now is the time to pamper yourself. Spend some time focused on the activities you enjoy. Give yourself a spa day. Spend a mental health day in bed with a book, a carton of ice cream, and a glass of your favorite wine. Do whatever it is that you have always wanted to do and make yourself feel good. You will get a confidence boost because you will feel clean and whole for the first time in a while.

Write Down the Reasons You Left

One final way that you can resist returning to the narcissist may be one of the most powerful ones there are. You must make a list of all of the reasons you chose to leave the narcissist and ensure that you have them for easy access if you ever feel like you are in a moment of weakness. You will be thinking about the entirety of your relationship with the narcissist, recording what he did, how you felt, and why you should refuse to go back.

Think back to when you realized that you were, in fact, ready to leave. You decided that you were no longer willing or able to accept the abuse in your life. You decided that you deserved happiness and escape from the abusive tendencies once and for all. What was that moment? What happened then that made you come to this realization? Why should you avoid ever returning to the narcissist?

It is best to do this step when you are newly out of the relationship and while the pain of what happened to end the relationship is still fresh in your mind. No matter what that final straw that broke the camel's back was, write it down. Email it to yourself. Scan it and keep it on your phone. Print out a copy and put it in your mirror that you see every morning to remind you of what happened.

When you have had time to begin to recover from what happened and your emotions fade, you are more likely to wonder if you made the right decision, and when that happens, you must have the reason why you left written right in front of you. You should also dictate other abusive tendencies that the narcissist had, what he did, and how it made you feel.

You must then read this; every time you start feeling like returning to the narcissist may not be that bad. When you start to feel like returning would be okay and that you would rather have the narcissist present than not at all, you should spend time reading this letter. Let it be your sort of guide to understanding why you must avoid returning. It is like your map that shows you clearly what has happened and where you will be going from there. It will keep you grounded and firm in your decision. All you have to do is remember to read it when you start doubting yourself.

HOW TO DEAL WITH A PERSON WHO HAS NARCISSISTIC TENDENCIES

Each of us tends towards narcissism. There are degrees of this condition and most people have normal levels of self-love as a characteristic.

However, some have very high levels of narcissism characteristics, and you don't know how high and how embedded they are until you've become extremely involved in a relationship with them. You begin to notice the qualities that made you attracted to that person are narcissistic features that have become annoying to you.

This person may be a parent, sibling, or other family relatives who have a narcissistic personality. You have to put up with those people but can't challenge or control them. You may have an employer, co-worker, student, teacher, or employee with narcissistic characteristics.

Although some people are narcissists, it doesn't mean that they're all terrible. Some individuals with elevated narcissistic characteristics can be charismatic, fun to have around, and excel in what they do.

- **Falling for the fantasy and why you shouldn't:** Narcissists are charming and magnetic. They sparkle and draw people into their sphere because they can with their attention-getting personality. They are good at exhibiting terrific confidence. Getting caught up in his sphere can be easy. We think that they will bring about our desire to feel alive and more important. However, it's all make-believe, and it's costly in the long run (Smith M. M., 2018).

- **They won't recognize or fulfill your needs:** Realize that narcissists are looking for admirers, not partners. And, for your information, the admirer needs to show obedience. The only value you have to a person with NPD is someone who tells him how great he is to feed his ravenous ego. You, your feelings, and your desires don't count.

- **Check out how narcissists treat others:** People with narcissistic personality disorder manipulate, lie, disrespect, and hurt others. If they do it to others, they'll do it to you and treat you just the same way and possibly worse because you are the closest person to them.

Don't even think that you're different and will not be treated in the same way. You're not special (nothing personal), and you will be treated the same way as others.

- **Focus on yourself:** Focus on things that you want to achieve for yourself. If you have a talent you want to develop or changes you want to make in your life, this is the path you should follow. Create your reality instead of living in someone else's fantasy.

- **Don't wear rose-colored glasses:** Stop looking at the narcissist in your life as who you want him to be and see him for who he is. His bad behavior and the hurt he causes you shouldn't be excused or minimized. Don't live in denial.
- **Narcissists aren't open to change:** It's a sign of weakness, and they don't want to appear weak; they want to appear superior to others. The real change needs to come when you question yourself whether you want to live with this personality type indefinitely or want to make the changes that will salvage yourself (Smith M. M., 2018).
- **Set healthy and firm boundaries:** Mutual respect and caring for the other person's feelings are based on healthy relationships. However, if you're involved with a person with NPD, they cannot reciprocate these feelings in their relationships. It's not as if they're not willing to return. They're unable to. They don't recognize you, see you, or hear you. You are someone who exists outside of their desires and needs. Your feelings, needs, and desires don't fit in. That being said, narcissists violate the boundaries of others regularly. They not only violate boundaries, but they also do it with a lack of empathy and an absolute sense of entitlement.

Narcissists don't think it's rude and invasive to borrow your possessions without even asking if they can go through your mail and your phone texts, arrive uninvited to your home, steal your ideas, and let everyone think they thought of it, eavesdropping on conversations and volunteering advice and opinions that are unwanted. Some narcissists may think they're your brain and tell you how you think and feel.

- **Develop a plan:** If you have a set of boundaries and have allowed others to violate them, you won't find it easy to retain control. The way to have firmer boundaries is to consider what your goals are and any possible hindrances.

Think of the questions you need to ask to develop your plan; are they the most important changes you want and hope to accomplish? In the past, has there been anything that has worked with the narcissist? Is there anything that didn't work? How will your plan be impacted by questioning the balance of power between the two of you? When your new boundaries are set, how will you enforce them?

When you can answer these questions realistically, they will help you make your evaluation of choices and the development of a solid plan, one that should work for you.

- **Unless you plan to keep a boundary, don't set it:** There may be boundaries that you have no problem setting and keeping while there are those you've set in the past, and then let it go and allow the narcissist to roll over it.

In setting your new boundaries, be prepared for the narcissist not to be so happy about them. They will test your mettle and limits in whether you'll stand firm by them or not. Let the narcissist know that along with the new boundaries there will be consequences, and be specific in what they are. Backing down is not an option. If you do, you'll be sending a message that you don't need to be taken seriously, and all your boundaries will be in jeopardy.

- **Prepare for other changes in your relationship:** You already know that the narcissist will not be too happy about your new boundaries. They'll feel upset and threatened by any attempts you make to have control of your life, with or without them.

Narcissists are used to having control over you and everyone else. They like to call the shots. They may step up demands in the relationship in other areas to make up for feeling they've lost control over you and the relationship as it was.

- **Taking a gentle approach:** In some cases, some choose not to give up on the narcissist person and want to give it a try to preserve the relationship. You need to do so. You need to step lightly and softly. Pointing out his dysfunctional or hurtful actions and behavior, you're doing the worst thing you can do to a narcissist. You're destroying his self-image of themselves and his perfection.

When you let them know that what they've said or done has hurt your feelings, make an effort to give them the message in a respectful, calm, and gentle manner. Concentrate your message on how their behavior makes you feel instead of focusing on their intentions and motivations. They may do the usual routine of responding in their defensive and angry manner. Try to keep calm. If you see you can't continue the conversation, walk away, and see if you can revisit it at a later time. (Smith M. M., 2018)

- **Try not to take things personally:** Narcissists always deny their mistakes, shortcomings, and inferiority complex to protect themselves from feeling shame and inferiority to others. One way they do this is to cast his faults on others.

One of the most upsetting things to feel is to be accused of something that's not your fault or has negative traits that you do not possess applied to you as your personality characteristics. Try not to take it personally as difficult as it can be for you. It's not about you.

- **The narcissist's version of who you are is wrong:** A narcissist's world is not one of reality, including how they view other people. Undermining the self-esteem of others is almost sport to them. Don't allow them to twist who you are into someone you're not or thrust Their blame game on you. Refuse to receive or accept any blame, criticism, or excessive responsibility. Those are negative vibes and accusations the narcissist can keep.
- **Don't bother to argue with a narcissist:** Usually, when we argue with a person who is not a narcissist, there is usually a back and forth and points made on both sides.

The key here is that the other person acknowledges and hears you.

When you're being attacked by a narcissist, your natural response is to defend yourself and argue rationally to prove to the narcissist that they are wrong. However, they don't hear you regardless of how rational your argument is. Fighting with them is a waste of breath. Just let the narcissist know you don't agree with the evaluation and move one. Don't entertain the argument if they try to revive it. To control discontinuing the argument, let them know you are over and out.

- **Let the narcissist know that you know yourself:** Having a strong sense of self is annoying to a narcissist. They see that if you have that sense of self, their insults and projections of their personality traits and weaknesses won't work. When you know yourself, your strengths, and your weaknesses, it is much easier to ward off any insults and criticisms that are unfairly leveled against you.
- **Discard the need for approval:** This goes hand in hand with knowing yourself. You need to draw your strength and approval of yourself from your own opinion and truths that you know about yourself. It's imperative to detach and let go of the narcissist's opinion of you and any wish to appease or please them at your own expense.

This is a boundary that you not only put in place for the narcissist to abide by but one that you should promise to keep for your self-respect and honor of who you are.

- **Look elsewhere for support and purpose:** Let's get real about a relationship with a narcissist. If you decide to remain in such a relationship, you need to be honest with yourself. You have to understand what you can fully and can't expect from them.

A narcissist isn't magically going to change into a person who will truly value you. That means you will need to seek out personal fulfillment and emotional support elsewhere. Cultivate new friendships—some narcissists want to control people's lives by isolating them. If this situation is one that you are in, you need to take the time to rebuild any friendships that fell away because of the isolation or begin to develop new relationships.

HOW TO DEAL WITH A PSYCHOPATH

D ealing with a psychopath is not going to be easy—at least, not at the beginning. Did we not see that a psychopath follows no logic when deciding to act? This is not a person you can reason with. In any case, from what we have already seen, a psychopath is a master of manipulation: they are always using lies and pretense to influence the way you behave towards them.

With that said, you can reduce the damage they bring into your life or even avoid getting entangled in their lives in the first place.

Great Principles that Can Help

Seek Professional Assistance

A psychopath is one guy who can transform you from one confident and flamboyant person to a withdrawn and unhappy creature. This emanates from the tendency of the psychopath to drum negatives onto you. To psychopaths, you are the cause of things going wrong in their life; and sadly, you seem vulnerable enough to believe it. That unwarranted blame then gets to seep into your skin, your heart, your mind, and the whole of you, messing with your personality a great deal.

That mess that has occurred in you as a person can only be undone with the help of a professional. Luckily, psychologists have studied the behavior of psychopaths and your situation will not be new to them, however serious you think it is. They will, hence, show you how to reclaim your person, as you have already been molded into someone else without you realizing it.

One thing you should know is that just as great professionals can be psychopaths, so can great professionals and people of means fall prey to psychopaths. In short, you need not fear stigmatization; it is not your fault you are a victim.

Beware: Psychopaths Try to Make You What They Want

Psychopaths want you to look up to them as your ultimate solution to problems as if they are the only ones who can bring happiness into your life. Well, they messed you up in the first place, and it would be great if they could restore your being. However, they want you to be their victim forever—bidding them every call. For all practical purposes, there is nothing more they want but to enslave your mind.

Suppose you take the example of cult leaders. In that case, it is easy to understand the manipulation of the psychopath and how, as the victim, you end up locking everyone else out of your life, particularly family and friends. See how one Warren Jeffs led a cult that practiced polygamy and abused underage girls and boys. Gladly, in this case, some bold victims testified down the line, and Warren got a jail term in Utah, US, in 2007.

Once you are aware of how psychopaths work, you can see the manipulation for what it is and stand firm, refusing to succumb to their control. If you had a plan to use a certain route, for example, and you refused to get influenced and alter the route, the psychopath realizes how difficult it will be to get you trapped. Often, that will be the end of that attempt as the mouth of the psychopath is always watering, longing for easy prey. If you are informed and wise in the ways of the psychopath, they will give up and leave you alone.

Do Not Be Generous with Information

Ever heard of the analogy of someone throwing you the rope with which you hang yourself? That is what happens with psychopaths and their pretentious concern for you. They use that feigned concern, sometimes in a dramatic way, to get information out of you. And then it is hallelujah as the psychopath uses the same information to manipulate you.

If, for instance, you volunteer information that you had some misunderstanding with your mum or dad, the psychopath takes that information and paints a picture of parents who loath you. Therefore, the psychopath will pose as your savior. And down the psychological decline, you begin, as you become easily brainwashed to review all your other relationships to end them. Every bit of detail that comes out of your mouth is fodder for the psychopath. If the psychopath is in your life in a way that you cannot ignore chatting with them, keep to facts when chatting, and avoid showing your opinion, this is because it is your stand that psychopaths are out to change to suit them.

Understand the Weaknesses and Strengths that You Have

This is important because the psychopath is already registering your weaknesses to capitalize on them. The same psychopath takes note of your strengths to know the best way to circumvent them when trying to manipulate you.

For instance, right now, you may not need to think long and hard to identify someone who has gone all out to misuse your generosity. Just because you make donations to the less fortunate and do shopping for your mum is no reason for someone else to manipulate you into buying stuff for them. That is the stuff psychopaths are made of.

Heed Your Instincts

If your senses tell you something does not feel right about someone, find your way out. If you are still strangers, make haste and purport to have company around or do something just as dramatic; get out of wherever you are and lose that company.

And in case it is a budding relationship you are having with someone, and your system keeps ticking caution, nip it in the bud before it turns out to be damaging to your person, your life, and the people around you.

Drop All Contact

If you feel you have been entangled with a psychopath and want to sever contact, suppress your urge to call even once in a while to say hello. Do not even send text messages. If you send those, the psychopath will jump onto that concern you have just shown and use it to resume the journey of manipulation.

One thing you need to know is that psychopaths have nothing of quality going in their life. They are idle for the most part, and when they are busy, it is in the business of seeking out victims. Of course, to them, anyone who is not their victim is their competitor.

Do Not Bother Trying to Change the Psychopath

When it comes to psychopaths, the solution is to part ways. Trying to reform them usually worsens the situation. And if you introduce them to a specialist, they leave there wiser and more cunning than before. They do not reform; they only get more ammunition for manipulation.

After all, we are talking of people who are full of themselves, selfish, and with no conscience. What professional can help with a conscience? That is a tall order.

Do Not Carry Any Guilt

It would be unfair to you to beat yourself up for falling victim to the psychopath. You were busy leading your normal life, and you had many people to interact with in a positive way when along came the psychopath unleashing all the manipulation.

Since you are a normal human being, you hardly realized that this person was not normal but a psychopath and a leech.

Get Informed

The more information you get regarding the thinking and behavior of a psychopath, the better your recuperation process. You will come to terms with the reality that it is not that difficult to fall victim to a psychopath when you have not come across one before. You can easily get apt information from books on psychopathic tendencies, videos, and also, movies.

And How Will Information on Psychopathic Tendencies Help?

You will understand:

- The characteristics that make you vulnerable at the onset.
- The whole process and how the charade continued the whole time.
- The tactics the psychopath used to keep you toeing the line.
- The reason you fell for those tactics.

Once you understand the whole process, you will feel a sense of freedom. And that is the only way you can undo the psychological damage done to you by your experience in the hands of the psychopath.

Set Your Conscience Free

It is easy for you to ask yourself why you could not see the manipulative tendencies, which brings about a great weight that comes from blaming yourself. You need to stop blaming yourself for not seeing through the psychopaths.

Now that you are not a psychopath, how would anyone have expected you to have identified one on the spot? The personal blame is not warranted, and you need to allow yourself a fresh start.

HOW TO RESPOND TO THE EX

It may be complicated at first but divorcing a narcissist is worth it. Isn't this a statement you tell yourself every day? It plays in your mind like a mantra, the self-affirmation reminding you that going in the right direction will be worth it in the end. It should be so easy—why stay with someone who has no empathy, care, or kindness towards you and who wants to see you suffer? Yet, it is not as easy as it seems, hence why you need to repeat statements such as this.

This is one detail that many people don't tell you when taking steps to divorce a narcissist. You need mantras or affirmation-like statements to keep you on the course, remind you that this is in your best interests and that it will be worth it in the end.

The psychological, mental, and emotional abuse and trauma you have suffered are real, and regardless of how many times you have been gaslighted or made to appear crazy, in the wrong, or losing the plot, you know the truth in the core of your cells. Being with a narcissist is entirely detrimental to your health.

Luckily, many steps can be taken. A covert narcissist is precisely this: covert; still in the shadows of his manipulations, delusions, and shady: hurtful character. He is not (yet) in the open or publicly acknowledged, and is this because you have not yet decided to allow him to be seen in his true light?

Taking a stand and choosing, with your free will, inner strength, and sheer conviction, that you will no longer allow yourself to be abused, victimized, or manipulated allows your partner to be seen, and for you to subsequently finally take the steps necessary to be free from his abuse.

Of course, all of this is something you know; see these words as a reflection of your psyche and conscious mind telling you exactly how it is. The fact that you are reading this and have chosen, consciously, to align with your true self and leave your narcissistic partner for good implies that you are already well on course. This is confirmation, and you are heading in the right direction! You are strong beyond measure.

Divorcing a Narcissist: Stop Reacting!

The reaction is not the same as the response. When you respond to someone or something, you provide space, wisdom, and awareness to connect on a mature and responsible level. Responding allows for authenticity, calmness of thought, and clarity in communication. Yet, reacting is something completely different.

The key to your narcissistic partner's success is in your reaction. He needs people to become emotionally entwined and engaged with his stories. There is no exchange if there is no reaction—no one is appeasing or empowering him. Power is a great word to be aware of here. The reaction provides a narcissist's empowerment or, more accurately, a false sense of empowerment. Causing pain, hurt, and manipulation to others is not empowerment. Regardless, reacting provides the sustenance that a narcissist needs, so the best way to heal and begin your journey of empowerment is to stop reacting and start responding.

Things to Be Mindful of How You May Be Reacting!

Your partner attempts to provoke a reaction, and you allow it. Instead of taking a moment to slow down, be calm inside and recognize the intentions of causing destruction, chaos, and harm, you play to his manipulations. Thus, a vicious and highly repetitive cycle can begin and continue for hours or even days on end. The key is to detach and not get caught up in his games. It can be easier said than done. However, the tips and techniques for effective response below can help with this.

'Snide remarks.' at this stage, your partner should know you very well and therefore understand your triggers. Snide remarks or specific comments are a very effective way to get a reaction from you and subsequently enable him to continue in his ways.

'Awareness goes where energy flows!' If you don't give your attention, time, or energy to something, how can it perpetuate? The answer is that it can't. The intentions and motivations of your partner require energy and attention. Otherwise, they are formless.

Watch out for the signs. Say you have been with your partner for a while. You will know the signs of when he is going to begin his games. If he is bored or displays signs of frustration, stimulation, or boredom, this is a sure warning that you will soon become his target for his stimulation. A narcissist's needs that 'spark' to feed his egocentricity, self-centeredness, and feelings of self-worth. Without it, his illusions start to crumble down, and they have no choice but to look within, seek help, and ways to change, which are, of course, very rare for a narcissist.

If you feel yourself becoming stressed, anxious, nervous, or heated inside, these are a sure signal that you are on the edge of a reaction. Unlike in partnerships where narcissism is not present or a key theme, and where most people are allowed a few moments of blowing off steam or showing weakness, in this relationship, you are not provided the patience, compassion, or support necessary.

This means that even if your partner does happen to be in a serene, kind, or non-narcissistic space, you may, unfortunately, spark them with your reactive behaviors. It is exceptionally rare for a true narcissist to see you becoming upset or worked up on your own accord and not use it as a chance for drama or further manipulation.

A Deeper Look into Divorce and Reaction

Divorce is a serious thing. The process inevitably means that you have decided to part ways, restart your life, and take back your resources, belongings, and physical necessities. Your partner's entire identity is merged in the reality that he can feed off you, use you as his hidden and subtle yet powerful supporting system, and bounce off your kindness, empathy, and positive attributes.

Once you started responding, this destroys the narcissist's world. He no longer keeps up the facade once you decide that his actions are not acceptable. This can only happen when you begin to respond.

How to Start Responding

The true response begins when you start to slow down and become an observer of both your thoughts and feelings and your partner's. This is best achieved through meditation and mindfulness. The significance of these two self-help methods cannot be overlooked. They are both extremely powerful in helping you to live your best life, be free from narcissistic abuse or targeting, and start responding.

Meditation

Why is engaging in meditation one of the best ways to learn how to respond and thus change the way you perceive and feel about the situation? Because meditation allows you to detach from overactive thoughts and feelings, further becoming the observer. When you observe, you are not caught up in the emotions or drama associated with your partner's intentions. You can calm your mind, control your feelings and responses, and feel more peaceful within. Clarity of mind and thought can also result, and you generally become more insightful, patient, wise, and loving with meditation.

Mindfulness

Linked to meditation is the power of mindfulness. It allows you to become more mindful or conscious, which means embodying a higher awareness and level of integrity. You won't want to react when you start to integrate the lessons and vibration of mindfulness, as you will not want to lower yourself to such levels.

There is an innate dosage of eloquence, self-respect, grace, and personal integrity associated and developed with mindfulness, and your viewpoints and perspectives will change for the better. Any action or behavior of your partner can be met with greater conscious reaction and response. Moreover, you will start to feel good about the situation, regardless of how testing it is and will see the positive.

In essence, mindfulness can help you see the light and recognize that your mind is a powerful tool. You are not responsible for your partner's thoughts, behaviors, or/actions, but you do have control over your own.

HOW TO DETERMINE WHETHER TO STAY IN A MARRIAGE/RELATIONSHIP OR TO LEAVE

Whether or not you feel like you have been the victim of narcissistic abuse, being in a relationship with such a character is not without its challenges. It may lead to an unhappy end, or rather, it could lead to you staying in it, even when it contradicts who you are as a person and your dreams and goals of successful relationships and a happy life. Whatever you are feeling at this moment, letting go of your relationship may not feel like your first choice, and that's okay.

Spend more time reflecting on the issues in your relationship from a more objective standpoint for a little longer about letting go and moving on.

For some readers, there is no question that it is time to pack up and go. It will depend on a person's wants, needs, and ability to be honest with what is going on in his marriage or partnership. Understand the dynamics of your narcissistic partnership after you have identified that you are in one.

Moving forward can be a challenge. Many people will struggle with ending this type of relationship, mainly due to the reality of narcissistic abuse and emotional manipulation. It is about who you are, what your experience is, and what is going on that will help you understand the best choice forward for you.

This will help you identify when it might be good to leave a narcissistic relationship and how to put an end to it so that you don't keep coming back to it. A lot of that experience requires getting help and support and eventually a period of recovery from the narcissistic relationship so that you don't end up with the same type of person again, repeating the patterns in an entirely new relationship.

When and How to End the Relationship

Trying to change a narcissist and help him work on growth and transformation will not get you very far. If you are trying to stick around and make it work, the best possible advice is to focus on his positive qualities. Even if your narcissist claims that they want to change, there will be little effort put forth and very little gain. They aren't going to be able to offer a change in the way you need or hope, and you will most often find yourself alone emotionally. You want to heal them, but only they can heal themselves, and so you might be waiting for a long time for them to figure that out.

The time is right for you to leave if you have undergone any emotional, mental, or physical abuse. Suppose you have identified serious cycles of manipulation or narcissistic issues that never change. In that case, you are sacrificing your power, integrity, success, and desires; you feel like you are being taken advantage of regularly to support someone else's fantasies of who they are. That narcissism within your relationship can affect in many ways your quality of life, personal views, self-worth, and more, and it is not worth it to stick around, hoping that your partner will change and be more what you need. They don't care about what you need. They will only ever care about what they need.

If you have tried for a long time to help your partner identify his issue and help him "heal" his problem to no avail, then it is time to let go and move on. It is important to recognize that you can never heal someone for them; they have to do the work to heal themselves. Being a supportive partner is always a good thing. Still, suppose you are familiar with how your supporting patterns have enabled your narcissistic partner to stay in his preferred role and behavior patterns. In that case, you need to admit that you are at the end of the rope to heal on your own and find a happier lifestyle.

The stages of detaching from your partner can go on for a while as you begin to identify the issues and start to pull away, changing your role in the situation and recognizing your readiness to end things. It can be uncomfortable for your partner, who will make it uncomfortable for you as a result, and so understanding some of the stages that you will likely go through will help you prepare for moving on.

Detachment from a Narcissist: Stages

First Stage

You stop accepting blame, guilt, or shame in your relationship. You begin to resurface and "wake up" to what has been going on. In the first stage, you are "seeing" more clearly all of the patterns, the covert and subversive ridicule, and all of the tools of manipulation to push you away and punish you, and then pull you back in and adore you. This is the stage of awareness of the problem and the first shift and changes in the situation.

Second Stage

You may still have feelings for your partner at this point, even a seriously deep love bond. The desire to please them will begin to be replaced with the feeling of anger and even resentment. They keep consistently and continuously demanding of your admiration, adoration, and pleasing them. The love may still be there, but you are not so "naïve" anymore.

Signals of the Second Stage

- Your partner's lies no longer affect you and they feel obvious and pathetic.
- You are no longer succumbing to the manipulation tools.
- You regain a sense of self-worth and feel you deserve to be treated better.
- You will begin to fight for yourself more and will create more conflict with your partner.

- You begin to regain and rebuild your self-confidence and self-esteem.

Third Stage

Your confidence is being reborn, and you are feeling better about yourself and your choices. You may have already joined a support group or started to see a counselor help you grow and feel more emotionally and mentally empowered. You can better focus on your wants and needs and start seeing how life would be if you are not involved with your narcissistic partner.

Signals of the third stage

- You cannot stand to be around your partner.
- You no longer feel an obsessive love or strong love bond.
- If they begin to push your buttons or act inappropriately, you will either have no reaction and not care or retaliate and lash out against them.
- You enjoy more time with friends, in support groups, engaging in classes, or group meetups that support your interests.
- You will start to make decisions to support yourself without concerning yourself with your partner's preferences or interests.
- You will begin to make your move to let go and move on by planning to get out and getting your ducks in a row.

Fourth Stage

This is the end of the relationship when your focus becomes facing your future without your partner. At this point, you may have cut the cords, moved out, separated, begun the divorce proceedings, etc. This is the stage when you will have cut them off and out of your life and when you can begin to feel new and like yourself again. You will not want anything to do with your partner, and in some cases, you may have to maintain some contact.

RECOGNIZING HIDDEN EMOTIONAL AND PSYCHOLOGICAL ABUSE TRAITS AND FINDING HEALING FOR THEM

You have been to hell, but how do you get back from there? What does your future look like? Can you destroy the trauma bond that you have become addicted to? Can you ever feel like yourself again?

These questions and more can come to the surface when you first manage to break away from your abuser. Life can seem strange and scary. You will feel yearnings to go back to your old relationship, even though you know all the reasons you should not.

For some people, the road to healing is not just about healing themselves, but they also want to find healing in their relationships and for their partners. There is a way to do this as well—it is hard and trying but not impossible. You can get there with work, dedication, and leaning on others for help.

Do not make the mistake of trying to do all of this on your own. There is no shame in seeking help. If you ask yourself: "Well, what is next for me?"

Where Do I Go from Here?

How Can You Heal After Being Subjected to a Relationship with a Narcissist?

Your recovery is an involved process. You know what abuse looks like from a narcissist, and you have explored the details behind his history. You have learned who the narcissist is, what his masks are like, how they manipulate you, and in essence, you have discovered what has been happening to you. This can be a lot to take in at first. But you need to learn these signs and identify the signals so that you can prevent yourself from being placed back into a situation like this.

Healing takes time and effort. You need to learn about yourself before you can try and heal the damage that your narcissist caused. For example, you need to learn about your childhood trauma that has made you susceptible to caring for a narcissist. Understand also how to create and establish boundaries that we need to make others adhere to. You need to understand that you are also accountable for your actions and the behaviors that you portray. These are all things you will learn on your path to healing so that you can find peace and a way forward after your traumatic ordeal.

Yes, the narcissist's behavior was heinous, but you need to analyze the other half of the equation—yourself. Ask yourself hard to answer questions like why you stayed and why you allowed the ill-treatment to go on for so long? Do not ask these questions to blame yourself but to analyze your behaviors. You are not to blame for the situation, but you need to understand how and why you stayed in an abusive situation. Or even why you continue to stay if you have not left your narcissist.

If your narcissist fails to get help, you need to make peace with the fact that he will never truly take accountability for the emotional turmoil he put you through. This is merely due to the way his mind works. You need to find closure for yourself without expecting it from your partner or ex-partner.

You will go through several stages on your journey to healing.

Stage One

Victim

When you first learn of everything you have been subjected to and realize that your partner is a narcissist, you will probably feel victimized. This is because you are coming to terms with the betrayal that your narcissist has created. The feelings that you have pent up inside you that add to this situation of victimhood are:

- Hurt
- Denial
- Rejection
- Confusion
- Shame
- Victimization by family members or friends that say you are crazy for your beliefs about your partner
- Anger at your narcissist

- Anger at yourself for not realizing or knowing
- Anger over the love that you gave
- Anger over the time that you spent in the narcissist's cycle
- Fear of what your next step will be
- Fear of being in an unfamiliar new reality
- Feelings of abandonment
- Feeling lonely

These feelings will run through your mind as you break ties with your narcissist or seek to change the behavior. It is a process, as you have also become addicted to the way they treat you.

Your next step in this stage is to acquire knowledge. You need to be prepared to learn about your narcissist and yourself. Once you have looked introspectively into your past and feelings, you need to study what factors made you his target. How did you allow them to creep into your life, and how did you become accustomed to the abuse? Write these questions down and try your best to answer them objectively.

Stage Two

Survivor.

Once you get through your feelings of being a victim and the shock of realizing what was happening to you, you will begin to feel like a survivor. You have a mental shift during this time. Your feeling will change towards:

- Rebuilding your life.
- Seeking out a counselor.
- Being unwilling to forgive your narcissist.
- Trying to find your way back to your old self.
- Navigating through your issues of trust.
- Learning how to understand yourself and participating in self-care.
- Re-evaluating and changing friendships as necessary.
- Weakening of your anger.
- Experiencing new hope.
- Manifesting anger or depression caused by a trigger.
- Discovering your trauma from childhood.
- Creating awareness for the flags of a narcissist.

You will need to actively work toward instilling change in your life at this point in your healing. This is where the real legwork of your recovery begins.

Before you do anything, you need to learn how to create boundaries and set limits that you do not want someone else to cross. This is how you begin taking your life back. Once you have established your boundaries, stop hiding.

Get back into routine and habits with your friends and family. Go out and have fun. Rediscover the freedom and joy that life can give you.

You might be struggling with forgiveness. That is not unusual, but you need to work on it. Your forgiveness is a pivotal step in your recovery. This act is not for your abuser but entirely for you. You need to let go of his control over your emotions and actions.

Stage Three

Surviving and Thriving

This is the stage where you have laid the foundation for your healing, and now you need to continue to build and work on it. You might feel troubled during your recovery, and some initial feelings of anger and resentment might surface.

- Feelings of anger toward the person that abused you.
- Inability to shake the emotions from your past.
- Shame and embarrassment at having been the victim of a narcissist.
- Lack of concentration in your life at work or even when part of a group setting.
- The sensation that you cannot move forward into your new life.
- Feeling bitter at the idea of forgiving your abuser.
- A concern of what other people might think as they see you struggle to move on.
- Desire to move on and create dreams and live in freedom.

It isn't easy to process what happened to you and to clear your mind to move forward. There are ways you can take to reinforce your recovery during stage three.

You need to refocus your perspective. You must learn about the dangers of keeping your emotional attachment with an abuser you left. There is the power to be found from releasing your abuser. Your focus needs to be on your recovery, not on the narcissist.

Find the self-confidence you are missing. There was you before your narcissist grabbed hold of you. Your confidence will help you move forward. Through your confidence, you should strive to learn to love yourself so that you can wash away the chaos and anxiety your narcissist left with you.

Change is important. With these steps, you can reclaim some of your former self back yet also forge a new identity. Learn to be mindful. Place yourself in every moment and be awake and active during it. As you practice mindfulness, your focus will keep bringing you to present moments, and you will be able to let go of the memories that keep surfacing from the past.

When you are ready, you can start building up healthy relationships. If you have let go of friends during your recovery, try to cultivate new and authentic relationships that offer you support.

SOLUTIONS AND STRATEGIES YOU CAN USE AND APPLY IN ALL RELATIONSHIPS TO RESOLVE CONFLICT

Conflicts can be resolved in relationships, but they must be committed to the process. If either or both couples are not willing to resolve the conflict, then the relationship may end. Couples must take some steps to resolve conflicts in the relationship.

Be Willing to Discuss

The first step is for couples to be willing to come together to trash pertinent issues to resolve them. But if the situation is that one of you is not ready to talk, then resolving the conflict won't be possible.

Dialogue is the way out of any conflict. The more you and your partner are willing to discuss issues affecting the relationship, the better the chances of resolving them. The couples involved must do well to make the discussion yield even when an arrangement is made. Both must do well to observe the following rules while the conversation lasts.

- Each partner should turn to talk and express his grievances. Both must not be speaking at the same time.

Otherwise, understanding will not be achieved, and another quarrel may start.

- Each partner must listen with keen interest when one person is talking. Phones must be off, and anything that could distract should be put off. Any attempt to interject when one is talking should be with consent.

- Avoid argument and use of insult words during the reconciliation conversation. You can show yourself and your views without ever insulting your partner or making him or her feel bad. Choice and usage of words must be selective and politely spoken with respect and dignity.

Be Objective

As you talk with your partner, you need to be objective. By this, you should try to see the issues raised from your partner's point of view, not just your own opinion. Failure to do so will render the discussion fruitless. Remember your partner is human and that you can't always be right in everything. Try to spot out what your spouse is saying that you are guilty of. Read through the lines when he or she is talking to understand the real issues.

Admit Your Fault

What happened in the garden of Eden that tore the first marriage apart was that both Adam and Eve never admitted her fault before God. The man passed the blame for the error to his wife. The wife passed the blame for her mistake to the serpent.

Who could the serpent blame? The blame game right from the beginning did not resolve the problem in the first marriage. Instead, it scattered it. They were thrown away from the garden of Eden. In any conflict, both will be at fault in one way or the other. To resolve the issue, both must acknowledge their mistake before God and each other. Only then the reconciliatory steps can be productive.

If you genuinely love your partner and have fate in the relationship, put your ego aside and admit you were all along wrong. You lose nothing when you do so. It is a show of maturity and forthrightness to admit your fault, which will begin the healing process in your relationship.

Apologize

One of the magic words that can heal and resolve conflict in your relationship is to say, "I am sorry," short but powerful, but unfortunately, most people won't say it to their partner out of pride. If you admitted your fault, it would be natural to apologize. If you need to kneel to apologize, do it to save your relationship from collapsing.

Forgive

Learn to forgive your partner. If you don't forgive your partner, then you are not ready for peace. Forgiving your partner not only resolves the conflict but also heals you physically, emotionally, and psychologically. It will restore you and your relationship. It is hard to pardon but is also possible by the help of God to forgive. Mutual understanding must take place for the conflict to be resolved. Let the offense go off your heart. You are better off when you do so.

Shift Ground

Parties must be willing to shift grounds on issues discussed. A situation whereby you still hold to your stand won't help the reconciliatory process. The win-win approach must be adopted. A little bend here and there between the parties involved is what will mend the broken bridges in the relationship. Don't insist it must go 100% your way. Be considerate and flexible in your decisions so that you and your partner can resolve the conflict and get along well again.

Make Renewed Commitment to Your Partner

After apologizing, forgiving, and shifting grounds, then the last step is to make a renewed commitment to your partner. Consider all the rights and privileges you deprived your couple of. Verbalize your love for your spouse once again and back it up with actions.

A warm embrace, kisses, and holding of each other's hands again will also bring back the lost emotional connection you both had before. Just laugh over everything, and all will be well again.

HOW TO IDENTIFY ISSUES WORTH FIGHTING, HOW TO FORMULATE THEM TO MINIMIZE ANY CONFLICT, AND HOW TO CHANGE YOUR THINKING STATE TO MAKE IT MORE POSITIVE IN ALL SITUATIONS

S lamming doors, angry words, silent treatment, and a host of other destructive behaviors become the norm if people in a relationship are constantly fighting. Verbal abuse can be just as damaging as physical abuse, so do not delude yourself that since you are just fighting verbally, it means you are not hurting each other. Human beings are naturally emotional. Sadly, it is the people we love who hurt us the most. That is why, in every relationship, conflict will arise.

When two people from different backgrounds and belief systems come together, you will find times when you disagree. The problem in a relationship is not that there is conflict but rather how it is handled. If you cannot resolve a disagreement without a shouting match, you have an unhealthy way of resolving conflict.

You should approach a disagreement to resolve an issue and not impose your will on another person. Absolutes like "never" or "always" can blind you and hinder you from making rational conclusions. Avoid making decisions when you are angry. Learn to step back from the situation until you feel calm enough to have a discussion.

Winning the Battle to Lose the War

Do you want to have a two-hour fight over who forgot to take out the trash? It is not unusual to find couples having blazing rows about the smallest of things. Constant bickering becomes a habit with time, and you start to find that the moments when you are in harmony with your partner become fewer each day. Therefore, it is important to know how to pick your battles.

While you do not want to let your partner walk all over you, working on minor issues is self-sabotage. Living with a nagging partner can be emotionally draining and will drive the other person away. There is a reason why some people will leave work and go straight to the bar instead of going home to their partners. Peace of mind is important, and when you cannot get that at home, you start to seek it elsewhere.

Nagging is perceived as disrespectful for most people, which immediately puts the other person on the defensive. Your partner will probably tune you out the minute you start talking if they have become accustomed to your nagging. Slowly they start to resent you because they feel personally attacked.

You have a better chance of success when you talk to your partner in a friendly and conversational way. Resist the urge to start harping on them the minute they walk in through the door. Wait for the right time to bring up issues, preferably when your partner is relaxed and open to communication. You can avoid aggravating differences and conflicts in your relationship by knowing how to disagree without hurting each other.

Living in Harmony

Do's

- It is okay to agree to disagree. Not every conflict has to end with both parties coming to the same agreement. On some issues, you will need to be okay with differing points of view.
- Keep the personal attacks out of your disagreements. Discuss the issue, not the person. Refrain from bringing up your partner's flaws to make them feel unsure of themselves or guilt them into agreeing with you.
- Keep your disagreement about the present and resist the temptation to dredge old issues and past mistakes.
- Stop combining all your problems and then linking them all into one big issue. Tackle matters as they crop up and find solutions to each. Do not stockpile all your grievances to be used later as some ammunition against your partner.
- Be responsible for your part in the conflict. It takes two to tango, and both of you have created most of the issues in

your relationship. By acknowledging what you may have done wrong, you also encourage others to accept mistakes. This enables you to resolve and move on from the matter. Stubbornly sticking to your point, even when you know you are wrong, does not resolve disagreements.

- Mind your language. Refrain from using derogatory terms or insults to make a point. Keep the discussion civil and avoid creating animosity. The more you attack the other person, the more closed off they become, and the less likely you will resolve your conflict.
- Make a safe space where you can retreat without needing to discuss the matter. It can be your bedroom or any other place you feel needs to be spared from the conflict. This will take some pressure off and give you a safe space and time to handle your emotions.
- Decide upon a time frame where you can discuss the issue and bring it to a close. Avoid revisiting the same issue for days on end. Set aside and decide that you should both reach a compromise by the end of that time and let that issue go. It could be an hour, thirty minutes, or if you feel you need to address the conflict and resolve it.

Don'ts

- Do not try to win by sticking to your point of view, no matter what. If you view conflicts as a battle for supremacy, it won't be easy to resolve anything.

- Do not view your partner as your competitor. No matter what, remember you are in the relationship together, and you still need to live with each other once the disagreement has passed.
- Do not be manipulative. Using threats, aggression, and manipulation to get your way means that the conflict is not resolved. This means you will find yourself having the same argument you tried to weasel out of sooner or later.
- Do not lie. Even when you are afraid of the outcome, resist the urge to be dishonest or mislead your partner. Be open and truthful.
- Do not let your emotions get into you. Getting angry or defensive will get in the way of effective communication if you need to pause the discussion until you are calm enough to engage constructively.
- Do not use the past against your partner or to justify your actions. Deal with the current issue without trying to make assumptions based on past experiences.
- Do not agree just to agree. Express yourself clearly and avoid saying yes to please the other person. If you make a habit of getting along, you will constantly be discontent because you are trying to suppress your true feelings.

The Art of Compromise

Compromise doesn't mean giving in to the other person. It means that you understand you each have needs, and the best way to meet them is to meet each other halfway.

Compromise is the willingness to recognize and accommodate the other person's needs without necessarily sacrificing your own. If you are in a relationship and do not know how to compromise, your relationship will be littered with conflicts. Everybody likes to get their way, but when you have decided to share your life with someone, you need to be willing to recognize that your way is not the only way.

When you make compromises a part of how you deal with issues, you increase the trust and security in the relationship. Both partners know that even when they have different needs, you will find a way to accommodate each other. This builds harmony and enhances the emotional connection.

To compromise in your relationship, you must be adaptable and flexible. You have to see and understand the situation from the other person's point of view and change your mindset.

Increasing Empathy for Your Partner

One best way to know someone is to walk a mile in his shoes. This means being empathetic and finding it in yourself to see beyond your needs and emotions. It is about feeling with the other person and looking at things from his perspective.

You understand where they are coming from when you increase your empathy for your partner. This is crucial in managing conflicts in your relationship. When you are closed off to the other person, your entire focus is on your emotions, which hinders you from feeling what the other person is going through.

Empathy enhances compassion and strengthens the bond between two people. What can be better than feeling understood and having your feelings validated in a relationship? While empathy is a trait that most people learn in childhood, not everyone can effectively use it.

The following are some tips on how you can increase empathy for your partner.

Be Present

When you are preoccupied and absent-minded, you cannot pick up on what your partner is feeling. Learn to be actively engaged in your relationship as opposed to just going through the motions. Switch off your phone and other distractions when you are spending time with your partner. This helps you to be present now and enhances your understanding of each other.

Switch Roles

When you are having a challenging time understanding your partner's needs, try switching roles. You can even role play if that will make it easier for you. When you put yourself in someone else's shoes, you get an insight into what they are dealing with and what it is to be them. It is easy to be selfish when you have no idea what your partner is going through. Once you put yourself in his situation, you can get valuable insight into his emotions and needs.

Do Not Be Judgmental

Even when you do not agree with your partner, disagree respectfully. Refrain from being judgmental or critical. Remember, everyone has had experiences that have shaped the way they see things. Never assume that your point of view is superior. Everyone is entitled to their needs, and the least you can be is open-minded and accommodating.

Stop Assuming

It is easy to misunderstand others when we assume, we know how they feel or what they need. Ask questions and encourage your partner to express themselves openly so that you clearly understand what they need. Sometimes simply having a deep conversation with your partner can change how you look at them and enhance your ability to identify with what they are feeling. Like we said earlier, nothing beats effective communication in a relationship.

Go Beneath the Surface

Know as much as you can about your partner's past. This can help you to understand his emotional triggers. We cannot deny the fact that past experiences influence how we relate to each other. Share your past experiences to deepen your understanding of each other's tendencies and weaknesses.

Be Compassionate

Not everything your partner is feeling must make sense to you. Learn to be compassionate even when you do not understand them. Compassion is part of being human. Acknowledging the other person's fears and insecurities does not hurt you in any way.

HOW TO IMPROVE MY COMMUNICATION AND PROBLEM-SOLVING SKILLS

In relationships, problems, or disputes consist of any circumstance, incident, or experience that affects or matters to those concerned. Several factors lead to conflict; some of which include topics such as finances, children and in-laws, personal issues like self-esteem, beliefs, aspirations, or priorities, or related problems, for instance, the amount of time together versus time alone, support versus power, affection, and communication.

Although there are seemingly endless reasons for conflict, they generally surround all humans' underlying needs, including physical, intellectual, emotional, social, and spiritual. Most significantly, the result is always decided by how we approach and interact with those issues.

The happiest couples also experience conflicts and problems. It provides opportunities for growth in both personal and relationships if handled well. Many skills can support people seeking to settle disputes safely. Communicating effectively is one of the greatest skills which helps in conflict resolution.

Most people know that we need to communicate to resolve conflicts, but negative communication patterns can often lead to greater frustration and conflict escalation. Consider the following communication challenges:

Body Language/Voice Communication

The tone is more than the words we choose to use. We sometimes speak our body language and voice tone louder than our words. Shouting, "I'm not angry," for example, is not a very convincing message. If we send a conflicting message where our voice and body language tone is not in line with our message, misunderstandings, and anger sometimes follow.

To surmount this communication challenge, we need to be mindful of what signals our body language and voice tone will convey to others. Speak calmly, give eye contact, a smile if necessary, and maintain an open, relaxed posture.

Differences in Style

Each of us has a specific way to behave, often based on interactions with our families, history, gender, and several other factors. For example, with our partners, we can appear to be noisier, outgoing, or emotional. While there's no right or wrong style, our past experiences mostly lead to expectations that are not usually communicated verbally with others, causing relationship tension and misunderstanding. For instance, if we came from a large family that tended to shout for being heard, we might think it's normal to speak loudly. But if our partners came from a quieter family environment, they might be uncomfortable or even scared by an elevated tone of voice.

Discussing our experiences and perspectives will help explain ourselves and others' expectations and help our partner appreciate our point of view. Knowing these details will also help in the process of problem-solving.

Communication Roadblocks

The roadblocks of communication arise when two people communicate in such a way that none feels understood. Research has identified four especially negative communication styles, sometimes referred to as "the apocalypse's four horsemen," because those interaction styles gradually become lethal to relationships if left unchecked. Criticism, disdain, defensiveness, and stonewalling are such types.

Criticism Assails the Other's Character or Personality

While it is common to have concerns about the actions of others, it is very different from putting them down as an individual. For example, a complaint may be, "I felt worried when you didn't call me that you were going to be home late." Criticism can be articulated in the same context as, "You're so unconsidered; you never call me when you're going to be late." Criticism focuses on certain behaviors; it focuses negatively on the motives and character of the person.

Contempt portrays disgust and disrespect by body language, such as eye-rolling or sneering, or by name-calling, sarcasm, and cutting remarks to the other person.

Defensiveness is an often-natural response to criticism and disrespect by individuals, but it also escalates the dispute.

When we're defensive, we appear to avoid listening to the other's perspective and shut down contact.

Stonewalling withdraws from dialogue and declines to participate in the discussion.

It's the adult equivalent of the "silent treatment" that young kids use when upset. Without touch, dispute resolution is unlikely.

Additional Examples of Communication Roadblocks Include:

- Order ("Quit making complaints!")
- Warning ("If you do that, you will be sorry.")
- Counseling ("You shouldn't behave like that.")
- Recommending ("Wait a few years before you decide.")
- Reading ("If you do this now, you're not going to grow up to be a responsible adult.")
- Agreeing, only to maintain the peace ("I think you're right.")

Acknowledging these roadblocks and making attempts to communicate effectively will help individuals resolve roadblocks.

Tips to Resolve Conflict

Ease the Startup

One of the skills to resolve roadblocks in communication requires a soft start to the discussion by beginning with the constructive, showing gratitude, reflecting on problems one at a time, and taking responsibility for thoughts and feelings. Furthermore, beginning the message with "I" instead of "You" will reduce the defensiveness and encourage positive experiences with others while presenting the issue. For instance, "I want to stay more involved in making money decisions" instead of "you never include me in financial decisions."

Make and Receive Repair Tentative

Another critical ability in resolving roadblocks in contact is learning how to make and accept attempts at repair. Repair attempts are efforts to prevent an increasingly hostile experience by taking a break or trying to calm the situation. This is critical because we often experience extreme emotional and physical stress when disagreements occur, impairing our ability to think and reason, leading to roadblocks in communication. Taking time away from the dispute to calm down (at least 20 minutes) can help us be more prepared to discuss the problem.

Speech and Listening Skills Are Important

It takes good speaking and listening skills to resolve roadblocks in communication. There is a method of speaking-listening to help individuals communicate more effectively. Every partner takes turns to be the speaker and the listener.

The Speaker Rules Include

- Share thoughts, feelings, and concerns.
- Use the "I" statements when you speak to express your thoughts and feelings accurately.
- Keep statements short of ensuring information does not overwhelm the listener.
- Halt after each short statement so that the listener can paraphrase what has been said to ensure he understands or repeats back in his terms. If the paraphrase is not quite correct, reframe the statement gently again to help the listener understand.

The Listener's Rules Include

- Paraphrase what the orator says. If vague, request clarification. Proceed until the speaker correctly indicates the message has been received.
- Don't disagree or give an opinion on what the speaker is saying—wait until you're the speaker, and then do it with respect.
- The listener should not speak or interrupt the other, except for paraphrasing after the speaker.

In each position, the speaker and listener should take turns so that each has an opportunity to express their thoughts and feelings. One can still ask for a time-out. This activity aims not to solve a problem but rather to have a healthy and constructive discussion and consider each other's opinions. Understanding and validating others' thoughts and feelings while we may not always agree with the other's point of view can improve relationships and build on common ground, leading to more effective negotiation and problem-solving.

HOW TO RECOVER FROM EMOTIONAL ABUSE

Emotional abuse is deeply damaging, and without going through the healing process, you make yourself even more vulnerable to entering into the same type of relationship. You have been violated psychologically, and you will experience anxiety, depression, dissociation, feelings of low self-esteem, low self-worth, nightmares, and flashbacks. You must seek counseling to assist you in the healing process; however, you can implement strategies in your daily life that will help you move forward.

Yoga

The effects of trauma live in the body. Yoga is a physical activity and mindfulness that helps to establish and restore balance. Research has proven that yoga alleviates anxiety and depression, improves symptoms of post-traumatic stress disorder in victims of domestic violence, boosts self-esteem, and improves body image. It involves a series of powerful movements that compensate for the feelings of powerlessness that abused victims are left with.

Dr. Bessel Van der Kolk has spent years studying the benefits of yoga, and he believes that it allows traumatized victims to take back ownership of their bodies. Trauma robs abused victims of a sense of safety, and yoga helps them reconnect through the use of bodily sensations.

Meditation

Trauma disrupts the area in the brain responsible for memory, learning, emotion regulation, and planning. Research has found that meditation benefits the same areas of the brain that are affected by trauma, such as the hippocampus, the amygdala, and the prefrontal cortex. Meditation gives abused victims their psyche back. It heals the brain and allows them to respond to life from empowerment instead of a place of trauma.

Daily meditation practice strengthens the neural pathways in the brain and boosts grey matter density in areas related to the fight or flight response and emotion regulation. Meditation also allows you to become aware of your need to make contact with your abuser. When victims are not aware of this, they make impulsive decisions which usually leads to them returning to the relationship. It will make you aware of your emotions in general.

Anchor Yourself

In general, emotional abuse survivors have been gaslighted into believing that they imagined the abuse they were experiencing. It is essential that you start anchoring yourself into the reality that you were abused but no longer in that situation. It is common for abused victims to idealize a relationship and spend time thinking about what could have been if only they were capable of pleasing their partner. Connecting to reality also helps when struggling with mixed emotions towards your abuser. As mentioned, one of the strategies of the narcissist is to show affection and then withdraw it; it is the affectionate side of the narcissist that victims are drawn to. The narcissist seeks to erode his victim's reality, but once you are reconnected with your reality, you can see your abuser for who he truly is.

Work with Your Inner Child, Self-Soothing

You didn't just happen to fall into an abusive relationship, some deep-rooted issues within you bring you to this point in your life, and they typically stem from childhood. Through therapy, you will discover that some fundamental needs were not met during childhood. In attempting to fill that void, you settled for an abusive relationship. Once you discover what that void is, you must learn what is required to fill it so that you do not leave yourself vulnerable to enter into another abusive relationship.

During the healing process, you will need to be extremely compassionate with yourself because of what you went through as a child, and the abuse you have endured is not your fault. Abuse has the power to open up old wounds that were never healed. The belief system that you have never felt good enough has always been a part of your psyche. Your abusive partner confirmed how you have always felt. When you are healing, you must change the narrative that is taking place in your mind, which is important in general, but even more so when you are recovering from abuse. Self-compassion can be the most powerful form of compassion, so you must be gentle with yourself during this time.

Exercise

Whether going for long intensive walks, going for a jog, joining a dance class, or joining the gym, incorporating exercise into your daily routine will help during the healing process. If you don't have any motivation, don't try and do too much at once; for example, you can start by going for a ten-minute walk and then increase it as time goes on.

Exercise lowers cortisol levels and releases endorphins, which help replace the biochemical addiction you developed with your abuser with something that will benefit you. This addiction was formed through chemicals such as cortisol, dopamine, serotonin, and adrenaline, which strengthen the bond with your abuser and form the cycle of highs and lows. Exercise allows you to build a wall of strength and resilience after leaving an abuser. It also helps to eliminate many physical problems associated with the abuse, such as weight gain, sleep problems, premature aging, and a depleted immune system.

Put Unhealthy Coping Strategies to Bed

You did everything possible to try to keep your narcissistic partner happy and to keep him from flying into a fit of rage. Your days were spent walking on eggshells—you learned how to be silent and submissive, to question your every move, and to start all your conversations with the words "I'm sorry." You learned how to dodge bullets, avoid landmines, and act as if parts of your dreams, desires, and needs didn't exist.

You learned how to devalue yourself and accept treatment from another unacceptable human being. The anguish you had to go through to experience even a little bit of peace and keep yourself, and maybe your children, safe from harm was astounding. All these terrible things you had to learn were unhealthy, but in a normal relationship, they are not skills that will serve you well; therefore, you must learn new and normal habits that will benefit you in a healthy relationship. Unlearning old habits involves a system of self-monitoring; there are two types, qualitative and quantitative.

- **Qualitative Monitoring:** This involves being attentive to the old habits you are engaging in—what do they look like, and how do they make you feel?
- **Quantitative Monitoring:** This involves counting the old habits that don't serve you to monitor how often you engage in them throughout the day.

Although both types of self-monitoring are effective, quantitative monitoring is most beneficial because, for the first time, you can accurately measure how you are behaving and the triggers that cause these bad habits to resurface. You may have had a slight idea of how bad your problem was, but now you can see it as well as have something to measure your progress by.

Learn to Love Yourself

It is essential if you will move on with your life and eventually get into a healthy relationship. No one can come along and try to convince you that you are anything less than the best! When you develop a certain level of confidence and self-worth, nothing can shake you. Here are some tips on how to love yourself after an abusive relationship.

- **Get in Shape:** You feel good when you look good! We have already known the benefits of exercise, so looking good is simply a bonus. Make a decision not only to improve your health but to transform your body. Whatever your ideal weight and shape are, aim for that.
- **Change Your Wardrobe:** Once you have achieved your ideal body shape, treat yourself to new clothes.
- **Have Fun Alone:** Take one day out of the week and do something that you enjoy. A lot of abused victims have difficulty being alone, which is why they are such easy prey for abusers—spending time alone will teach you how to enjoy your own company. Things you could do might include going to the movies, out to dinner, or finding a new hobby.
- **Try Something New:** Do things that you wouldn't normally do. Try something new and crazy like skydiving or bungee jumping. That's a bit extreme, but you know yourself better than anyone else, so you can

choose something that you know will add an element of surprise to your life.

- **Go on Vacation:** Even if you don't make it a regular activity, take a vacation somewhere. Go to a country that's completely out of your comfort zone. If you are not brave enough to go alone, invite a friend. Experience a different culture, new food, different activities, and have fun.

- **Journal:** Writing is one way to release any negative emotions you are feeling. It is also a good way of tracking your progress. When you come out of an abusive relationship, you will have more bad days than good ones. There will be better than others; however, after some time, you will notice that your emotions will begin to stabilize.

- **Learn to Say No:** Being submissive is a survival mechanism for women in abusive relationships. You would never dare say no to your partner in fear of what might happen. However, now that you are not in an abusive relationship, you mustn't carry this submissive nature into your friendships or feel as if you need to say yes to everyone to please them.

- **Celebrate Accomplishments:** No matter how small you think the accomplishment is, celebrate it. Going through a whole day without thinking about your ex is an accomplishment, as well as being consistent with your daily exercise routine. Pay attention to these points and treat yourself for them.

- **Challenge Yourself:** Is there anything you have always wanted to do, but you have never gotten around to doing it? Make a list of these activities and start doing them. You may have always wanted to compete in a triathlon or to get some additional qualifications. Decide that whatever you put your mind to, you are going to achieve.

- **Learn to Trust Yourself:** Before you got into an abusive relationship, your instincts told you that something wasn't right, but you chose to ignore them and pursue the relationship hoping that things would get better. Familiarize yourself with that feeling because sometimes something isn't right, that is how you will feel, and this isn't just about relationships. It's in all areas of your life.

HOW TO OVERCOME A TOXIC RELATIONSHIP, DEAL WITH AN ABUSIVE EX, AND GET RID OF THE CONTROLLING SOCIOPATH

Toxic relationships let out the worst in you because the other person knows exactly what buttons to push to get you to toe the line. You will find yourself often doing things you would never consider just to keep the other person happy. This dysfunction, if left unchecked, becomes a self-repeating cycle that takes over your life.

It poisons you from the inside out. In extreme cases, they may even drive you to coping mechanisms such as addictions to help you process your unresolved issues. This potential for self-harm is one reason why freeing yourself from codependency requires that you eliminate any toxic relationships from your life.

Whether you are dealing with a narcissist who thrives on attention and being the center of the universe or with more covert manipulators, the damage to your self-esteem is hard to repair. Toxic people will come in many different shapes and forms, and you need to identify them by their characteristics. You need to be aware of some warning signs to identify toxic people and weed them out:

- They like to control you.
- They like to shift blame and never take responsibility for their actions.
- They are overly critical and always trying to find fault.
- They use threats and intimidation to manipulate you.
- They try to gain sympathy by playing.
- They are always complaining.
- They often use emotional abuse to make you feel worthless.

Perhaps the most toxic relationship for a codependent is one with a narcissist. They have no consideration or interest in other people's feelings or needs. The narcissist is the polar opposite of the codependent when it comes to compassion and empathy.

The following are basic signs that point to a narcissistic personality:

- They lack empathy and never try to meet your needs.
- They manipulate you to get what they want.
- They await you to cater to their every need and whim without question.
- They demand to have the best of everything.
- They are continually making you feel inferior.
- They have a compulsive need to be the center of attention.

Tips for Freeing Yourself from Toxic Relationships

Build Boundaries

Identify your limits and do not compromise on your boundaries. Be very clear on what is and isn't acceptable. Always be ready to enforce the consequence of the other person crossing your boundaries. This means you should be ready to permanently cut off ties with this person if they are unwilling to change.

Stop Taking Responsibility for Other People's Problems.

The only person whose happiness you are responsible for is you. Stop trying to fix other people's problems. Never feel obligated to rescue or support someone unwilling to take responsibility for his actions.

By trying to fix the other person's problems, you become an enabler and promote dysfunction and codependence in the relationship. People tend to be more conscientious when knowing they will be responsible for the consequences of their actions.

Discover Your Triggers

Identify the triggers that make you vulnerable to manipulation. Whether you have unresolved issues with guilt, blame, or shame, know your triggers. Be vigilant around anyone trying to use these triggers against you. For instance, someone trying to force you into doing something you do not want might exploit your guilt issues.

Build Your Emotional Intelligence

Emotional intelligence enables you to manage your responses effectively. It allows you to stop being reactive to other people and have more control over your behavior and feelings.

This also increases your social awareness and the ability to recognize other people's motives. It will be easier to see manipulators and energy vampires and give them a wide berth.

Find Safety and Security in Yourself

When you are secure in yourself, you no longer feel the need to be validated or approved by others. This leaves you free to make decisions based on your needs. Freedom from the need for validation also means that you no longer have to please others to feel loved or accepted. This frees you up to be true to yourself without fretting about other people's opinions.

Surround Yourself with Positive People

When you build healthy relationships, you will be less likely to get back into a dysfunctional one. Focus on making new emotional connections with people who share your values. A good relationship will help you get over a bad one that much faster. It will also give you a chance to experience what a good companion should be.

PROTECTING YOURSELF DURING A DIVORCE FROM SOMEONE WITH BORDERLINE OR NARCISSISTIC PERSONALITY DISORDER

No divorce in the world is easy; however, divorcing a narcissist can be a terrifying time. You may be worried about the safety and well-being of not only yourself but also your children. If you have decided to divorce your narcissistic spouse, you need to know some things. This will lead you to the process of divorce and what you should expect. You will need to find help and create a good defense. We will also know how to deal with a narcissist in court as it is not as cut and dry as other divorce situations.

After realizing that they are married to a narcissist, many people find that divorcing is the best they can do for their overall safety and well-being. Making the decision may be difficult, but it is often the best choice for themselves, as well as their children. It takes bravery and knowledge to venture down the road of divorcing a narcissist.

A variety of stressors surround a "normal" divorce. People worry about the financial aspect and the difficulty and pain it causes to everyone involved. Many couples won't ever have to go to court, and they can work it out through mediation and other techniques. When fighting with a divorce from a narcissist, situations are more complicated, and you can almost guarantee a judge will end up being involved.

Divorcing a narcissist can become a real mess. People usually work together to stay out of court and find alternatives to the tribulations that divorce can entail. When dealing with a narcissist, they will do their best to make things as dirty as possible.

While no one wins in a divorce, the narcissist will strive to feel like they have won. More often than not, when handling divorce, people hope for things to be split down the middle. It includes assets and responsibilities. The narcissist is not going to see it this way at all. They are excellent at playing the victim and will have no intention of meeting you in the middle. They will not take the route of mediation or negotiation.

The narcissist's goal will be to be the one seen as being always right. The truth of a narcissist is anything but truthful.

They will do all means to make themselves look good and sway everyone's opinion, including a judge, to see things from their point of view, even if it is tragically skewed.

The narcissist is also a master game player. They will likely up their game because they are genuinely after a win. They love to hold power, and they do this by keeping other people off-balance. Unfortunately, narcissists tend to be charismatic and charming. It can win favor with a judge or other people involved in your divorce. They will do whatever it takes to wear you down or win the favor of the ones that are making decisions. It makes them dangerous to deal with, especially when kids are involved.

One of the worst actions you can do when dealing with a divorce from a narcissist is to say, "I give up." It is precisely what the narcissist wants. They will ensure this to make it happen. It not only gives them the win but also enables them to feel good about besting you.

They will use this to their advantage with their "friends" and other people to continue making you look bad and making them look like the victim. Stay strong.

You will likely end up in court when divorcing a narcissist as they will refuse to talk on reasonable terms.

One of the reasons why narcissists prefer court is that it helps them avoid accountability. When a judge decides, the narcissist is more comfortable as they don't have any responsibility for turning out. Narcissists don't want to be accountable, so the court system can be blamed rather than whether they win or lose. They also find some illusion of control in putting the decision into the hands of the court.

Planning and Creating a Secret Account to Fight in Court Against a Narcissist

When dealing with a narcissist, you always want to be proactive. When you are reactive, you are giving them exactly what they want.

You will certainly want to talk about some points with your attorney. You should likely also get a therapist involved. When you have been in a relationship with a narcissist, it takes a psychological toll, so does divorce. The two together can break a person apart, so enlisting a therapist is simply a smart decision. It can help you keep your feelings steady and allow you to be productive while working through this challenging journey.

Consulting with a professional can be helpful in many ways. It shows that you are working hard to do your best, and they will be able to give you an unbiased opinion on many points. Remember, you should not be looking for legal advice from your therapist; that is what your lawyer is for. When looking for professional support, finding someone specializing in PTSD and narcissistic traits or narcissistic personality disorder will be your best avenue.

Take your time and do your research. Find a lawyer who will handle the extra difficulties that come with dealing with a narcissist. You may have to talk to several attorneys before finding the right one, staying patient, and not being afraid to ask questions. Eventually, you will find the perfect fit to ensure you use the strategies needed to handle a narcissist.

You will also need to take the time to be psychologically prepared. To do this, learn everything you can about narcissism. Learn how to recognize the traits and find the ability to prove that your partner is indeed suffering from a narcissistic personality disorder. You should also seek out a therapist, counselor, or psychologist.

As noted, finding one specializing in narcissistic traits and narcissistic personality disorder will be the most advantageous. If they are also familiar with PTSD, you have found yourself a winner in terms of psychological help. Several damages can be done to the partner of a narcissist, and the support of a professional can get you on the appropriate path toward healing and recovering from the abuse you have endured. They can also keep you focused on what is essential.

How a Specialist Divorce Attorney Can Help You

One thing you need to do when dealing with a narcissist is to let your attorney know. As stated, narcissists tend to present themselves very well, easily fooling someone who does not know them. They are talented at pulling the wool over the general public's eye.

By letting your lawyer in on who your ex is, you can both be better prepared with how to deal with them.

Even though few narcissists will show their true nature while working through divorce proceedings, they will just likely keep their masks on. When you offer your lawyer the narcissist patterns and how you have dealt with them, it can explain how to deal with him. It leads us to a perfect point when looking for an attorney; it may be best to ask them right upfront if they have ever dealt with a narcissist. If they have not, you should probably keep looking. When you are in such an unsafe position, making sure the people fighting for you are well-versed in your problems is the best course of action.

Collect Evidence for the Defense in Court

Keeping good records will also work in your favor. From simple conversations with your narcissistic partner to a list of expenditures, all information is useful. When a narcissist starts to play games with the words said, you want to prove them wrong. Being organized and keeping the storyline straight and accurate is a significant bonus to your side. This evidence can help show the true nature of your soon-to-be-ex and discredit the ridiculous strategies they try and get others to believe.

Maintaining control over your emotions will also be a critical element to your success. The narcissist will try to get you angry to act out, which helps give them more power. Do not allow this to happen. They are doing this on purpose to try and gain power and control. Do your best to minimize communication as this will leave less opportunity for you to lose your cool. Remember to just talk about your spouse to a minimum. It is true when it comes to speaking in front of your children or other people that also hang out with your soon-to-be-ex. The things you are saying may open up a door to the narcissist. From there, they will do everything they can to use your words against you.

The narcissist will likely try and use his children as pawns. They will try and gain the upper hand in all things through them. It is likely they will even try to turn their children against the other parent. Please do not participate in the same behaviors, and your children will quickly see that you are a trustworthy parent and genuinely care about them. They will also eventually see that the narcissistic parent is merely trying to manipulate them. It can be a hard situation to face, and you must, above everything else, stay patient and resist the urge to badmouth the narcissist.

No matter how ready you are, there is likely going to be damaged and fallout. It is true of regular divorces, so it is even more real when dealing with a narcissist divorce.

You will be facing high levels of stress, and it will be a test of your endurance. When children are added to this mix, it only makes it more challenging. Know that it is not impossible; you need to be prepared. Take the time to prepare truly. Take notes of what has transpired throughout your relationship and be prepared to talk about all of the horrible things that have occurred. Note the help of your friends and family so that you have the emotional support that you need.

TIPS ON WHEN YOU PERCEIVE THE PROBLEM AND WHEN YOUR CHILD DOES

Many parental separations occur when children are small and emotionally unable to understand what is happening. It can be a scary experience for your children who are just learning to express their feelings. There are helpful ways to communicate simply so that your children will understand.

Explain the separation in easy-to-understand terms: "mommy and daddy need to live apart for a while" or "mommy/daddy will be moving away for a bit." If they ask why to explain in simple terms: "sometimes we fight, and we need to spend time away so that we can get along better" or "we need to live separately to be a better mom and dad to you."

Let children know that the decision to separate, and divorce, is about the parents and has nothing to do with them. Make it explicitly clear that they have no fault or reason for the split. One of the most painful effects that separations have on children is when they fear they are the reason. A narcissistic parent will make them feel this way at some point, either by blaming the child or the other parent. Keep explaining that they are not to blame and make a point of reminding them as often as needed.

Provide space for your children and allow them to express themselves. It is essential for them to feel safe in venting or showing their emotions, as holding it in will only cause them more grief later. If they feel angry and vocalize this to you, validate it for them. Let them know that they have a right to feel this and other emotions.

There is an instinct as a parent that wanted to protect our kids from harm, including emotional hurt and abuse. When a parent reveals his true narcissistic form, it can be difficult to shield children from them, even following a divorce where they are expected to visit the other parent or live with them as part of a custody agreement. When your children are in your care, exercise as much care and kindness as possible. Show your unwavering support for them in all they do and make sure they feel comfortable talking to you. They may want to express frustration about the other parent and explain the pain they feel, though maybe resisting because they fear you may tell the other parent, or their statements may reach them somehow. For this reason, reassure the kids that anything they divulge is safe with you and that they have no reason to fear any backlash or retaliation at the hands of the other parent. While it may seem easy to convince them, children worry when they don't understand how a process works.

What happens once the separation becomes permanent, and the divorce proceedings begin? Children will need more of an explanation at this point, including what to expect next. Even when kids understand what is going on, they may not comprehend life outside of what they are used to if they (and you) viewed the separation as a temporary circumstance. A simple explanation could suffice; however, more information is needed when there will be a significant change in the way the kids attend school, live, and interact with family and friends. It's important to "fast-forward" to possible results of the divorce so that they know what to expect and to prepare for it.

Where are we going to live? In the early part of the separation, temporary arrangements are made. Usually, one parent will leave the household and live separately for a period, during which both will decide if there is a chance of reconciliation. While the family home remains occupied, change is minimal, and no major upheaval is needed, such as a change in school or living arrangements. The parent who lives apart may agree to pick up the children according to a temporary arrangement or find a way to meet with the other parent for access and visitation provisions.

What if one of the parents is abusive? In severe cases, you might be the leaving parent. If you've encountered abuse at the hands of your spouse or have reason to believe they are abusing the children, this can lead to a quick decision, such as seeking refuge with family or friends, or living in a temporary shelter or living situation, until permanent housing can be found. Children may already understand what is happening, though it can be a frightening experience, especially when they are not in a stable home and may have to move more than once following the split. During this time, it's important to stress to your children that the reason for the separation is their safety and well-being. Make it clear that their safety and health are a priority, above all others. It is also essential to impress upon them that moving is temporary and that soon they will have a new home and feel better again. Keep hope and positivity alive as much as possible, even when you don't feel it yourself. Let the kids know that it is not easy for you and them but everything will get better in the end by working together.

Stay in contact with friends, family, and arrangements where a transfer in school is necessary. This can be a difficult realization for your children, as they will lose contact with friends at school and family and friends who live nearby. When you have to move, it's important to make arrangements in advance to stay in touch with the people they love, even if it's through online social media and arranging visits now and again. Make a point of calling them regularly and video-calling in real-time to keep your kids connected to the people they will miss once they move. This is an invaluable way for your children to see that you care about their connections with family and friends by keeping the communications open and continuous. This will also help them understand the importance of bonding and caring for others, which is not something their narcissistic parent will teach them.

It is essential to understand that while every child and situation is unique, most children will need comfort and understanding to feel valued and wanted. This is especially a must when the other parent is a narcissist and tries to manipulate the kids into a state of codependence. They will attempt to make children feel incapable of doing anything on their own, and they must rely on the opinion and direction of the toxic parent for all their decisions. This can be done in subtle, minor ways, by criticizing or making them feel incompetent or their opinions unworthy. Comments like "don't be silly/stupid," "you won't make it on your own," and "you are not capable" are just examples of how a toxic parent can make your child's life miserable and cause him to hurt. It will significantly impact his confidence and ability to feel capable of accomplishing goals on his own.

There are ways to build a protective barrier with your child to help them cope with a narcissistic parent. The following examples are ways in which you can foster a strong bond with your children while combatting the negative behavior of your ex and its effect on them:

- Praise them for hard work and encourage them to work towards goals. When they fail or fall short of achievements, reassure them of capabilities and give them as much time and effort as possible to accomplish them. Even where they need assistance, assure them that they can do it on their own.
- Show empathy and explain it to them. Demonstrate the importance of caring for others by inviting them to volunteer and listen to other people's thoughts and feelings. Prioritize to help them understand the value of feeling empathy for other people and how to gauge their responses when handling delicate situations. A narcissist

parent will not provide any guidance on empathy, as they are incapable of it.

- One meaningful gift you can provide to your children is unconditional love. This is defined as a love that prevails above all else, regardless of your kid's decisions and how they live. It is not an easy road for those who co-parent with narcissist ex-spouses, as some children will grow to exhibit signs of narcissism of their own. This can lead to another level of difficulty and conflict. Despite this, you can continue to show love, even if you don't agree with your children's behavior or how they handle situations. You can constantly reassure them that you love and support them while disapproving actions. It can be a challenging yet rewarding way to communicate with your children in the long term, as they will always know that you are there for them.

- Change is inevitable during a divorce or separation; whether it involves major overhauls or smaller modifications, it's going to impact your children in many ways. Being a supportive, stable parent will help children anchor their lives throughout childhood, as they progress into adulthood. While the ex-spouse connection will be volatile, it's going to be easier for them to cope with you by their side.

HOW TO HANDLE YOUR EX WHEN HE DENIES YOU ACCESS, INSULTS YOU IN FRONT OF YOUR CHILDREN, OR DOES ANY FAMILY WRONG. TIPS ON HOW TO DEAL WITH AN EX WHO SIMPLY DOESN'T PLAY BY THE RULES

There are several reasons why victims might want to maintain a Low-Contact relationship with a narcissistic abuser. However, suppose a relationship with a narcissist makes you feel that your health, sanity, or safety are under threat. In that case, there is usually only one sensible path to take and move forward, which is to cut them off entirely.

You must set boundaries for yourself and hold yourself accountable for enforcing consequences when a narcissist refuses to recognize or respect them. Never get into the practice of making hollow threats; if you tell a narcissist that your departure is a possible repercussion of a certain behavior, then you must be prepared to leave when they try to test your resolve.

You cannot force a narcissist to respect your boundaries or treat you the way you deserve to be appreciated. Therefore, you are responsible for respecting your boundaries, setting an example for others, and treating yourself well. If nothing but abuse is being served, your best option is to leave the table and show the abuser that you can cook up something far better for yourself.

Going No-Contact

Going No-Contact is not a tactic, strategy, or mind game, though a narcissist may retaliate by accusing you of harboring these intentions when you employ it. The end goal is not to encourage the narcissist to turn around and chase after you. The end goal is to prevent any further opportunities for abuse, period. Once and for all. When you decide to go No-Contact, you must embrace the notion that this is a non-negotiable state, with no grey area and no more second chances.

That being said, you mustn't expect it to be easy, nor beat yourself up if you find it difficult to maintain zero contact with someone you love, admire, or rely upon. This is challenging for most victims; you would not be the only one to go back on the decision. Experts estimate that victims of narcissistic abuse usually rack up several failed attempts at establishing a boundary of No-Contact before they can successfully maintain it. Seven failed attempts are average; for some people, the cycle lasts much longer.

You may feel the urge to announce your decision to the narcissist or ask them to respect your wishes and stop

141

contacting you. This is understandable, but unfortunately, not likely to work as intended. Narcissists often see all forms of contact as a foot-in-the-door; they may interpret your declaration as a thinly veiled invitation to pursue you further or make an over-the-top gesture to get back in your good graces. By contrast, the most effective way to go No-Contact is to disappear and stay gone. Block the narcissist's phone number and email address; stop following them on social media; not invite yourself from gatherings or institutions where you might run into them by chance. Take power into your own hands, and don't give the narcissist any opportunity to try and steal it back from you.

Remind yourself that you have reached this point because you've already given the narcissist far more than enough chances. Ask yourself: "Is there really anything this person could do to convince me that they've changed, and this won't happen again?" The answer, most likely, is no. You don't owe the narcissist another chance or an explanation. You owe it to yourself to be set free.

Protecting Yourself and Maintaining Resolve

Set yourself up for success by informing your support system first—ideally shortly before or after cutting the narcissist off. Choose people that you feel are trustworthy, meaning no potential members of the narcissist's harem. It's important to be brutally honest with yourself about the characters and values of the people in your life when you do this; if they are susceptible to seduction by the narcissist, eager to advance in the same career field, envious of the narcissist's trophies and wealth, or just similarly shallow in value structure, they may be better suited to the harem than to your support system, and they'll be reluctant to see what you are trying to show them. The people you choose to share this with will not only be able to hold you accountable to your declaration; they also may be called upon to protect you from the narcissist's future attempts to discredit, devalue, or hoover you back in. Choose them wisely.

Next, get to few mutual acquaintances you know these people will be curious about the split. It's best to get to them before the narcissist has a chance to spin his side of the story, but you also want to appear calm and unhurried, so don't trouble yourself to rush this step. What you should tell these people is a detail-free, bare-bones version of the story--no blaming either party or requesting pity, just a statement that things didn't work out. Afterward, you'll go on to explain that you've decided not to be in contact with the narcissist (whom you should reference by his name, not the term "narcissist") anymore and that you'd appreciate his support of your decision. You can even further clarify that they can show this support by not passing messages between either of you, not putting you in a room together without warning, not trying to encourage reconciliation, and so on.

This may certainly arouse their curiosity, but no further divulgement of information is needed for them to respect your stated boundaries. If any of these people are unable to respect these reasonable requests, you have discovered in them a flying monkey who cannot be trusted. Let them go, along with the narcissist; these people were never really on your side.

How to Handle Smear Campaigns

When a narcissist tries to retaliate by spreading lies about you, his ultimate goal isn't just to change other people's opinions of you; they are also aiming to throw you off-balance.

As difficult as it may be to embrace this reality during a vicious attack on your character, the best way to respond to a smear campaign is not to respond at all. Narcissists are masters at this game, and you probably are not their first target; they may have set things up purposefully in such a way that any reasonable emotional reaction from you will only serve to prove their point. Furthermore, people tend to disbelieve victims who are frantic, furious, or panicked, thinking that those who make a spectacle of themselves are much more likely to be liars than those who appear calm (and the narcissist will appear quite calm, in comparison to your reaction).

Do not engage in arguments with flying monkeys or harem members. Recognize that anyone who buys into the smear campaign is a lost cause and can never be fully persuaded to be on your side or believe you. You're probably better off without them.

It might feel shameful to walk away from this situation without trying to stand up for yourself but you need to have faith that the truth will prevail if you leave it alone. The more you engage, the more energy you are giving to the narcissist. Instead, use that energy to build new and better relationships or invest in your self-care routine.

How to Respond to Harassment

While it's best to ignore smear campaigns, forms of harassment that pose a viable threat to your safety are another story altogether. Timestamps, photographs, and messages sent to members of your support system may come in very handy if you decide to file a legal complaint. Don't try to be a hero and impress other people with your independence and self-sufficiency; you need witnesses and support.

Though it may be tempting to retaliate, seek vengeance, or try to scare them off, do everything in your power to resist this urge. Narcissistic abusers are extremely likely to flip the script and accuse you of abuse, pressing charges even if your reaction is minor compared to their behavior. Understand that this harassment is a baited trap set just for you. The awful thing you can do is walk right into it.

If you cannot involve law enforcement, for whatever reason, realize that there are other ways to back yourself up with institutional power. Allow your family and friends to know that they should never reveal your location or details of your personal life to this abuser and agree upon a code word to use with them if the situation ever becomes dangerous and you need immediate assistance. If possible, try not to get too emotional or cry when making your case to outside parties. As unfair as it may seem, people in your workplace may not take your claims seriously if the report appears dramatic or if you seem wishy-washy about the state of this relationship. Make it clear that you want to prevent this person from even interfering with your work again, and that you would like to have his support in maintaining your privacy. If your dedication to the job is made plain, there is a better chance that you'll get the support and protection you need in that environment.

If you feel that your safety is being threatened or stalking and harassment behaviors have continued to escalate despite your best efforts to deter them, please consider contacting the police and pressing charges. It may help to remind yourself that you are not the only person in danger here; the narcissist is liable to attack other people who interfere in his quest to control you. Call for law enforcement is the best way to keep yourself and your loved ones protected.

WAYS TO BUILD RESILIENCE IN CHILDREN WHEN CO-PARENTING WITH A NARCISSISTIC EX

Co-parenting with a narcissist can be an especially difficult endeavor but knowing how to build resilience in children is essential if they're going to survive and thrive while still keeping their sanity.

Children and narcissists are often thought of as "soul mates" or, at the very least, his mirror image. They have all of the same characteristics, and in many cases, those who've co-parented with a narcissist have found themselves constantly identifying with them. Naturally, survival instincts kick in, which leads them to want to "fix" the narcissist before he can do any further damage to his children.

Unfortunately, this dynamic is often an ill-conceived one. While you may feel that you can't survive without the narcissist in your life, it's important to remember that if you do choose to stay with them, the children are going to be expected to endure as well.

Children Build Resilience by Finding Their Way

Resilience comes from within and is based on a child's will. There are no shortcuts, only a willingness to recognize the truth and to pursue that truth with all of his heart.

Once you've recognized the truth, you must begin by gaining knowledge about narcissism and narcissistic abuse. You can't fix someone else unless you understand how they think and why they behave the way they do.

Many people who've co-parented with a narcissist have been able to let go of desires to fix their ex, once they truly understand how deeply hurtful and malicious they can be. They've also learned that they can never control anyone else.

The Golden Rule applies especially well to narcissists because they always do unto others as they would have done unto them. You must realize that what you're about to endure is coming directly from the narcissist's heart. You must expect the unexpected and then let it go. Otherwise, you will find you are engorging yourself with hate and shame.

Those who have managed to survive (and even thrive) after co-parenting with a narcissist are those who've learned to forgive themselves for not being able to change them while also forgiving them for having done what they've done.

You can never completely rid yourself of pain or the desire to seek revenge, but you can learn to get a clean break from the narcissist and do what's best for your children.

Children Build Resilience by Internalizing and Releasing Their Power

There is no particular thing as achieving perfection, only a willingness to evolve and adapt constantly. Don't be afraid to change your mind.

Don't let the narcissist have power over you anymore by giving them ground or giving into them through self-criticism. As they say, "Confidence is never a substitute for competence." Empower yourself by trusting your instincts and being persistent. If you don't succeed at first, keep trying until you figure it out. Build resilience by using adversity as fuel for change and growth.

When narcissists feel threatened or "outraged," they can become incredibly vicious and vitriolic. Don't let them steal your joy.

Children Build Resilience by Forgiving Others, Their Parents and Themselves

Children who've survived while being co-parented by a narcissist are those who've allowed themselves to be loved even when it didn't make sense to them, and they know what love is now. They've learned to rely on their guts and make decisions based on what truly matters to them. They know how to be show their feelings, and they know that their growth is far more important than any conflict derived from a narcissist's actions.

While it's unlikely that you'll ever achieve true peace with a narcissist, knowing how to build resilience in children will help them cope better, even if they've never come face-to-face with one themselves.

The Only Thing a Narcissist Fear Is a Child Who Has Built a Resilient Foundation

Easing your son or daughter into the process with physical coping strategies like drawing, coloring, or reading can be a good start.

Resilience building may seem overwhelming and even impossible but remember that you're not alone. You have many resources at your disposal.

The National Domestic Violence Hotline welcomes calls from anyone in an abusive relationship and provides a plethora of resources for those in need.

You can also reach out to the narcissist's family members if you think they might be willing and able to help you.

While it's impossible to reform anyone else, you can change your perspective on his behavior by learning how to build resilience in children. Remember that you don't have to feel powerless or hopeless.

HOW TO SOLVE REAL PROBLEMS AND COMMUNICATION TRICKS FOR DEALING WITH AN EX WHO ACTIVELY UNDERMINES YOUR ROUTINE, DISCIPLINE, VALUES, OR DOMESTIC TRANQUILITY

We will explore how to manage an ex that still shows up in your life. How do you get through to them and communicate with them? How do you deal with a divorce or separation going on that has the potential to ruin your routine, values, and domestic tranquility? In addition, we will also learn some communication tips for dealing with difficult people.

The struggle is real for most of us in love relationships. The pain of separation and the confusion of pursuing or even maintaining the union is complicated by stress, drama, and relational baggage. Stress levels can rise above normal due to uncertainty, anxiety, over-thinking, etc.

It is challenging to remain calm and focused when dealing with the stress of the breakup. This is because of the intense emotions involved in a divorce, separation, or ending a long-term relationship. Of course, this creates additional stress and confusion in dealing with how to cope with your ex. These exes are often very close to you emotionally yet can also be very confused about the situation. Often, they don't know what they want now or what they want at all.

Most people don't like the idea of being told what to do, but if enough communication can be established with the ex, you can find a path forward; and this is very important to feel confident and maintain your sanity. Many tools can be used to communicate well with an ex.

Dealing with an ex, especially when they are contacting you a lot, can be very difficult in these challenging times. Managing the process can be extremely hard if both parties don't have the money for lawyers or amicable resolutions. It is possible to solve the most complex issues and personal cases without raising your family in arms.

Communication Tools

Consider what you want to discuss with your ex. Are you trying to get basic information, make plans, or find out more about the reasoning behind the breakup? Communication tips are very important to determine what you need from them and formulate a plan to meet your needs.

Consider writing or sending an email. However, do you want to have a conversation with your ex? Consider the time of day because some people cannot have phone conversations due to work, family issues, etc. Therefore, texting or emailing is better to start.

In addition, you can consider writing a letter by hand. This can be extremely personal and private, but keep in mind that it isn't secure like a digital message. Think about how you feel and what you want to say. Don't send it via email or text messaging because others could see it or could be forwarded to the other party without your permission.

The question of whether it is better to meet your ex for lunch or just text or call is a very common one. This question can be confusing because many people do not know the best way to communicate with an ex, so they err on the side of caution and want to stay away from their ex. However, other relationships require frequent interaction, and this may not be possible in cases like this. If you're going to see your ex and to talk, then meet them for lunch. If you don't want to meet them, then just text or call.

Some basic rules will help you communicate effectively with an ex and avoid conflict and confrontation. These rules are very simple but effective in dealing with difficult an ex:

- Don't always accept calls or messages right away. It is best to let him know that you will send an email or message. This will save you both times, and it will give him a hint that you don't need to deal with the situation.

- Don't let them ruin your life. Tell them to back off and leave you alone unless there is an emergency or problem. This is what they want but being responsive to their concerns can lead to a big problem.
- Be patient and collected because communication can be difficult when dealing with an ex. Always use good manners and think about what you are going to say before responding.
- Never let your frustrations defeat you. This will only derail your communication and lead to significant conflict that can spoil your ex's visit or interaction with you.
- Always be very polite in your communication. Even though you are angry, try to write your message or email in a very friendly tone. This will allow the other party to know that you care enough about them to communicate correctly and effectively.

After you have decided that divorce is the best option for you, it is time to move forward and start planning for the future. The process of getting a divorce, drafting a separation agreement, and deciding on how to manage the finances are all critical issues that need to be settled quickly.

In this situation, you have to keep your emotions in check because you don't want to make any hasty decisions or cause any financial harm. Making sure you think through every aspect of your upcoming divorce is crucial to moving forward with your life.

Consider the future you want to live in now. Do you want to be a single parent, or would you prefer to share custody with your ex? This is an important aspect of the divorce and needs to be planned out before discussing it with the other. The reason for this is apparent; everyone's life changes after divorce. Therefore, the details of your life will change, and disagreements could occur if these details are not worked out first.

In addition, make sure that you are open-minded when it comes to parenting decisions. Consider if the kids would benefit from joint custody or even a shared custody arrangement. Both of these arrangements have pros and cons and will affect everyone involved. However, taking time to think through all of the potential options is essential.

Additionally, it is not always easy to know what your ex will agree with, so be sure that you work together towards a mutually agreeable resolution. If you decide to go back to court, consider this process as well, as there are different laws concerning child support and other financial arrangements.

Divorce is also about dealing with the financial aspects of your separation. The first step is to get an attorney that can help you with this process. Make sure that you and your attorney come up with a strategy for both getting through this part of the process and possible objections. This will give you the best chance at getting what you are seeking from the divorce settlement.

If you find it challenging to communicate with your ex, consider hiring a mediator or consultant who can talk with both parties without conflict. This will allow for the conversation to be productive and not hurtful. An intermediary will speak directly with your ex and help maintain a healthy and productive dialogue.

WHAT TO DO WHEN YOUR EX-SPOUSE TRIES TO TURN THE KIDS AGAINST YOU

There has been a great debate over the claim that parental alienation is a phenomenon that rises to the level of a psycho-emotional syndrome. The parent is then perceived to have malicious intent or serious psycho-emotional pathology.

In parental alienation, one parent works out of neediness or rage to prevent the kids from having a fine relationship with the other parent.

However, as in all human conflict, it takes two to tango.

Is one parent, suffering at the hands of the alienating parent, equally responsible for his predicament? No.

Are they unconsciously contributing to the problem and playing into the toxic parent's hands? Likely, yes.

The Court Provides a Framework

Take note that the family court does not have a case management function. That is, once you are done with your basic order, you are expected to make it work—despite the complications of family schedules and parenting children in general. At best, the court can only provide the parents with a framework or foundation to construct the ongoing co-parenting relationship. It's up to both mother and father to fill in the numerous blanks that occur in raising kids.

This means the court does not monitor or amend the custody orders as situations on the ground change from day to day. Judges deal with discrete issues that are brought before them. These include:

- Formal filing of a motion to create a custody label (legal and physical custody.)
- Custody timeshare orders (percentage of time in each parent's care.)
- Modifying existing orders.

If a parent fails to live up to the letter or intent of the orders, returning to court via the filing of a new motion is your ultimate recourse.

What Parental Alienation Looks Like

Here's a rough sketch of how parental alienation plays out. A needy, envious, or angry parent creates a "special" bond with the children. This is usually characterized by a peer-type relationship with the kids.

The alienating parent creates a dynamic in which the kids become overly dependent on the parent by treating them as if they are still babies that need care only this parent can provide. At the same time, they treat the kids as peers making them feel entitled to do whatever they want, especially at the other parent's home.

A child will then want to be in the care of the "nurturing" (alienating) parent while simultaneously talking to his other parent as if they were equals.

When the disrespected parent responds with anger or discipline, the children run to the alienating parent, claiming to be treated harshly. The targeted parent feels they are being perceived and treated by the kids the same way by the alienating parent. It's true. The kids will indeed disrespect and devalue the mother or father in the identical way the alienating parent does.

In a healthy post-separation dynamic, a parent, presented with reports of harsh treatment by the kids, will communicate with their co-parent, then, if appropriate, support the co-parent's response to the acting out behaviors. This scenario is quite different in the case of the alienating parent. They will concur with the kids that the other parent is mean and doesn't understand them. They are allowed, even encouraged, to stand up to the other mother/father as their equal.

Compounding this situation, the alienating parent has shown the kids that his undivided loyalty is required to maintain their "special" relationship. This is communicated by subtle nonverbal cues that the kids recognize. They are not told in so many words. The children know it by seeing how the parent responds to anyone that the parent dislikes.

Understanding the Hidden Emotions

What's going on emotionally for the kids is not as it appears on the surface. Despite their cruel, disrespectful attitude toward the alienated parent, feeling compelled to choose between their parents causes them a tremendous amount of stress. Children's identities and sense of self-esteem come from their attachment to both parents. The kids' hurtful behavior masks many conflicted emotions, including anger at having been put in the loyalty bind by the alienating parent.

The healthy parent needs to realize the kids are compelled to behave inappropriately toward them to avoid rejection by the alienating parent. The solution to this is twofold. First, realize that any emotional reactivity will trigger more resistance from the kids regardless of how justified it is.

Responding to the kids or the alienating parent harshly out of anger and exasperation will be used to show what a horrible parent you are. It will prove to an objective observer that all the flaws the alienating parent has accused you of are true. Again, we see that acting out of righteous indignation and anger not only doesn't get us the resolution we want, but it also makes matters much worse.

Often, this is when the alienating parent files a motion to gain sole custody of the kids. The alienating parent will have created a situation where the kids tell the court they no longer want to be with the healthy parent because that parent is mean to them. And from the kids' perspective, this is an accurate depiction.

In this dynamic, the children are not deliberately behaving inappropriately but rather doing what they instinctively know is necessary to keep the alienating parent's "love." So, when the victimized parent reacts angrily, all the kids see is anger and not the rationale behind it.

Measure Your Responses and Focus on the Kids

Once again, the solution is to change your mind. Think before you respond. Imagine a judge or family court services mediator reading every email and text that you send. More critically, shift your focus away from the toxic parent and back to maintaining the best possible relationship with your kids. This may require you to pick your battles with the kids more carefully. Don't impose punishment that's going to push them away. An authoritarian approach will play into the alienating parent's hand.

Does this mean that you adopt the same approach as the toxic parent and let the kids get away with behaving poorly? No, but if you focus on changing your kids' behavior through discipline, you risk driving a wedge into your relationship. It's healthier for your connection with the kids to let an occasional infraction slide.

This is what it means by it takes two to tango. You can choose to defuse the clashes with the children or become so rigid in your responses that you unwittingly contribute to the toxic parent's plan. I've seen parents become so exasperated that the children end up having no privileges, including cell phones and other electronics. Unfortunately, the children end up hating and disconnecting from the healthy parent.

Neutral, Therapeutic Support

The second part of the solution is to enlist clinical support. Without the input of a neutral third party, the dynamic can never rise above the level of "he said, she said," in the opinion of the family court. Therapeutic intervention allows removing the kids from the center of this destructive co-parenting pattern.

A typical clinical program would involve therapy for the children and family to facilitate communication between the kids and the alienated parent. This intervention is helpful to the kids and gives the alienated parent some support for those relationships. Also, if requested, the clinical specialist can provide objective input about the family dynamic to the family law court.

As a rule, the alienating parent will pay lip service to the idea of therapeutic intervention, then proceed to sabotage all efforts to implement it. The alienating parent's strength is in seducing the kids to take his side in an attempt to manipulate the court system. This correctly implies that they have encouraged the kids to become directly involved in custody. Remember, this kind of parentification of the kids is often a key characteristic of alienation.

The alienating parent will share the details of the case as if the kids are peers rather than children that need protection from conflict. They also encourage the kids to confront the other parent on issues that the alienating parent wishes to dominate. For example, the alienating parent may deliberately sign the kids up for extracurricular activities that occur during the other parent's custody time without getting advance consent as mandatory by joint legal custody requirements.

If the healthy parent objects to this intrusion, the kids become furious at that parent's lack of support for their interests. The parent is put into a no-win situation. The kids are effectively put in control through the alienating parent's behavior, and any attempt to set appropriate, healthy limits results in an angry backlash. This scenario can lead to the kids stating their preference to live with the alienating parent.

The ability to change your mind and focus on your relationship with the kids rather than reacting to the other parent's provocation is crucial. The biggest challenge is tempering their reaction to the feelings of loss, helplessness, and exasperation that naturally come from being run over by a self-centered or narcissistic personality.

The relentless focus on the healthy parent's /toxic parent creates the perception that they are unwilling to look at their contribution to the process. It's also a waste of energy as you will certainly not be able, nor will the family court endeavor to, change the alienating parent in any fundamental way. You can only hope to create a strong bond with your children that will withstand the constant barrage of intrusion and undermining by the alienating parent and enlist the support of professionals and the court.

PARENTAL ALIENATION SYNDROME

This is a deep and often misunderstood phenomenon that occurs when one parent purposely manipulates, threatens, punishes, or brainwashes the child into showing and feeling anger, hatred, or resentment toward the other parent. It can destroy a family by hurting children and creating emotional instability.

Parental Alienation Syndrome (PAS) is not simply a parental disagreement with each other on how to raise a child. Nor is it evidence of normal arguing between parents who have split up.

PAS occurs when one parent uses manipulation and brainwashing techniques to get a child to reject the other parent with bad feelings. A parent having difficulty adjusting to his separation or divorce may be vulnerable to creating this situation.

The problem with Parent Alienation Syndrome is that it poisons tender emotions, leading to confusion and serious emotional problems.

When a child feels responsible for his parents' separation, it leaves the child feeling guilty and shameful. The vindictive parent then exploits this guilt and shame to turn the kid against the other parent.

People who want to help must realize that the PAS situation is a cyclical pattern of behavior with no apparent end.

PAS creates stress internalized by the children, or it may manifest itself in aggressive acting out behaviors. This type of emotional and physical stress can lead to a wide range of symptoms, including irrational fears, depression, anxiety, panic disorder, and dyslexia. These situations are immensely difficult for children as well as adults.

In the United States, several lawsuits against alleged PAS have been filed over the last few years. Some have resulted in settlements of over $100 million. Other cases are working their way through the court system.

One case involved a custodial father who temporarily took his son away from his estranged wife while he and the boy were on a vacation trip. When he brought his son back, it was evident to everyone concerned that something had changed dramatically in the child's attitude toward the mother and her new husband. The boy began to refuse visitation with his mother and her husband, started getting bad grades in school, became violent, and began using drugs.

The child's behavior was explained as being due to the problems of the custodial father. An evaluation was ordered, and a therapist recommended that the child should live with his mother.

No one found out that the child had been warned that living with his father would result in physical punishment from his stepfather. This warning was given in the presence of a social worker.

The custody order was appealed, and a federal court-appointed guardian ad litem supervise the case. The judge requested that both parents be brought before the court. When they arrived in court, the child began screaming at his mother and throwing things at her. The judge then ordered that the child not see his mother again until he could behave properly in the court.

The child's mother then contacted a lawyer who filed a lengthy appeal alleging that the child's problems were due to custody. The appeals court agreed and ordered that the boy lives with his mother until he was fourteen. When he was fourteen, the judge finally decided that the boy should choose which parent he would live with. This means that both parents will have very little control over their life from now on.

The point of this is to show how a Parental Alienation Syndrome situation will not go away, and in fact, gets worse. The child's current problems directly resulted from a separation that did not have any real basis.

The boy's stepfather was clearly at fault for creating the PAS situation in the child. However, you could also blame the judge who failed to see what was happening and who ordered a custody evaluation before it was warranted.

The problem was that the judge did not see the whole picture in its entirety. Both parents were emotionally blind to what was happening to their son. One of them had a mental problem, and the other didn't recognize it. In addition, both parents were blind to their weaknesses.

If you look at this situation, you will see that it could have been avoided if one or more people (or parties) involved would have recognized the problem and taken action before it got any worse.

Figure out what brought about this problem. Then we need to look at the people involved, including ourselves, and see if there are any other situations like this anywhere else in our lives.

In most cases, when you follow the money trail, you will find that PAS cases are caused by someone who wants to use children for some purpose that has nothing to do with their welfare. In other words, someone wants something and will go to almost any length to get it.

Because of this exploitation, the emotional problems created by PAS can be devastating for the child. The kid's self-worth is diminished, and he feels sad and angry. He hates himself for being manipulated and brainwashed into believing that his mother or the father is the one to blame for everything wrong in his life.

ADVICE FOR EACH AGE OF YOUR CHILD

Parenting one size doesn't fit all. The same is valid for talking with your children about the divorce. Every child is at a different developmental stage that requires you to adapt what you say to meet individual levels of maturity and understanding. In every developmental stage, these constants apply:

- Shield children from parental hostility and conflict.
- Give frequent reassurances of your love.
- Create and follow a predictable parenting plan.
- Remain engaged in parenting.

Older Toddlers: 18 Months to 3 Years

If you have a toddler, you are undoubtedly quite familiar with his strong need to be independent. They test limits and begin to express opinions. A primary developmental task for toddlers is to learn to be unique and separate individuals. Temper tantrums are common. From a developmental standpoint, a lot is going on at this stage.

It is difficult for parents to recognize whether the uproar is related to the divorce or is developmentally normal. Signs of distress may include acting sad or lonely, changes in eating or sleeping habits, fears of once-familiar activities or things, and regression to behaviors from an earlier stage of development such as thumb sucking, baby talk, fear of sleeping alone, asking for a bottle, or wanting to wear a diaper again.

As with infants, providing a consistent, predictable routine where needs are met will help your toddler adjust to the many changes divorce brings. Your toddler will need frequent reassurance of your love through your actions as well as your words. A parenting schedule where they regularly spend time with each of you is optimal. Toddlers do best to go no more than three to five days without seeing one parent.

What to Do

Since toddlers don't have a good concept of time, helping them know when they will be at each house will ease transition jitters. Make a calendar where they can see it and use stickers or colored pens to designate "Mom time" and "Dad time." Help them count the number of nights of sleep. For example, "You have three nights of sleep with Mommy, and then you go to Dad's house. Let's count them together, one, two, and three, Daddy." The more light-hearted and matter of fact your tone, the better for your toddler.

Children love books about themselves. Make a small book with photographs of familiar items and routines at each parent's house and read it together before changing homes. I've known children to carry these books until the paper is nearly worn through. Check your library or bookstore for age-appropriate books about divorce.

What to Say

Toddlers need a short and simple explanation about the divorce. You will have to repeat it many times as they work to understand what it means.

Preschoolers: 3 to 5 Years

Preschoolers experience a huge boost in cognitive and physical abilities. They are more self-sufficient than before and can carry out basic self-care tasks. Their vocabulary has increased, allowing them to understand better and express feelings and ideas. Preschoolers can be big talkers! Even with this growth in cognitive ability, there are still areas of confusion. For example, if they overhear parents discussing or arguing about parenting time, they are very likely to make an inaccurate conclusion that they are responsible for the divorce.

Preschoolers benefit from routine and a predictable schedule. They can feel overwhelmed by the multiple changes that accompany divorce. They are sometimes afraid a parent will abandon them.

Preschoolers may show signs of distress like clinginess or fear of exploring the world, regressing to earlier developmental stages, feeling responsible for the divorce or a parent's feelings, acting sad, showing uncharacteristic outbursts of anger, and trying to control their environment.

What to Do

As you talk with your preschooler about the divorce, assure him of your love and abiding presence in his life. Breathe calmly, smile, and relax as you describe what's going to happen. Gently touch a hand or rub your child's back as you talk.

What to Say

Reassurance and comfort are the keys to the game with preschoolers. Tell them what's going to happen without turning it into a crisis.

Early School Agers: 6 to 8 Years

School-age children are becoming quite savvy about the world. Their cognitive abilities are growing by leaps and bounds, giving them a much broader understanding of feelings and the ability to regulate them better. Family relationships are important and provide a strong base from which to venture into the world of school and friends. When the divorce disrupts this secure base, it can affect the normal developmental milestone of moving away from the family as the primary source of social interactions.

Children at this age are well aware of rules and become very disappointed when they believe a parent isn't following rules. They deeply miss the parent they are not with and sometimes side with one parent against the other.

Signs of distress include major changes in grades or attitudes about school, increased physical symptoms like headaches and stomachaches, exaggerated emotions like moping, crying, acting sad or lonely, and a general lack of enthusiasm.

What to Do

Provide a loving environment for your children. Maintain a predictable routine with clearly communicated expectations for behavior. Be a good listener, accepting all feelings while you help your children attach words to the feelings they share. Keep your kids away from any conflict you may have with the other parent. Be that secure base they need as they go out and explore.

What to Say

At this age, your children will want some details. They've probably noticed the conflict and may anticipate your news about the divorce. Even so, they will need a gentle explanation and reassurance of your love.

Preteens: 9 to 12 Years

In this developmental stage, children become even more independent, and friends play an important role in their lives. Preteens are much more aware of what other people think, especially their peers. They might feel ashamed or embarrassed about the divorce, sometimes to the point of keeping quiet about it. They are selfishly and appropriately focused on their own lives, and they don't like it when they see the divorce messing things up for them.

Preteens have made huge leaps in cognitive ability and are better able to understand the nuances of parents' problems. They are likely to feel torn between parents, and they worry when they believe a parent isn't okay. Conflicts tend to occur when they don't get something they want. They are usually very good at pushing guilt buttons, blaming parents and the divorce when things don't go as they'd like.

Signs of distress about the divorce show increased physical symptoms like headaches, stomachaches, or general "just not feeling well", a dramatic change in grades or attitudes about school, fighting with peers or siblings, acting like the divorce is no big deal, and premature sexual activity.

What to Do

Your preteen will vigilantly watch how you handle things and will be reasonably quick to judge your actions. Parents need to model good self-care and healthy ways to express emotions. Preteens need to involve and alert parents to help them with the increasingly complex issues they face in the world. They will want to know what's going on and will push for details. Be cautious about how much you share. They can handle more information than younger children, but they must be protected from the specifics of adult problems.

What to Say

Your preteens will hold you accountable for your actions, sometimes brutally so. When you talk with them about the divorce, it's essential to keep it real and be honest without sharing too much.

Adolescents: 13 to 19 Years

The primary developmental task for adolescents is to get ready to leave home and live in the adult world. Yet, they aren't entirely as prepared as they may think. There are developmental milestones to achieve. They have their version of "magical thinking," where they believe bad things could never happen to them. Part of their parent's job is to compassionately help them learn responsibility for their actions as they gain experience to leave the nest successfully.

Like preteens, adolescents are focused on themselves. They resent the divorce when it disrupts their lives. Because of divorce, they may have greater responsibilities at home, less money, and overworked and unavailable parents. Teens' cognitive ability has increased to make them think like adults, although they aren't quite there yet. They are good at figuring out what's going on with their parents and will endlessly push for details. Be cautious about sharing too much because it isn't in their best interest.

Teens that are getting ready to leave home feel anxious about this huge step and will need compassionate parents mentally and physically be available as they work through the fear and excitement. They may feel some responsibility for the breakup because of things they did or did not do. It's important to reassure them the divorce is, in no way, their fault.

Signs of distress include premature sexual activity, excessive drug or alcohol use, problems in the school including truancy or suspension, negative attitude, criticisms of parents, leaving home prematurely, or showing reluctance to leave, canceling college plans, and moving out.

What to Do

Maintain stability in your teen's living arrangements with a few life changes as possible. Teens need reasonable limits with clearly articulated expectations and consequences. Parents must stay attentive and keep on top of monitoring daily activities. There is a great need for excellent communication between parents around rules, curfews, homework, cell phones, Internet use, and cars.

What to Say

Teens will be very interested in the logistics of your divorce and will do best when they have a say in the schedule. They want to know you are taking their needs into account. If possible, reassure them that their activities and interactions with friends won't change. They need to be told they aren't responsible for the divorce. Because their social lives are busy, teens do best with plenty of warning before changes occur in the family schedule. Offer multiple times to talk about what will happen and then compassionately answer their questions. The sample script for preteens also works for adolescents.

POSITIVE PARENTING APPROACH IN DEALING WITH A HOSTILE EX-SPOUSE

Y ou have learned that taking things personally and losing your control feeds into your narcissistic ex's behavior. They will continue to do things to spite you, manipulate you or your children, and always have their best interests at heart—not your child's. By limiting contact, setting parental guidelines, providing structure for yourself, modeling healthy communication, and ignoring the narcissist's attempts to abuse you, you can focus more on your child. In this co-parenting situation, your child's development is of crucial importance.

Encourage Individuality

Children are influenced by everything and everyone in their world. A narcissist will make them believe they have to please everyone or "bow down" to their peers to feel loved or appreciated. The child of a narcissist is not an individual but a reflection of them. Being a non-narcissistic parent, you can counteract these habits by helping your child realize that they are their person. As all children like to follow their parent's lead, make sure to model positive mannerisms to help them figure out the difference between impolite behavior and kindness. Seek opportunities for your child to grow independently, such as:

- Providing creative activities.
- Asking them which sports or summer camp they would like to join.
- Journaling their thoughts and feelings.
- Letting them choose their clothes and toys.

Encourage Self-Esteem

Self-esteem is built through unconditional love and acknowledgment. Build positive reinforcement through the milestones your child accomplishes in his life. Give him praise when it's needed, not when he does something to gain your affection. Narcissists have a high, self-absorbed image, and so their love will only ever be conditional as long as your child serves them and their needs. More ways to counteract this are:

- Tell your child that they are smart or good (when they are good) to remind them that they have good traits.
- Praise them for things like going potty on their own, winning third place at the fair, or displaying good behavior with their friends.
- Be careful with what you tell them, like: "you are so awesome in my eyes" rather than "you are the most awesome person in the whole wide world."

Help Build Self-Confidence

Your child is always taking in new information and building skills to boost his self-confidence. Reward them by saying things like, "wow, you are good at that; show me again." Or "some things take practice, why don't we try again?" In doing this, you allow your child to figure out his strengths and weaknesses, which encourages independence and teaches them to develop confidence in the things they can do while letting go of perfecting what they can't. Try this:

- Enlist your child up for a sports team.
- Encourage them to try new things.
- Explain that being fearful is their body's way of reacting to change and that change is a good thing.

Allow Mistakes to Be Opportunities

A narcissistic parent will ensure that his child strives to be the best and only rewards them when they are the best. This promotes perfectionism and results in temper tantrums when your child can't impress. Teach your child:

- Mistakes will happen but are needed to grow into happy individuals.
- Make a mistake on purpose before your child, and don't make it a big deal. Like paint together and "accidentally" color out of the lines. Say oops and laugh about it.

- Challenge them to do things they don't enjoy doing or are not good at, then applaud their efforts and say, "good job for trying."
- Do not exaggerate their accomplishments, as focusing too much on this can put pressure on them, encouraging perfectionist behavior.

Create Positive Influences and Environments for Your Child

Creating a stable environment for your child—one where they will feel safe, secure, and confident—will keep their minds at ease during the switch between parents. As hard as this is for you to co-parent with your ex, it is even harder for your children to adapt to such change. Building a community of support can help aid you in this difficult transition. This can also help your child make positive connections and learn from others—not just you.

Teaching Your Child Empathy

All children and teens are selfish individuals, which is part of their development to independence and individuality. However, it doesn't become a problem unless there is no remorse or feelings behind their actions. You can teach them empathy by:

- Always remind them that other people have feelings, too.
- When reading or watching TV, ask your child how they think the person feels.

- When your children do something good or bad to someone else, ask them how they would feel if it had been done to them. This will help them realize the other person's feelings.

Explaining the Importance of Friends and Family

Narcissists are usually lonely and sheltered. They rarely have friends come over, and they rarely let their children have playdates. Children can pick up on these patterns and use their friends in the same way through manipulation or exploitation. To counteract this:

- Inspire your child to make healthy bonding relationships.
- Role model healthy interaction.
- Host a get-together and invite friends for your child while modeling laughter and fun times.
- Demonstrate loyalty, sharing, and effective communication skills.

Discipline and Explain Manipulation Tactics Used by Your Child

Every child will push limits and boundaries to see what they can and cannot get away with. This is where positive reinforcement and discipline come in. Catch his malicious acts, pull him aside, and explain at eye level how unhealthy this type of communication is. Tell him a better way to handle the situation and ignore or overlook negative tantrums. When you feed into the positive, you develop positive attitudes. When you give attention to the anger and negativity, it allows them to continue because even though throwing hissy fits, they are still getting a reaction out of you.

If your child tries to manipulate his friend by saying, "if you don't do xxx, I won't xxx," catch his behavior and tell him that holding something over someone else's head is inappropriate and will not be tolerated. Let him know that he cannot control someone else, but he can do his own thing if a friend isn't playing nicely.

Role model to them that the kinder you are, the more beneficial rewards you will get.

Explain to them that through effective communication and being polite, people will likely want to help you rather than fear you.

Every time they do something positive on their terms later, pull them aside and tell them how proud you are of handling the situation the way they did.

HOW TO WORK WITH THE THERAPIST

Whenever you are healing from any form of abuse, it is always advised that you work with a therapist who can help you completely recover from the abuse you have faced in your life. Especially in a situation as complex as healing from narcissism, having a therapist can help you work through the challenging emotions and realizations and have compassion for yourself. They can also support you in developing healthier coping methods and self-care routines while keeping you accountable in your commitment to living a healthier life.

It is recommended to combine self-help with professional therapists. Read as much as you can, surround yourself with supportive people, and do everything you can to educate yourself on what you are going through and how you can successfully get through it. Then, consult a professional therapist who can help you in ways that you cannot help yourself, which would not be available through loved ones or books. The therapist will help you understand your unique situation, create custom strategies for healing and coping based on personal needs, and ultimately support you in feeling safe and comfortable during the entire experience.

Self-Validate Your Right to Seek Help

It is an excellent time for you to practice self-validation as you understand that you have a right to seek help and that you deserve the support you desire. This opportunity can prove your commitment to yourself and your needs, assert boundaries in your mind to the thoughts that tell you that you do not need assistance, and forgive yourself for your fears around help. You can even use this as a time to label and work through the emotions you are having around the idea of hiring a therapist in the first place to seek help.

Find a Trauma-Informed Therapist

In finding a therapist, you need to find a trauma-informed professional. These days, many psychoanalysts make an effort to be trauma-informed, which means that there should be no shortage of therapists available to you to help you with what you are going through. With that being said, make sure that when you are looking for a therapist, you ask them what sorts of trauma they have helped people heal from and their philosophies on healing from suffering. Knowing that your therapist understands your unique type of situation and what you might be going through, can help assure you that they will believe you and be helpful to your healing experience.

Create a Sense of Safety in Your Client-Therapist Relationship

When you work with a therapist, always make sure that you pick one who helps you feel safe and supported right from day one. It might be challenging to tell if you are particularly afraid of visiting a professional in general. Still, typically you will know because you will speak with a psychoanalyst who seems to help you feel better. You should pick a therapist who helps you feel more comfortable and supported from the start, as this is a professional with whom you are likely to develop a good relationship. If you find a counselor with whom you do not feel comfortable, recognize that this is likely a mismatch between you and your therapist's personality and not evidence that the treatment will not help you.

If you are afraid of visiting a professional, even if you think that fear sounds silly or strange, do not be afraid to open up about this. You could even make this your first area of focus so that you can test the waters to see how your psychoanalyst responds to your emotions and your needs. In many instances, sharing this will help you feel more confident and allow your therapist to understand your needs while also showing you that they are there to help you, not judge or hurt you.

Lastly, keep the topic of your therapist away from your partner unless you truly feel the need to tell them. Telling them that you go to therapy, or saying that you go because of them, could expose you to being abused for your choice, which could compromise your willingness to continue going. Keep some things to yourself. You can do so by asserting the boundary that you are not required to tell your mother everything can be incredibly helpful in establishing a sense of security in your client-therapist relationship.

WAYS TO PROTECT YOUR CHILDREN FROM LOYALTY CONFLICTS

U nfortunately, even with a detailed child arrangement plan in place, there will be times when disagreements and conflicts will be unavoidable. You may have to accept the likelihood of this, as well as the fact that it will largely fall upon you, as the non-narcissistic parent, to shield the children from such conflict as far as you are able.

The narcissist is likely to:

- Treat the children sub-optimally because they know no other way.
- Badmouth and lie about you to them to punish you.
- Use the children as a means through which they can legitimately maintain contact with you and keep some form of control. The children are likely to be your 'Achilles' heel' and, therefore, an excellent button to repeatedly press.
- Use them to cause pain to you with no regard whatsoever to the consequences of the children being caught in the middle.
- Make numerous court threats via the children.

You have a very difficult line to tread—between enabling the narcissist's bad behavior and openly denigrating it. Neither is ideal and in truth, there is no perfect answer to these dilemmas.

What You Can Do

Try to avoid a 'knee-jerk reaction to the narcissist's behavior in front of the children. Count to ten, go into another room, rant in your journal, or to a friend. Only once you've got things off your chest and returned to a place of rational thinking can you respond logically and calmly.

Pick your battles carefully. Do not give your kids a childhood in which the predominant memories are friction and litigation between their parents over them.

Accept that the court system is unlikely to be your salvation. It might be the only option in extreme situations, but in most cases, it will only fuel narcissistic supply and make matters worse.

Carefully consider if discussing the narcissist's behavior directly with them will have any positive outcome or whether it will just feed the drama. There are occasions where you may have to accept things as they are. You can only be responsible for your parenting and asking the narcissist to cooperate with you in adopting a certain parenting style is likely to be met with deliberate opposition.

Shield the children from the disputes between the two of you as much as you can by not offloading on them or trying to get them to see your point of view rather than the narcissists. Stick your nose in the air and try to take the moral high ground.

Try as hard as you can not to allow the children to become aware of how annoyed you are by the narcissist's manipulations via them. The effort required to maintain an outward image of calmness may well be Herculean. Again, offload on your friends, not on them.

Expect times when your children will be unfairly turned against you and run with it. If the children are old enough, you can calmly suggest that if they would like to know anything about you, they can ask you directly. An explanation that if a person is angry with another person, they should not tell stories about them may also be helpful to younger children here. It is fine to contradict stories that are being told about you without specifically accusing the narcissist of lying—clarify what is true about you rather than directly labeling the narcissist's fabrications as lies.

In situations where you can see the narcissist manipulating children against one another, try to provide support and reassurance, but don't involve the narcissist again. This will be exactly what the narcissist wants—to create chaos within the family and, consequently, be firmly placed back in the center.

If you can demonstrate equality between children and show no favoritism, you will be teaching them by example that no one child is better than the other in your household. Again, showing empathy and encouraging them to talk about their feelings will benefit here—something that the narcissist will not be able to do. All you can do is lead by example.

If the narcissistic parent refuses to pull his weight as Mum or Dad, for example, not turning up to the school concert, sports day, or parents' evening, try not to leave the children feeling that the other parent doesn't care, but at the same time avoid making excuses for the narcissist.

While you might want to avoid discussing the other parent's behavior with children, even if they are teenagers, you can still discuss with them about reactions and feelings. You can treat the situation as very 'matter of fact' without using it as an opportunity to highlight to the children how useless the other parent is. A response such as "That's a shame for you—I understand that you are disappointed" doesn't judge the other parent but does acknowledge that the child is allowed to have feelings (something which, of course, the narcissistic parent will be invalidating or ignoring).

When it comes to poor behavior, compensating for it or excusing it is a no-no, and so, of course, is exploiting it and using it to work in your favor. But they were completely ignoring it or pretending that it is okay when the risk is that the children may normalize the behavior. You can act consistently in a way that naturally contrasts your actions with the poor behavior of the narcissist without specifically talking about it. Be on time, show empathy, encourage the children to develop their interests, celebrate who they are as individuals, support them in their ambitions and dreams, and teach them how to have boundaries. Listen to them, talk to them, and get to know them. Be a grown-up—all things their narcissistic parent patently will not do.

As they grow up, they will form their view and develop adult relationships with both parents. They may decide not to have any relationship with one or the other parent, but that should be left to their adult judgment.

There is, sadly, an element of crossing your fingers regarding the amount of emotional and developmental damage that will be done to them while not in your care. But remember that even the best parents inflict some damage on their children. It is part of everybody's life journey to overcome that damage. This is something you have limited control over—some acceptance and self-compassion may be necessary here.

HOW TO AVOID PARENTAL ALIENATION SYNDROME

Many children in divorce or custody disputes face parental alienation syndrome when one parent or relative actively attempts to damage the relationship between his child and the other parent. This is a potentially life-threatening situation, as it can lead them to be the target of ongoing psychological abuse from that person.

The most common form of parental alienation syndrome is caused by a child's grandparents, as this can range from feelings of rejection and anger to physical violence. The child will generally be upset and frightened at attempting to wreak havoc on the relationship between them and the other parent.

As this usually occurs after a period of alleged negligence on the part of the couple involved, they may decide to take action against them. They will want the court to find that the parents have been mentally unfit to raise their children. Evidence might include statements by the child of being regularly beaten or verbally abused, and these will often be picked up by the courts later.

Parental alienation can be difficult for parents to deal with because it is often very subtle and hard to recognize.

In many cases, children can maintain contact with one parent while being alienated by the other parent or relative, and they can describe experiences accurately.

To avoid parental alienation syndrome, parents must remember it is extremely important to communicate with their children so that they can feel comfortable speaking about any issues that may arise.

The basis of the solution for avoiding parental alienation lies in good communication between the parents.

If a parent does not feel comfortable communicating with the other parent, they should turn to the child and discuss his feelings.

It may be necessary for them to communicate with a third party, such as a therapist.

They should be aware that while they may feel that they are not getting their point across, children will eventually see through any attempt to alienate them.

If the parents can work together and keep an open dialogue, they will be less likely to fall victim to parental alienation syndrome.

Parents may need professional help from a therapist if they cannot resolve issues with one another. They should remember that this form of alienation syndrome can worsen if no effective action is taken.

Techniques for Talking to Your Children in Ways that Foster Honesty and Trust

No matter how small the issue, it doesn't hurt to hold a family discussion at the beginning and end of each day. Just be sure you start with something positive—something such as "I love you, and I'm glad we're together."

Make a list of your favorite features about each child on separate pieces of paper.

Let them pick one thing they can share with their partner—even if it's something so small as loving to eat an ice cream cone.

Periodically, ask each child to talk about what they love most about the other parent.

This is the best way to help them maintain their relationships with each parent separately and your relationship with one another as a family.

Do everything you can to keep your children in contact with the other parent financially and on holidays, even if this is difficult for one or both of you.

One common strategy for resolving conflict in custody battles involves "parenting coordinators" who are trained to offer their services at no cost. They offer to facilitate communication between parents and children and mediate between parents, but custodial parents or his attorneys do not hire them.

These mediators are trained to listen actively to the children. They are required to adopt a non-judgmental attitude that maintains the child's sense of being valued in his own unique identity and life.

If parents have difficulty working out their differences through an informal meeting between themselves and their children, they may find these services helpful. Some believe that the involvement of these services does not make a difference.

In some cases, judges have ordered that these therapists be paid with public funds through the custodial parent. In others, the court has ruled that they are a family matter, and only parties involved can decide what is best for their children.

A further strategy involves a social worker or psychologist who both parents hire.

This person will evaluate all of his interactions with his children and make recommendations on how to resolve conflicts between parents without involving the courts.

For example, such a worker might suggest that one parent set aside a certain time to meet with the other parent in a neutral place.

They may also suggest that the parents take turns speaking alone with his children about their feelings and may offer other suggestions.

Sometimes these workers will offer to mediate between parents to get them to agree on a specific arrangement or schedule for parenting time until they can resolve their conflicts independently. If they cannot get the parents to agree on such an arrangement, the court may appoint a guardian (or assign a mediator) without their consent.

WHEN YOUR EX IS BRAINWASHING YOUR CHILDREN

The parent that has the least amount of time with the child is always going to struggle with his lack of involvement in the child's day-to-day life. After all, this interaction has been a staple of most parents' commitment to their children and with their families. Keep in mind that your kids are also adjusting to this change and may have real issues with the fact that one parent is no longer in his life as much as before. Typically, this is true of children of all ages. However, older kids often feel a stronger sense of abandonment or loss since they are more aware of the divorce issues.

When both parents work together to understand that divorce is an issue between adults and not between the parent and the children, this anger and anxiety will fade away. Again, both parents have to help the children understand the dynamics of divorce. Facilitate the kids understanding that both Mom and Dad are important people in their life and that both parents will continue to work together. This is the non-toxic side of divorce that children need to be exposed to.

But when one parent intentionally minimizes or prevents the child from not spending time with the targeted parent, it steps across the line into alienation. Sometimes—although rarely—these controlling parents even go to jail for non-compliance with the court-ordered visitation times. Then they will twist this around to how much they love the child and how worried they are about sending their kid into a "harmful" environment. In addition, they aren't above putting the child on a guilt trip about their stint in jail since they constantly talk about how they would do anything to "protect" the kid from spending time with the other "unsafe" parent.

Take advantage of all the time granted in your divorce decree. Don't allow long-time gaps between contact. Even if you can't spend physical time together, making phone calls, sending text messages and emails, and cards to the kids is essential. This helps thwart alienation since you continue to be the same caring parent even though you aren't around as much as before.

Unfortunately, alienating parents use this time away from the other parent to systematically coach, manipulate, and reprogram the child's thinking. This intentional mind molding occurs over weeks, months, and years.

Child therapists working in Parental Alienation Syndrome and brainwashing indicate that increased, positive contact with the targeted parent is the key to breaking the negative cycle. Even if the alienating parent continues to use negative messages and align with the child to try to undermine the parent, kids can begin to see that the targeted parent is not a bad person. This is the benefit of recognizing alienation and working with your kids to show them that you are still Dad or Mom and that you still love them with all your heart, no matter what the other parent is saying or doing. Be aware, however, that this recovery from the damage done by the alienator often takes years—if ever, in severe cases.

For many parents, negative brainwashing activities start immediately after the separation; so, parents should have current legal representation for the temporary and final orders regarding the children. In other cases, the actual alienating behavior doesn't begin until after the final orders have been signed.

In situations where you no longer have an attorney since the divorce is completed, it is essential to talk to a lawyer regarding your concerns as soon as you notice the issues developing. Talking to the other parent is the first step, especially if you have previously had at least a civil or calm relationship when working in the best interests of the child or children. Parents that are naïve alienators may be willing to listen to your concerns, especially if you speak to them without attacking or criticizing them.

It is essential to talk to an attorney for the other types of deeper alienation, including active and obsessive. Your lawyer will provide information on:

Documentation

Document all examples of brainwashing or your ex's mental state. For your attorney to start helping you with your mental abuse case or having access or contact with the child or children, it will be important to start documenting. This can include several different issues such as canceled or no-showed visitations, changes in the duration of your time with the child or children, negative messages, or statements that your ex-spouse makes about you in front of the children, or your child's outbursts at exchanges. Your attorney can provide outlines on how to document your ex's actions and your child's expressions showing emotional damage.

Some ways to document these outbursts by both your ex and your child:

- A smartphone's video camera.
- iPhone users: your Voice Memos application.
- Android users: your Voice Recorder application.

If your lawyer doesn't object, start recording or audio taping disturbing events (your son leaving screaming voice mail messages, crying at visitation exchanges, etc.). It's one thing for you to talk under oath about how your child is mentally abused. It's another thing to let the judge hear it for him or herself.

Another element to document is all the troubles and incidences that happen from week to week. Why? Because one day, there's a good chance you'll need some reminders of your ex's performance. Also, it's helpful to fully document every ugly utterance, denied visitation, and outburst one day. Once your child is an adult, let them know that you documented every action because it concerned you so much. Then be prepared for your adult child to want to see it.

Options

Many parents dread going back to court and facing the extreme costs of a prolonged custody dispute. Since this can run into the tens of thousands of dollars in legal fees, your attorney may be able to provide less costly options.

Referrals

Attorneys especially established in any area, often have other professionals they work with to help reconciliation between parents and children of alienation. Don't hesitate to ask, as you may be surprised at the results of these referrals.

Avoid getting angry and upset at your child.

It is common for brainwashed children to only talk about the negative side of the targeted parent. They may make extremely hurtful comments to you as a parent, ones that you can't believe you're hearing. However, no matter how much it hurts to listen to put-downs or disrespectful remarks, do not take out your frustration on your children.

It is essential to remember that the other parent has entered into his campaign of negativity to block your child or children's love and affection for you. These kids will have lots of negative memories, images, and thoughts about you. This is particularly true if you have had several weeks, months, or years with minimal contact with the kids.

Often brainwashed children are extremely hostile towards the targeted parent. Their behavior may include:

- Disrespecting actions: includes eye-rolling, swearing, and yelling. Indicating they "hate" the target parent and cannot see the effect of this hurtful language, nor show any signs of remorse.
- Remaining extremely rigid in their inability to see anything positive or loving in your behavior.
- Talking about the alienating parent as the sole victim in the divorce.
- Interpreting past incidents inaccurately.
- Speaking negatively not just about you but even your entire family tree.
- Speaking in a disrespectful, indifferent way mirrors the alienating parent's tone (especially if the parent is narcissistic).

These statements and actions are hurtful, and the targeted parent has to learn to avoid taking them personally and acting out on them. It is entirely acceptable to let the child know that the comment hurts you and makes you very sad to hear that. But then follow up with a concise, unemotional statement that explains the truth. The key while doing this is not attacking or blaming your child or the alienating parent in any manner whatsoever.

An example:

Your son: "That's not fair... my mom is right about you."

You: "I understand why you're upset. But such acting out against your sister won't be tolerated."

The "wrong" you: "Of course, there you go again siding with your Mom's hatred of me. It is fair, and I don't care what your Mom says about me."

Text (SMS) Messages

Like email, text messages, or SMS messages are a great way to gently and positively tell your kids that you are thinking about them. The messages need to be relevant to the child, knowing you are interested and aware of his life. And they can be as simple as, "Just wanted to say I'm thinking about you :)."

Of course, texting "I love you" is a great way to let your child know you are thinking of him, but it can also be seen as routine if this is all that each text message is. You should also text questions about his upcoming game, something they are doing outside of school, or anything else that they're up to.

However, avoid sending too many text messages; otherwise, you risk making the children feel trapped between the brainwashing parent and yourself. A few text messages a week is a great balance; more is just needy or self-serving.

WHEN YOUR EX INTERFERES WITH CONTACT AND COMMUNICATION

Everyone needs boundaries but narcissists more than most because they are essentially still children inside. Therefore, when communicating with them it is useful to think about how you would communicate with an infant rather than the adult they present as.

Be clear when and how communication can take place and enforce the consequences of not adhering to this. If you have agreed on calls with children that are in the other parent's care, set clear times when the children will be available and on what platform. This can be agreed on weekly, monthly, or annually depending on the lifestyle of the parents. Do not accept calls or texts outside of these times.

Equally, if you have calls agreed to the children when they are in their care, do not deviate from the times arranged, even if they don't answer. A huge part of boundary setting is you maintaining them as well because the second you breach; the narcissist will see it as evidence that they can breach too. Yes, it will be hard but think about the bigger picture and the long-term peace you will get if you stick to it.

It is recommended to have one main platform for communication with the children with a backup platform just in case. Facetime is the preferred platform but if there is an issue with that, Skype. Nothing else unless agreed to by both parties.

The absolute best thing you can do here is to remain "no contact" and ride it out. Give them nothing. A strong sense of self is needed here and if this is something you struggle with; it is highly recommended to get professional help from an experienced therapist.

When you step out of the abuser, victim, and enabler triangle, the narcissist has no choice but to find someone else to fill the spot you left open. They may use your children, so it is important to help build their resilience to withstand the pressure.

- Limit your contact with them as much as is humanly possible. If you have children, use a mediator or communication app. This reinforces the idea that their behavior is not acceptable, and they will get no attention from you when they "misbehave."

You will struggle to go no contact but there are ways for you to give yourself the space to heal whilst maintaining open communication about the children. Or the narcissist may be a family member who you aren't ready/willing to cut out of your life completely but recognize you need to limit your contact with them.

- Set up a clear strategy for dealing with "emergencies," but define what constitutes an emergency

You know the narcissist will do anything and everything to trample all over your boundaries and using the children is easy pickings for them. They will go against your requests but use the "it's about the children" or "it's an emergency" to lure you into breaching your boundaries. This just provides them with the confirmation that they are powerful and in charge.

Emergencies

Emergencies Could Include

- Health issues
- Unable to collect/return children
- Urgent appointment

Both of you need to agree to these but if they are unwilling, have them as your standard.

Also clearly state what and how the other party will be notified about the emergency. Again, narcissists love to keep control so they will often keep you in the dark about situations or communicate through a channel never used so that they can say "I tried to notify you, it's not my fault you didn't check." Make sure it is something you can access but isn't intrusive. So, phone calls for example might be a definite "no" but a text is OK.

Things to Consider in Case of an Emergency

Are they to be returned to the primary caregiver?

Does the parent they are with deal with the emergency and notify the other parent on an hourly basis?

Remember to consider your boundaries whilst ensuring that the children's needs are met.

Also, be aware that going no-contact triggers a deep trauma within the narcissist and so this will be the most active and dangerous time. They will try:

- **Hoovering**—narcissists hate to lose supply and so they will attempt to lure you back in. It will start innocently enough with some form of contact. Maybe a "can I collect my stuff?" or "my friend told me you weren't at work, just wanted to check you are ok." It's bait to see if you are serious about no contact. If you are, you will probably skip ahead to smear campaigns. If not, love-bombing comes next.

- **Love-bombing**—they will lavish you with loving messages, gifts, promises of how they realize the error of their ways and you are the only person they love. It will be like music to your ears after the pain of separation and it will trigger your abandonment wounds. But it is the same lies they told you in the relationship; no one can change in a few days or a week or even a month. Especially when it is a lifetime of behaviors. I know you want to believe them, but the reality is NPD requires years of specialized therapy to address the disorder. If they have been through that the likelihood is that they

210

won't contact you because they understand now how much they hurt you and would never want to re-open that wound for you. So, if they are back, they still lack empathy and simply do not care about the pain they caused.

- **Smear campaign**—you have resisted them so far and now they experience narcissistic injury. You have wronged them so badly that they have to punish you and they will use every means possible. Children, friends, family, professionals, pets... They will triangulate everyone into the drama and paint you as the abuser. They will use your firm "no contact" rule as "evidence" of how abusive you are being— "they won't even talk to me to tell me what happened." This is designed to weaken your resolve and make contact as well as give them a clear narrative that they aren't the problem: you are. Nothing you do or say to any of the flying monkeys will change the story.

YOUR CHILD REFUSES TO SEE YOU AT ALL

It can be difficult for children to adjust when a parent has just left the family home. If your child refuses to see you or talk to you, you can do a few things.

First, do not get angry or upset. Your child may be punishing you for leaving them. They need to understand that you will be there for them, no matter what happens.

Do not give up hope of being able to see your child again. It could take a long time—you may need patience and understanding and plenty of love, but eventually, your child will realize this is important for both of you.

If you are worried that your request will be refused, try not to show this. Children can be very wise, and they will soon work out that you are upset about the situation. You need to keep your emotions hidden until your child is ready to see you again.

If you feel it is necessary, try to talk to someone close to your child about his behavior.

- **Send cards or letters**—it may seem simple but telling your child that you love them and thinking of them often can go a long way in making someone feel wanted and cared for. Even if they don't write back, they might keep the card or letter as something of yours that they treasure and remember from their past.

- **Help support the children financially**—if you have left the family home with a child of your own, you can ask a court for maintenance payments or arrears from your child's father. If your child is not living with his father, then there are no automatic rights to receive financial support, so you need to talk to a solicitor about whether this would be possible.

- **Consider mediation**—there is information on mediation for family disputes that might help you talk to your child and work out a way forward.

- **Keep yourself safe**—keep in mind the legal rules that protect you from harassment and abuse. You might want to get some advice if you feel threatened by your child.

- **Consider approaching the Child Maintenance Service (CMS)**—they may be able to help you with a maintenance application for your child.

- **Make an application for enforced contact**—if you have left the family home and have tried to communicate with your child by using the courts, local authority, or CMS that will order contact between your child and yourself.

- **Consider contacting a support group**—it may be that you are not alone, and other parents have left the family home and will be able to give you advice and support.

- **Consider whether it is necessary to make a criminal complaint against a parent**—if you have already left the family home and have had no contact with your child, you may want to speak to the police or social services about making a criminal complaint or assault or harassment.

- **Consider taking out an injunction against a parent**—if you are not comfortable with making an application at court, you may want to consider applying for an injunction against another parent.

HOW TO PROTECT YOUR CHILD FROM ALIENATION AND LOYALTY CONFLICTS

Every parent worries about his child's future and whether they will find happiness in life. Some parents are also concerned about whether their children will withstand peer pressure or develop a sense of belonging around them.

As you try to protect your children from the surrounding environment, you become worried about how much effort it takes to shelter them from social evils such as drugs, peer pressure, and abuse. Some parents find it difficult to understand that a child can have different values than theirs. Some fear that their kids might even be viewed unfavorably by their peers.

As a parent, you are willing to try and understand your child's values, but it will take a lot of effort. Some parents try to put their children in situations that they deem ideal for them, but this can cause other problems such as "enforced alienation."

Some parents believe that their children should be protected from opinions and situations that conflict with them. However, this can cause a child to feel alienated from society and lose his sense of belonging. As children try to form an identity for themselves, they will develop different opinions and feelings about the world around them. This is an important process for healthy development.

Loyalty conflicts occur when parents create extreme or strict rules, focusing on every aspect of their lives. Because the child has been exposed to this type of parenting from a very young age, they feel confused and unable to cope with other situations that involve peers.

Many parents try to shelter their children from abuse and bullying. Some focus on every little aspect of their lives, such as what they wear, who they talk to, and how long they spend on the computer. This kind of parenting can ruin a child's independence and self-esteem.

By avoiding these strategies, you can help your child develop independence and self-esteem by making them feel safe in the world around them. Children should be encouraged to spend time with their peers and become involved in activities that help them develop an identity for themselves.

When children feel alienated from the world, they can feel sad and withdrawn from society. These behaviors can cause them to lose the motivation to spend time with his peers and participate in social activities. If you are anxious that your child is feeling this way, you should seek mental health assistance immediately.

Parents should create a positive and healthy relationship with their children without trying to shelter them from the world.

Kids should be encouraged to develop an identity for themselves rather than conform to their parents' ideal image.

Children who are afraid of abuse or bullying should be encouraged to speak about their concerns. Parents should help their kids discover ways of dealing with these situations immediately, rather than shelter them from these types of actions forever.

Parents should try to understand that anything you do for their child is an investment in their future. No parent can guard his kid against all peer pressures and social problems, but you will be doing your best to guide him into healthy choices when he faces these types of situations as teenagers.

A loyal child can gain the trust of others; it means he is faithful to his parents or other close relatives. They can be loyal to friends and neighbors and loyal to a country, religion, or school. A child loyal to his parents and friends will make the right decisions later in life, have a positive attitude towards others, and have self-esteem.

A child loyal to his parents and friends uses good judgment and is committed. A child with good judgment knows what he should do in different situations; he can think clearly about different circumstances without letting emotions get in the way.

CAUSES OF LOYALTY CONFLICTS IN DIVORCED FAMILIES

Several children of divorced parents are forced to deal with loyalty conflicts. One parent plans to have the child's complete loyalty, while the other attempts to discredit this same child. The child's primary loyalty is towards the parent without custodial care, but he or she wants to make it so that person feels isolated and alone. This is not only displayed in domestic situations but also social circles such as sports teams and clubs.

Children of divorced parents attempt to find a balance between these two worldviews. They learn to see both sides, regardless of how difficult it is, and come up with solutions that make everyone happy. They try to understand each parent's motivations and feelings. For example, a child may be interested in the parent who has custody and demonstrates loyalty, but the other parent may feel threatened by this new interest. On the other hand, if they fail to show interest in the parent with custodial care, this parent may feel abandoned and isolated.

To resolve the problem, a child of divorced parents must balance these two conflicting interests. They must observe and understand each parent's emotional life while maintaining his

218

loyalty to them both. This can be difficult for kids who have been exposed to years of conflict among their parents. They do not know how to deal with family relationships without causing tension or upsetting any party.

Causes of Loyal Conflicts in Divorced Families

Loyal conflicts can be caused by anyone or several of the following:

Family Structure

Family structure is an essential aspect of loyal conflicts in divorced families. A typical structural pattern is the presence of an absent parent. One or both parents may choose to have little contact with or even be missing from the child's life; however, they maintain a close relationship with each other as an ex-spouse. The result is a long-standing issue in which one parent feels abandoned, and the other feels rejected.

A new dynamic is often created between a parent and his child following a divorce. This new dynamic is powerful to the kid as they may feel obligated to act in a certain way because that is how they learned behavior from his parents. They may begin to emulate his parents' relationship, or they won't, but they will learn how to deal with divorce by observing his relationship with his parents.

One of the significant reasons why a divorce leaves an impression on children is that they feel deprived and rejected by one of the primary caretakers. This has been shown to lead to significant mental health problems.

Children of divorce need to make sense of what they have experienced. They need to know why it happened, what it means for them, and how they fit into the picture.

Parental Conflict

Parental conflict is an essential aspect of loyal fights in divorced families. It can be seen that children are being denied some contact with one parent because of this issue. This rejection is often a result of an ongoing parental feud that escalates into physical violence.

Parental conflict can be divided into several categories, such as:

Children are often left confused and frustrated by these various types of conflict. They are also very aware that his parents are fighting, but they do not understand why. Parents may try to justify his behavior by saying it "isn't the child's business," but this only causes more confusion and frustration because they want to speak up but can't.

Children of divorced families are often left with a feeling of helplessness in this situation. They hear both sides arguing through walls and doors. They feel trapped in the middle of the struggle. Children are not the cause of conflict, but they often become the victims and are made to take sides.

Social Stigma

One of the major causes of loyal conflicts in divorced families is social stigma. This is caused by "a social perspective emphasizing how people should behave in response to moral or legal standards." This includes, but is not limited to:

When a child becomes aware of this stigma, it often makes them feel that one parent is more important than the other. They are forced to decide whether they want to run and live with the parent who seems more socially acceptable or stay with the parent who appears less socially acceptable.

Child's Behavior

Children of divorced families sometimes experience a change in behavior as a result of his parent's separation. This can be attributed to the fact that they are attending two separate households. Therefore, his time is divided between the two families because they have to deal with his internal struggles.

The most important factor affecting children's behavior is the extent to which children feel isolated from one parent due to conflicting loyalty. Kids feel isolated from one parent when they refuse to be loyal to them.

Behavior of Parents

Parents are the role models for children. They educate his kids on how to treat people and also how to behave in various situations. Therefore, if a child's parents are divorced, they may have trouble deciding who they should respect and admire more, as each parent is likely to have different principles upon which they govern his lives.

Child's Relationships with Siblings and Peers

The relationship between siblings and peers can be affected by loyal conflicts as well. The struggle between being loyal to one parent or the other may make a child develop a hostile attitude towards his siblings. They may begin to see his siblings as enemies. Also, if his parents separate them, one sibling may be required to live with the parent who is seen as less socially acceptable. This can be quite damaging for the sibling's relationships with the other children in that household.

Family or Social Events

Another cause of loyal conflicts in divorced families is family and social events.

A child may feel uncomfortable at family or public events as they may expect to see his parents in an argument or don't want to choose between them. They may refuse to participate in the event so that they do not have to make this decision.

CONSEQUENCES OF LOYALTY CONFLICTS IN DIVORCED FAMILIES

Family relationships are the foundation for healthy functioning. When they are strained or severed, it has a trickle-down effect that can negatively impact all family members. Research has identified several consequences of divorce on children and adults.

The children of divorced couples have to deal with the harsh reality that his parents are not together. They often feel left out and misunderstood. They may have to deal with resentment on the part of one parent and hatred toward the other.

Non-custodial parents often take a back seat to financial support from his ex-spouse. Helping children adjust to parental divorce and loss can be a taxing experience for them.

Loyalty conflicts among parents can arise in divorced families because of issues ranging from finances, living arrangements, visitation rights, and child support to how work schedules will be handled.

Parental conflict can lead to behavioral problems in children. Kids who witness or are exposed to parental conflict may turn to negative behaviors such as substance abuse, violence, or other unhealthy activities. They may express his feelings through aggression toward others, violent behavior at school, depression, and anxiety disorders.

Children whose parents are involved in bitter custody battles are more likely to have increased symptoms of depression and anxiety than those who live with non-custodial parents. The high levels of stress that both parents experience may raise the risk of depression for children residing with the custodial parent.

Children who live in homes with volatile family environments struggle with emotional, behavioral, and social problems. His world is often cut off from other people or events because of the two opposing parents' competing claims on his time and attention. Children in these situations are more likely to have feelings of insecurity, anxiety, loneliness, and withdrawal. They start to believe that they cannot make his own decisions. They often have difficulty in school and may develop a victim mentality.

Children who experience parental conflict are more likely to demonstrate behavior problems such as acting out, aggression, anxiety, depression, bedwetting, sleep problems, and poor peer relations than children who do not. They also tend to have a higher negative self-image and low self-esteem rates than those who live in non-conflictual households.

When parents cannot express feelings and emotions without arguing with one another, it can have a detrimental effect on the children. These kids grow up with the impression that they are not as important as his parents, leading to low self-esteem and feelings of insecurity.

Children who have suffered parental divorce may be more likely to experience delayed onset of puberty because of the increased time they spend away from home while his parents are fighting over custody and visitation rights.

Adolescents and young adults struggle with peer rejection, ostracism, and even bullying due to the divorce. They believe that they have to choose his friends carefully or leave his school altogether.

Adults that have experienced divorce often struggle to bond with his children. Although bonds are made and strengthened over time, they are still affected by the end of the marriage. They may suffer from depression and anxiety or find it difficult to trust a potential romantic partner again after the divorce.

Some separations are the result of domestic abuse. Although this is not common by any means, it does impact divorce when children are involved. Like all victims of domestic violence, children can suffer from psychological trauma that can last a long time after the abuser has left home.

Regardless of the severity of the conflict, children who live with both parents have a more secure relationship than they would if only one parent was still living in the home.

When there is a divorce, children may even be pressured by his friends and peers to go for the parent they want to live with. This can be problematic for many different reasons.

HIGH CONFLICT CO-PARENTING SITUATION

C o-parenting with a high-conflict person is exhausting, and just keeping up with the documentation of all his bad behavior will seem like a second job some days. Some apps take some of this burden off you and have protections to prevent some dirty tricks. You can even request that using one of the co-parenting apps is part of your parenting agreement.

Important Components of the Plan

Your attorney or a quick Internet search should be able to provide you with the parenting plan guidelines for your state or local area. You will need to establish an agreement around the following items. Refer back for more information about custody and visitation. It should include:

- **Child support**—Which parent is the payor, the amount, and how it will be paid.
- **Legal custody**—Who will be in charge of decision-making for the children.
- **Physical custody**—Who is the residential parent.
- **Parenting schedule**—Specifically when the children will be with each parent.

- **Medical, dental, vision insurance, and expenses**—Which will cover the children, and how non-reimbursed expenses will be shared and reported.
- **Other expenses**—Who will pay what, and how reimbursement or expense sharing will occur.

When dealing with a high-conflict person, a verbal agreement is never sufficient. If you have young children, think ahead, and include all expenses that you believe might come up for your child, such as:

- Clothing
- Daycare
- School tuition, uniforms, and supplies
- School lunches
- Extracurricular activities, fees, and equipment/supplies
- Auto insurance, fuel, and maintenance
- Haircuts and personal expenses
- Cell phone
- Prom, homecoming, and other special-occasion clothes and expenses
- College entrance exams
- College visits
- College tuition, books, and expenses

It's important to detail how the expense is to be shared and how the parties will notify each other of the cost, how payment will be made, and within what time frame the payment should be made—the more specific, the better. Leaving things too general opens the door for the high-conflict person to find a loophole and will leave you frustrated.

Without a legal agreement in place, it will be difficult to get a high-conflict person to negotiate or even agree on anything.

Set a Firm Schedule

Make sure that you promote a relationship between the children and his other parent. Suggest a schedule that you believe is reasonable, and then stick to it.

If you or your spouse work unusual schedules (police, firefighter, shift work), then suggest a time split based on the number of hours per month and schedule that month (or every two weeks) as soon as the work timetable comes out for the next period. If that person fails to communicate his work schedule within X days to coordinate a parenting agenda, they will forfeit his parenting time for that period.

Be specific. That is critical with high-conflict people. Allow no wiggle room because they will keep pushing.

Communicate in Writing

If you cannot use a co-parenting app, e-mail is your next best option. Phone calls with a high-conflict person can easily get out of hand, and you'll have no documentation as to your agreement. You must be able to show written proof that your partner agreed to the visitation schedule or the expense sharing that they are now not complying with.

See Sharing Information for ideas to communicate about the children.

Document

Document the efforts you have made to come to an agreement and to follow the temporary court orders. Also, register any behavior by your spouse that is uncooperative or not in the children's best interest. Make notes if your partner picked the children up or dropped them off late, if they took them out of state without approval, or failed to pay expenses. Write down any nasty comments your partner makes in front of the children or anything your kid relates that they experienced at his other parent's house.

You Can Say No

You don't have to agree to schedule changes or other variations to an agreed-upon parenting plan. Yes, you should demonstrate that you are cooperating, but continued requests for changes, particularly last-minute ones, do not need to be agreed to. You won't decrease his anger or high-conflict behavior by being accommodating. You'll set a precedent that they can continue to do whatever they please without regard to the agreement.

Don't Take the Bait

Your spouse will try everything to get you to react, back down, or give up. You deserve a fair settlement, and your children deserve to have you in his lives. Keep cool, speak assertively, and respond. The way to win with a high-conflict person is to manage your emotions and not give them any fuel for his arguments.

Kids First

Every action and decision in divorce should be made with the best interest of the children in mind. That includes your language, behavior, parenting, and cooperation with your co-parent. Unless proven otherwise, the court will work under the assumption that civil co-parenting and equal time with each parent is best for the child. They assume that because it's usually true.

Regardless of how your spouse is behaving, it's still critically important to take the high road for your children and advocate for yourself in divorce.

How to Resolve Common Issues in Co-Parenting

Co-parenting with a high-conflict person is bound to be filled with struggles. My advice to you is this: Your high-conflict partner will not follow the rules of decency when it comes to co-parenting. Decide right now that you will stop fighting to change things you cannot change.

You can either take the conflict up a notch or dial it back. Escalating the conflict isn't good for you or your kids. If your spouse always sends the clothes back dirty even though you asked them to send them back clean, let it go. Choose your battles. Only fight the ones that matter.

What are the issues that matter, and how can you attempt to resolve them?

Schedule Changes

You must be flexible with them so they will be flexible with you. What if you get the chance to go on a great boating trip and want to swap weekends? Shouldn't you extend the same courtesy? Ideally, yes.

Assume best intentions and accommodate his request. Then ask them for a parenting time change and see how they respond. If you're not getting what you're giving, then the schedule stays the schedule. Period. It's harder on you with no flexibility, but it's one less battle you have to fight with them.

Expenses

If you've gotten temporary orders or made an agreement, the types of expenses and how they will be paid should be clear. Otherwise, the best practice would be to scan the receipt and attach it to an e-mail explaining the expense, the other parent's share, and when/how you are requesting payment. Typically, 14 to 30 days is reasonable for reimbursement. If you don't receive payment by the date requested, send a brief e-mail reminder asking for payment. If they owe you more than one outstanding receipt, continue to send monthly statements listing each item and the total amount owed.

If you have court orders outlining your partner's responsibility, you can show them to a school, doctor, or sports team, so you are only financially responsible for your share. Some will honor this arrangement and hold the other parent accountable for the remainder of the balance.

It is, unfortunately, common for high-conflict people to be financially abusive. They don't care that it hurts his children. If the behavior continues and what they owe becomes excessive, you may need to ask the court for relief.

Information Sharing

The other parent should be sharing information with you just as you are sharing it with them. If that isn't happening, arrange to add yourself to the school or activity e-mail or notification system. Call and explain your situation.

Involving the Children

You know it's best not to bad-mouth your spouse or put the children in the middle, but that may not stop your partner from doing it. They may tell the children untrue things, use the children as spies or messengers, or say things about you in front of them.

Exceptions to Co-Parenting

If your partner has been abusive, has an addiction or mental illness, or otherwise puts the children's safety at risk, act surely and quickly. Talk to your attorney and look for steps you need to take. Request sole custody and a protection order. Ask for supervised visitation only. Request these at least temporarily until the court has a chance to investigate. Prepare your documents and be ready to prove your case. "He said/she said" may not be enough to win the day.

Ask that guardian ad litem be appointed. This is an attorney who will act as a neutral third party on behalf of your child and may testify as an expert witness.

Without the court's backing, it's dangerous to prevent your spouse from seeing the children even if you have concerns. The court may view this as uncooperative or adversarial on your part.

PREPARATION FOR A CUSTODY EVALUATION

I f you seek permanent guardianship of your children, your case will be stronger if you have custody when you file for divorce. The laws of most states say that whoever has custody when the divorce papers are filed, keeps it until the court orders something different. This is to avoid parents stealing the children back and forth from each other.

There are two kinds of custody in most states, often called Physical Custody and Legal Custody. Physical custody is where the children are, which parent they live with most of the time. Legal custody involves the right to make or participate in decisions such as medical care for the child or which school a child will attend. Most states also have the concept of Joint Custody, in which each parent exercises some custody rights over the child after the divorce. The alternative to Joint Custody may be called Separate Custody.

There are different kinds of custody in more detail because they usually come into play when the court enters the final order. Speak about "custody," unless the context indicates otherwise, I'm talking about Physical Custody—which parent the child is living with, where the child's principal residence is.

In contentious situations, to make sure there is no question of who has custody at the time of filing, I've had my client take the children and a friend with him to the courthouse. The friend sits with the kids in the car outside the courthouse while my client goes inside to file the divorce papers I prepared. However, if you plan to ask for custody, don't allow your wife to take care of the kids for six months of separation, then snatch the kids the day before you file.

One final warning: It is best to have custody when you file. If you effectively try to kidnap the children or do anything that will seriously upset them to gain early custody, that will come back to bite you later. Talk to your attorney before you plan anything tricky.

You should not do the following unless your attorney approves before you take any of these steps:

- Move the children out of a school they have been attending.
- Start the children with a new daycare provider.
- Take or send the children across a state line.

Divorce is very upsetting for children. For the kid's benefit and to demonstrate that you are a careful parent, pay close attention to his emotional reactions. Phone his teachers and daycare providers and tell them about the family situation, so they are in a better place to assist your child.

If you have the guidance of your children and have any reason to believe your spouse might try to snatch them, school and daycare are some of the most common locations for such a move. You need to notify the school principal, your children's teachers, and the daycare provider about the situation and make certain who is to pick up the children. Deliver a letter stating you are in a divorce proceeding and instructing the school or daycare center to release your child only to you or someone you designate in writing.

If the events leading up to the divorce have been nasty and it has affected any of your children, you should consider professional counseling for them. Your attorney can recommend possible counselors.

Quite frankly, some of the counseling is for the benefit of the children, but some are also to inoculate yourself against accusations that you're a careless parent.

If the laws of your state are that whichever parent has custody when the divorce papers are filed keeps custody until trial, and you have such custody, you're not going to be asking the judge to change that. But, if your spouse has custody and that's not what you want, your attorney will need to file a Motion for Temporary Custody.

The Motion for Temporary Custody will state why custody should be changed, so this is often the start of mud thrown in the divorce trial.

After a motion is filed, it will be set for a hearing. A temporary custody hearing is no different than a permanent custody hearing. Each side presents evidence relevant to what custody arrangements are in the children's best interests, and the judge makes a decision. However, after a temporary custody hearing, the judge's order is temporary and continues only until the judge enters a permanent order at the end of the case.

Usually, an attorney will want to file a motion for temporary custody quickly. Suppose the children have been living with one parent for three months after the separation. In that case, the parent with temporary custody has a powerful argument that switching custody will upset the children after so long. If the final custody order switches them back, this will cause unnecessary emotional burdens.

Many judges are not excited about hearing custody testimony twice for temporary custody and a second time for permanent custody. (They like the idea of multiple temporary custody hearings even less.) Sometimes, a judge will respond to a motion for temporary custody by moving the entire divorce proceeding to an earlier date on her trial docket so that permanent custody can be determined. Sometimes, a judge will respond to a motion for temporary custody by ignoring it or setting and postponing a hearing several times.

If the judge sets a temporary custody hearing quickly, it's not easy to organize compelling evidence within a few days. If you're asking for temporary custody, make sure you have a good chance of winning because losing such a hearing may put you in a disadvantageous position in a later permanent custody trial.

On the other hand, a quick temporary custody hearing is just as hard for the other side to deal with. If you have some smoking-gun evidence—a cell phone video of your wife in bed with her lover with your five-year-old daughter lying between them, for example, or testimony from your wife's landlord that he is evicting her because the kitchen is full of rotting garbage—you stand a better chance of ambushing your wife's lawyer at a temporary custody hearing when he is unprepared to respond to such evidence. He has had much less time to discuss damaging evidence with his client than he will have before a trial in permanent custody.

Sometimes, a Motion for Temporary Custody provides a basis for negotiation between attorneys for the parties. A hearing is going to cost both parties some significant attorney's fees and make the entire divorce more expensive. Maybe the custodial parent is discovering he or she doesn't like being the sole caretaker of the children. Perhaps the parties can agree on an arrangement that puts the spouse who started without custody of the children in a better position to ask for permanent custody later. Maybe the wife will give up custody if the husband agrees to pay credit card bills.

As a general proposition, more Motions for Temporary Custody are settled by negotiation than by trial, but you can't be sure that will be the outcome in your case.

You can see why beginning your divorce with custody can be so important. While each parent has an equal right under the law, if the children have been living with a parent for one year and nothing terrible has happened to them, it's hard for the non-custodial parent to make a case that leaving the children in that situation permanently is a bad idea. It's also easy for the custodial parent to argue that the children have already gone through enough trauma without adding another move and, perhaps, different schools or daycare providers and different friends in a new neighborhood to that mix.

If you want permanent guardianship of your children, starting your case with custody is important enough to defer the formal filing of papers until you have custody. Usually, it's safer if you file first than wait for your spouse to file. Your spouse can drive to the courthouse with the kids in the car just as easily as you can.

Suppose you anticipate a disagreement with your spouse about custody. In that case, your best bet is to keep quiet about any divorcing ideas and hire a good lawyer to help you plan a strategy that will strengthen your chances of a good custody outcome.

THE CHILD AND THE CUSTODIAL PARENT: POSITIVE AND NEGATIVE ASPECTS

A custodial parent is a parent who has custody rights over his child by going into an agreement to work in exchange for having the child live with them. A non-custodial parent is usually a mother but can also be one of the two male parents in a blended family.

Generally, people in a blended family favor a shared custody arrangement and are unhappy when the other parent wants to end the agreement or deny any visits.

Custody is defined as having legal rights and responsibilities over a child. It is often very emotionally charged and controversial. Many cases go through the courts over custody disputes of children. When parents separate, they usually have joint custody arrangements, which means both parents are equally involved in his kid's life.

The relationship between a child and the custodial parent cannot be perfect. In other words, there are both positive and negative aspects to being in the custody of one parent compared to two. These differences may arise for many reasons, but they may also stem from the fact that the laws concerning custody, in general, are more lenient on mothers than on fathers.

After all, it seems logical to award custody to the parent who demonstrates a greater ability to provide care through employment or income, is more stable, and takes care of the children.

In other words, mothers have a distinct advantage in determining the custody arrangements in family cases. This is a product of the fact that children are more likely to be dependent on his mothers than his fathers, whether it is due to age, work, etc.

Positive Aspects

- The child has one home and one family identity.
- The custodial parent can spend more time with the child.
- There is reduced financial strain on the custodial parent.
- There is a reduced risk of conflict between divorced parents about dividing his assets because all resources are in only one name (the custodial parent's name).

The child may be less confused about why one parent is absent or missing in his life and how they feel when they are away.

The kid may be more satisfied with his role relationship with the custodial parent than the rest of his family, despite his closeness to other family members.

Parents who have been rendered a single custodian of his children typically feel closer since they are now forced to rely on each other for all parenting responsibilities and decisions regarding children's arrangements.

No custody orders are completely negative. There are, however, many more negative aspects to it than there are to joint custody arrangements. Custodial parents tend to be isolated in his homes and become quite lonely since they have no outside social contacts, especially when they have very young children. They may even feel imprisoned or trapped by the child's behavior because his power as a parent is severely limited by decisions made by childcare agencies, such as those concerning schooling and medical care for the child.

Negative Aspects

- The child may have trouble adjusting to a new family situation.
- The child may function better with two parents.
- There is an emotional strain on the custodial parent to balance a new relationship with the child with the other parent.
- If there are two divorces, both parents will be asked about the assets and debts of each, which can be very harmful to both parents.

Custodial parents can be overbearing to control his children, especially as they get older. The kid may no longer listen to the parent because they think of themselves as an adult and not a child. He or she may rebel against authority after being raised by one parent and following only his rules. This can create a tense relationship between parent and child.

There are also many cases where custody is given to a parent who is not fit for the task. The parent that has been given custody may be unfit mentally, emotionally, or physically for the task. In many situations, this can lead to neglect and abuse or the inability of the custodial parent to properly provide for the kid, especially if they do not have jobs or stable lifestyles.

Psychological problems in children can also stem from being raised by one parent. This is the case if the mother believes the father to be a threat to her or the kid or has feelings of insecurity towards him. In these cases, the child will likely grow up believing his parent's fears about his father.

Children raised by only one parent often have low self-esteem or feel that they cannot live up to the standards of one parent if they are unable to do so for both parents. The child's feelings of disappointment grow as they realize that there is not a second parent to lean on when life gets complicated.

Kids who are sent to live with extended family during their parent's divorce usually stay with the mother's side of the family. They will feel that they do not belong in their father's family, or they may feel scared about staying in a different home than where they were accustomed to.

Custody disputes are frequent and can be quite emotional. Children may not acknowledge why they have to move or why their family is split up. This can cause insecurity in the child and make him feel he is losing his childhood.

If the child moved multiple times while growing up, this could be an even bigger source of insecurity; this is more common than we would think.

When both parents are involved in raising a child, they have been exposed to the same influences; therefore, this helps them learn about each other's beliefs and values.

HOW TO DEAL WITH PARENTAL ALIENATION

Contact Is Important

I t is crucial for you, as an alienated parent, to show your kids, you're there for them. Don't wait and let them come to you. Keep trying to contact them.

It may mean texting your kids if they have a phone or sending emails. It may mean that you turn up at arranged pickups, regardless of whether or not your ex intends to let the kids go to your contact.

Don't wait for your kids to contact you. You need to be the one who is reaching out and making an effort. They need to feel that you haven't given up and that you're still trying to be there for them.

When you speak to them, don't mention the other parent negatively. This isn't about getting your kids to understand your side or turning them back to you by pointing out what their other parent has done wrong.

Positivity

Always be positive about the other parent. You can think that your ex is the living embodiment of Satan himself, you can even say it out loud, but you really shouldn't say it in front of your kids.

Even in the most amicable of separations, children can feel that they're caught in the middle. With an alienating parent, this is escalated to extremes. However, you should always try to be positive about the other parent in front of your children.

Your family and friends will want to help, so talk to them about your frustrations, but never do it in front of your children.

If you can't be entirely positive about your ex, and as long as it's age-appropriate, you could say something like 'I'm sorry you had to hear negative things about me,' or 'I'm sorry that you're caught in the middle of this adult stuff, but you should know that both of your parents love you.'

Letters, Emails, and Gifts

While almost all of our lives seem digital, kids will get a kick out of receiving something in the mail. So, send cards, letters, and small gifts.

Keep your letters positive and happy. Don't say that you miss them or that you can't wait to see them. Instead, tell them that you love them, and you're excited they're having a good time with your ex.

Many alienated parents don't do this because they fear that his ex will intercept anything sent in the mail. If this is the case, send everything by recorded delivery. You can say to your ex that you had sent something, and could see it was delivered, so you want to check if your children got it or enjoyed it. This may be enough for your ex to give your letters to the kids. If not, give all the evidence of delivery to your legal representative, and let them deal with it in court.

Whichever route works for you, be aware that this is not the time to go off on a tangent about your ex in general. The problem is around your children receiving mail, so make sure you stick to that issue.

Be Interested in His Interests

You can ask a person about any extracurricular activities, friends, or even just how his day was at school. However, some alienated children don't react well to even the most innocent of questions and can become shut down, avoidant, or even hostile.

If that describes your children, there are still ways you can show them you're interested. If you have friends who have kids a similar age, ask what they are into. You could pick up magazines, browse websites, and look at the trends for video games, TV shows, movies, music, and apps.

Be Involved at School

Alienating parents don't often share important information about the school, events, sports games, or anything else going on in your child's life. One way you can circumvent this is to talk to the school directly and ask them to keep you updated.

When you have the information, attend the events. If the alienating parent has told the kids that you don't care but still come to his events, they will start to question the idea that you don't care. They will start to realize that you do care as you keep coming to support them.

Many alienated parents don't go to events because they don't want to have any confrontation with the alienating parent or embarrass their child by causing a scene. You can still attend without it needing to be a drama. You should speak to your legal representative about the best way to do this.

For some, these issues can be worked out in mediation. For others, it can be agreed in court that both parents attend and sit at opposite ends of the hall, field, or wherever the event is. Some may need to arrange a schedule for one parent to attend on one date and the other parent to attend another.

Technology

Depending on the ages of your kids, technology can be your best friend. Social media, email, and messaging apps can all help you keep in touch with your kids.

You could use an app to create an album and keep adding photos and videos to it. Incorporate family pics, but also photos or videos that your kids would find interesting. You can keep the album private so that only you and your kids have access.

Video Games

You also shouldn't discard video games. If you're a gamer, many games allow online co-op play, so you can play and talk to your kids.

Kids like playing video games because they're fun, they're challenging, and they can be creative in them. They can also get a sense of achievement from a video game, such as when they beat a particularly difficult level or create an amazing building.

If you're involved, either in person or online, they will remember how they beat the level and that you were there to help. This also helps create a disconnect in their minds between their memories and feelings of you and your ex's feelings about you.

Text

If your kids have their phones, then text them. Don't text too often but send messages to let them know that you were thinking about them and love them.

Don't send the same message all the time either, as they can begin to think that it's a routine for you, and you don't mean it. Ask about school or an activity they enjoy or share something you've seen and thought they would like or news about their favorite band.

You should still text a few times a week, even if your child doesn't reply.

The Extended Family

You need to keep your extended family involved in your children's lives. It will help your children realize that they have a wider family than just your ex and his family members. It will show your kids that not everyone shares your ex's opinion when they hear your family members speaking positively about you.

However, before you throw your kids in at the deep end, it might be a good idea to talk with your family and set out some ground rules.

The first thing you need to be certain of is that nobody will say anything negative about your ex. They're allowed to think that your ex is the devil, but they absolutely cannot say it in front or on earshot of the kids. Everyone should know that those conversations are only to be had when the kids aren't there.

Make sure that your family knows that if they have to talk about the other parent, they do so respectfully and without hostility. Remind them to call your ex by his title—use 'mum' or 'dad.' They'll need to avoid calling your ex by his name.

You also need to be clear that your family shouldn't ask the kids questions about your ex or anything that happens at that house. There's no way to ask these questions without it looking like your family is snooping, which will not go down well with your kids.

Spending time with you and your family must be positive and completely free from any 'them vs. us' mentality.

Don't React to Hurtful Comments

Kids can be very matter of fact, and they might not notice that the things they say are hurtful. They won't understand that saying something like 'mummy says I can't love you' causes painful emotions.

You must not react in a way that shows you feel angry or upset. Instead, remain calm and explain that, of course, your child can love both parents.

Hostile Children

Some children are so alienated that they have many negative memories of you. These memories can be entirely false and planted by the alienating parent, but your child has been taught that they are true.

Extremely hostile children can be very disrespectful and entirely unable to see anything positive about you. They can tell you they hate you or speak to you in the same way as the alienating parent does. They can idolize the alienating parent and believe that this parent can do no wrong. They can make similar comments about your extended family.

These children don't show any remorse for what they're saying or see that it hurts them. It's incredibly important to stay calm; however, you should tell them that what they've said has been hurtful. After following up with a short factual statement — for example, 'it hurts me that you feel that way, but I love you and only want what's best for you,' or 'I understand you feel angry, but you still need to be nice to your cousins.'

Never say negative about the alienating parent. Telling your child that the alienating parent is lying will only serve to further alienate your child.

DEALING WITH FALSE ALLEGATIONS OF CHILD ABUSE AND DOMESTIC VIOLENCE

As a parent, you know that allegations of abuse are taken very seriously by Child Protective Services. These allegations can have major implications on your child, family, and personal life. You might end up in court with no safety net fighting for custody of your children and a restraining order against you, which can impact your professional relationships as well as personal associations.

In circumstances where you are in a family dispute, and the court is taking allegations of child or spousal abuse seriously as a parent, you should prevent your children from being taken away from you. Be prepared and in a position where you can defend yourself against false allegations and be able to win the case in court if all else fails.

Step 1: Demote the False Allegations

You can question the credibility of your accuser. In most cases, the person making the accusations seeks financial gain or revenge and will not be truthful in his accusations.

For example, how long have they known you, their true intentions, and what do they stand to gain if these allegations go through.

Step 2: Monitor Your Alleged Victim

You should also be aware of the character of the person who is making false allegations against you. If it is someone who has a history of telling lies often, that can be used to dispute his credibility. You can hire private investigators to get information about him and present that in court as evidence.

If you observe people who are supporting your accuser, be wary of them. They are likely to be the ones who have given false testimony against you.

Step 3: Consult With Your Lawyer

You must consult with your lawyer in steps 1 and 2 as they can help you strategize on winning the case and not fighting it just for the sake of fooling people into thinking that everything is fine. They will know what steps to take and how to make a strong case in court.

Step 4: Document Everything

Your lawyer will know that the most important thing is to document everything and anticipate the kind of questions you may be asked in court so they can get the answers for you. Listen carefully to your lawyer and follow his instructions.

If there is something you do not understand, ask them to explain it to you so that it will benefit your case. You will be better at defending yourself and winning back custody of your children when you know more.

Step 5: Don't Make a Statement or Answer Questions Without Your Lawyer

Never make a statement in the case without consulting with your lawyer first. If you are asked to answer questions outside of when you and your lawyer are present, refuse to answer them as it can hurt your case later. The only one who can help you in this situation is an experienced attorney familiar with these types of cases.

Step 7: It Is Possible to Win a Case

If you are not guilty and have taken the proper steps to prepare and defend yourself in the first few hours or days after it happened, you can win a case with allegations of abuse.

Step 8: Seek Counseling for your children

False allegations are very traumatizing for your children as they suffer the negative impacts when they are removed from their families. Do everything to get them the help they need to cope with or recover from the trauma of being separated from you.

Step 9: Seek Counseling for Yourself

Do not be surprised if you are traumatized by what is happening and have difficulty coping with everything. Suppose you think you cannot manage this and your children, seek counseling for yourself so that you can get better and fight back.

Sometimes false allegations can be made against you or your child, in which the person who is accusing you is the one who is guilty of abuse. You will need to have a solid case that will show that they are not credible, and this needs to be supported by evidence and witnesses.

You should think about hiring a private investigator to watch the person making the allegations. You can also get them to expose their private life on social media so that it will be easier for you to assemble evidence against them.

You should also present this information in court so that the judge and lawyer know that they are not credible and there is no real evidence against you or your child.

TIPS FOR DEALING WITH YOUR ABUSIVE EX IN A CUSTODY HEARING

We know that just the mention of your abusive ex can set off a stress mechanism in your brain that leads to some serious anxiety. You may also worry about what will happen at the custody hearing and how you'll react when seeing them. There are some tips on how to cope with this challenge and strategies for dealing with your abusive ex at a custody hearing.

When you first had the child in your safe and protective care, you likely felt an immense amount of stress as they were also under incredible levels of stress. You may have already developed coping mechanisms which are working well for you. The anxiety surrounding the custody hearing is typically not similar to the stress from early on in your relationship while fighting for custody. Rather than feeling anxious about future events, you might be experiencing anxiety symptoms as a result of deep-seated insecurities stemming from the abuse you suffered while in your relationship.

To prepare for the custody hearing, you need to know what you will say and do when in court. This is best done in advance, giving you time to prepare yourself, so prepare ahead by doing some practice runs. Get some information from someone who knows a lot about this process who can help you understand what will happen. It could be a family member or your lawyer. Here are some other tips that can help you when you get to court.

Be Informed

You need to know all the facts of the case from both sides. Considering how volatile and emotional this process can be, it is best to get as much information as possible in advance so you'll be prepared for what will happen. Your lawyer can give you some tips on what a judge will be looking for and how they may question the parties. You can also read the materials that were prepared for both sides if they are available.

Stay Calm

It is easy to get emotional and, when you do, you'll likely have problems doing what you need to do in court; so, it's important to keep your cool and stay focused the whole time. A patient approach will help you get through this process without any serious stress or anxiety.

Don't Be Afraid of Your Ex

They may bully you a bit, but you need to keep in mind that they are not in the right mind and are probably trying to manipulate you into doing things they want. Remember that underneath all their anger, abuse, and aggression is someone who cares about you very much.

Be Prepared to Be a Witness at the Custody Hearing

The court will likely ask your ex some questions, so it's important to be prepared for these kinds of situations. It will also help if you have a list of requests you want to ask your ex or his lawyer. Keep in mind that being in the position of questioning your ex's character may not be the best tactic to use. This isn't the time to get into a battle for who is right or wrong, but rather focus on what is best for your child.

Don't Try to Be Perfect; Just Be Yourself

You will likely do better and find it easier to concentrate when you're more relaxed. You need to do some things when you're in court but try not to overdo it and let the stress get to you.

Don't Be Terrified to Use Your Lawyer as a Consultant

During the decision-making process, you may have problems deciding what actions to take. You can ask your lawyer for help with this, and they will give you good advice about how you should proceed.

Now that you understand some tips on how to deal with your abusive ex at a custody hearing, it's time to get prepared for this challenging process. Putting together a strategy in advance will give you the best chance of moving forward without fear.

PREPARING FOR TRIAL, TESTIFYING, AND DEALING WITH THE TYPES OF QUESTIONS ATTORNEYS ASK DURING CROSS-EXAMINATION IN THE UNITED STATES

Many people have a hard time preparing for trial. The thought of taking the stand and being questioned by an opposing attorney can be disturbing and intimidating. Jurors have similar feelings as witnesses and often feel overwhelmed during trial preparation. You must know what to expect when you come face-to-face with your opponent in Court. Narcissists are very controlling and manipulative, and they want to win. They are good at spinning lies and making other people look bad. It is important to have a plan and stick to your guns. Narcissists are very persuasive and can play the "victim" very well. It is for this reason that you mustn't take their comments personally.

The narcissist wants to win and will use any sneaky means to do it. Remember, they are pathological liars and can stage Oscar-winning performances in courtrooms.

Pathological narcissists are the most poisonous and dangerous opponents that can be faced in any court.

The types of cases in which you may be involved are the following:

- Criminal proceedings in which you have fallen victim to a crime committed by a pathological narcissist.
- Divorce proceedings, in which goods/money are at stake.
- Child custody cases.
- Return procedure for goods/money due.

If it is a divorce case, the narcissist will appear confident and calm. At the same time, the subjugated former partner will have already been severely trampled by this ruthless individual in the months and years preceding the trial and will often appear stressed and lacking self-confidence and the law.

If you are in this situation, not having conversations and avoiding eye contact with the narcissist inside or outside the courtroom will be essential for you. Better to find a place on the sidelines where to sit outside the courthouse while waiting or at intervals so that the narcissist and his lawyers and followers cannot intimidate you or make you nervous.

Many people who face a narcissist in court fear that he will be able to manipulate there too and that the lies told are believed. It is essential to ensure that the legal representative of your choice is aware of what Narcissist Personality Disorder is. A lawyer who knows nothing is likely to be manipulated by the narcissist and can advise you to negotiate when it is not in your best interest to do so.

If the narcissist pushed you to the limit in the past, now it's up to your lawyers to play hard.

Narcissists are likely to react when their lives are exposed, and their bad behaviors brought to light. Eventually, you reveal information that they had no intention of letting the world know, so their anger can become uncontrollable. Often their lawyers do everything to keep them "good," calm, and content (a rather tricky, if not impossible task).

They probably have hidden or diverted goods: they are very skilled in concealing their earnings.

Is it possible to empower a narcissist in Court? Of course, one must be well prepared. It is essential to be armed with irrefutable, undeniable, and corroborated evidence.

Avoid giving the narcissist credible alternative scenarios to the facts. A skilled lawyer knows how to put a narcissist in trouble with the right questions, to remove the wind from the sails subtly but effectively.

Example:

- I am led to believe that you are entirely qualified in your profession. Excuse me, what is your highest academic qualification? So, it doesn't have a formal qualification, I understand. "

- Contradicting or diminishing the narcissist's inflated vision of himself and his fragile self-esteem will shatter.
- A trained lawyer knows how to play with words so that a narcissist understands that he has no control over everything and everyone.
- When we are in the confines of the courtrooms, we must stay as far away from the narcissist as possible and never look in his direction. The fact that never being looked at causes a narcissistic wound: they hate being ignored!
- As we know, the narcissist believes he is above the law and not subject to the limitations of ordinary citizens. As for them, they are superior to anyone in the courtroom, including the judge and lawyers. Nobody can have the audacity to make them responsible for their actions! Anyone who testifies against them will be labeled a liar and corrupt.
- Avoid showing any reaction to their words or behavior. They knew how to step on your Achilles heels first, and they will try again. Make sure these attempts are accepted with indifference.
- It can be challenging to communicate to magistrates and lawyers how unacceptable the behavior of a pathological narcissist has been.
- The goal of a good lawyer will be to snatch any information from the Court and lead them to discredit themselves when their explosive fury makes its appearance.

- Always remember to tell the truth. Never be tempted to beautify the truth or paint a fake picture.

And remember never to drop to the narcissist level.

CONCLUSION

I t is unfortunate that many people in this world are narcissists. It is a debilitating condition that can cause severe pain to the narcissist and those around them. When it comes to co-parenting with a narcissistic ex, both parties must make choices that will allow for an environment where his child can thrive.

For this to occur, the non-narcissist must make certain sacrifices, and the narcissist must repair his damaged self-esteem. While this process is an ongoing one, the narcissist must choose to do what it takes to repair his relationship with others and themselves.

It is important to note that you cannot control another person. It is your job to take care of yourself. You cannot change the actions of another person. You can choose, however, how you will react to those actions. It's essential to remember that you played no part in forming the narcissist's disorder, nor can you cure it. Abuse is not about power and control; it's about pain and disempowerment. A narcissist may use emotional and physical abuse to feel powerful and in control.

As difficult as it may be, you must set healthy boundaries. This is your life, and you should be treated with the same dignity and respect that anyone else would expect. You are not your children's property or the property of your narcissistic ex. You must make choices that will allow for a healthy environment for everyone involved. It is also important to realize that narcissistic behavior will always be a part of the relationship you have with your ex. There are years of pain and dysfunction that your ex must deal with to become well again.

Remember, you must take care of yourself as well as your child. You must protect both parties from the emotional chaos that may be occurring. It is recommended to seek therapy for yourself to heal from this difficult situation and make decisions based on what's best for you and your child.

The goal is to form an environment where the narcissistic ex can learn how to treat others to respect and honor them.

You must also protect your child from the negative effects of co-parenting with an ex who has such a severe disorder. It will be essential for you to teach him what it means to have boundaries and what it means to respect themselves. This may take some time, but in the end, you will both be glad you did.

Keep in mind that the non-narcissist is not responsible for the narcissist. You are the victim of abuse and must make choices that best suit you, your child, and your family unit. The narcissist's actions have nothing to do with you; they are merely symptoms of an underlying problem.

I hope you have found these statements to help you come to terms with your situation. It is my sincere goal for you to also gain insight into some of the behaviors that may be occurring in your relationship. And when you feel like there is no way out, remember this: You are a worthy individual and deserve a deep sense of self-respect, happiness, and love.

BOOK 2
PROTECT YOUR CHILD

The Powerful ABC Guide For Raising
Resilient Children To Secure Their Future
Relationship Development When A
Borderline Or Narcissistic Parent Is
Involved In The Picture

INTRODUCTION

It is a difficult task to be a parent, but it is even more challenging to be the child of a borderline or narcissist.

Borderline parents often give mixed messages of love and abandonment, are highly sensitive to situations, and may react with anger if their children don't live up to their expectations.

Raising children with narcissistic or borderline parents is difficult because they are unemotional. They say and do cruel things without any emotion, and children have a hard time understanding why they are supposed to love them or treat them in that way. They often feel that they are the cause of the parent's rage, and they tend to take on a lot of responsibility for all the parents' feelings, which leads them to feel guilty.

Loving a narcissist or borderline parent is like loving a wild horse. It is often challenging because these parents are always looking at what can go wrong or how they can be disappointed. They lack trust and, therefore, don't have loyalty to others. They are never satisfied, and they become outraged when others aren't pleased with them.

Narcissistic parents are materialistic and competitive with their children; they demand perfection and only praise them for extraordinary accomplishments. This makes the situation·even more challenging for children trying to heal the wounds inflicted on them by their narcissistic parents.

It is not our plan to make excuses for narcissists or borderlines, but instead to encourage children of these parents to recognize their pain and its source to heal the wounds.

Children of narcissistic or borderlines parents have a difficult childhood and adolescence because they feel that they have two moms or dads, one that is emotionally stable and one that is not. They don't know which parent to emulate since there is an extreme shift from the love; they feel from one parent to the abandonment by the other parent.

Children are confused by their narcissistic or borderline parents who are unaware of their inner pain and can't empathize with their children. The narcissistic or borderline parents often abandon their children after an argument that may have nothing to do with their child. The child feels like a ball being tossed around by the parent, and they lose respect for the parent and themselves.

To heal the wounds of being the child of a narcissistic or borderline parent, you must first acknowledge the pain within you. This acknowledgment will help you recognize self-accusations made by the narcissistic or borderline parent and take responsibility for your self-hatred.

Sometimes, adults who have been abandoned by their parents have those memories of feeling rejected, even though years have passed, and they might still be angry at their parents. You might even wonder what your parents could have done to love and accept you. It is essential to know that children are always innocent, and they did not do anything wrong. Sometimes, the parent's pain is causing them to reject their child because their parents denied them.

It is not uncommon for adult children of narcissists or borderlines parents to become narcissistic or borderline themselves when they have children of their own. They often repeat the same pattern that was used with them. They reject their children, are demanding, and are never satisfied.

This guide is designed to assist children of narcissistic or borderlines parents on their journey towards healing. It is written for adults, but it is also meant to be used by children of all ages. It can help children better understand what happened to them and how their parents felt about them. By recognizing that your parents abandoned you, you can move towards healing the wounds that are holding you back from being the person you want to be.

NARCISSISTIC PARENT: DEFINITION AND BEHAVIORS

Narcissism is also something that you may encounter in your immediate family setting. This is because you may have a parent or a sibling with a narcissistic personality disorder. It is quite challenging to deal with this type of social disorder within your immediate family setting compared to other places, such as in the workplace. The family setting constitutes your primary social space, and, in many cases, we have to spend most of their time within such a setting.

Furthermore, you can choose to work in another company or attend a different college to avoid being a narcissistic person. For instance, you may decide to quit your company and look for another job opportunity in case you find your current employer a little bit too narcissistic for you. However, you cannot choose your family, and at the same time, it is almost impossible to walk out on the family. You should know how to go about identifying and dealing with someone with a narcissistic personality.

Parents are supposed to be the primary caregivers of their offspring. Your parent should ensure that you are brought up in a good environment and one that is devoid of any physical or emotional threats. Parents are also tasked with instilling self-confidence in their children and ensuring that they have the mental and emotional strength to face the world.

However, many parents do not have what it takes to properly raise their children. You may have a narcissistic parent, but you are not sure if this is the case. These are the signs and symptoms of narcissistic behavior among parents.

CONSTANT RIDICULE

In many cases, narcissistic parents seek to be the only ones on top and are afraid of perceived competition even from their children. For this reason, narcissistic parents will do anything to ensure that they can bring down their children. Notably, this involves constant ridicule from the parents targeting the children to make them feel as if they are not good enough. For instance, a parent will ensure that they can constantly remind the child about a failure that they had in the past to make it difficult for the child to try again. Secondly, the ridicule might take the form of criticizing the child based on their physical appearance. For instance, a parent who keeps telling the child that they are too fat and ugly is considered narcissistic since they know that the only effect of such constant ridicule is that they will lower the child's self-esteem.

It is important to remember that the driving force behind narcissistic parenting is high insecurity on the part of the parent. Only extreme insecurity can make a person fear competition from their siblings. All the same, as a child subjected to narcissistic parenting, it is essential to remember that there is nothing wrong with it, but there is something incredibly wrong with your parent. You should, therefore, not try to change who you are to please your parents, but you should instead let your parents know that they have a personality disorder and it is undermining your relationship with them.

INFLATED SELF IMAGE

Most narcissistic parents also exhibit a sense of inflated self-image. They tend to believe that they are more important than other people, image is extended to the family setting. In many cases, parents will feel that they are more important than others, including their children, based on what they do. Those in mainstream professions such as medicine, finance, or engineering tend to believe that their profession gives them the status of being the most important people in society. This might result in them frowning upon the career choices that their children have in mind. For instance, you might be having a parent who is a doctor and becomes highly disappointed that their daughter or son has picked a career in acting. Such a parent will go out of their way to convince the child to pursue a career in medicine since they think that this child will end up being someone important in society.

It is worth noting that most narcissistic parents with inflated self-images will extend this characteristic to the child. The parent might, for instance, convince the child that they are more important than their friends at school. As a child, once you notice that your father or parent is trying to material wealth as

277

justification for your perceived superiority over others, you could be alive to the fact that they may be having a narcissistic personality disorder. Probably, you can do very little regarding their condition, but on your part, you should never give in to the fallacy that you are more important or superior to others. In the end, you must appreciate the fact that we may be different in many ways, but everybody is essential.

MANIPULATION

It is quite unfortunate that many parents manipulate their children on account of narcissistic personality disorder. Manipulation in this context can take many forms, but it mainly aims to make the children feel a little bad about themselves. The parent, in turn, derives some satisfaction by knowing that they have brought their kid down a notch or two.

Many parents with narcissistic personality disorder use guilt as a tool to manipulate their kids. Such parents will constantly remind the child of something good that they did for them to ensure that they feel indebted to them. A parent might, for instance, keep reminding the kid of the new bike that they bought for them so that the child is forced to keep expressing their gratitude for the parent. This is because the regular expression of gratitude is one of the things that will make the parent feel important.

Manipulation can also take a blame game whereby the parent apportions blame the child for things that have nothing to do with them. For instance, a parent might lame the child for their state of unhappiness, anti-social behavior such as alcohol addiction, and many other things. The goal in many such cases is to make the child feel worse than the parent for things that they know nothing about.

Comparison is also another form of manipulation that parents with narcissistic personality disorder use. The parent might compare one sibling to another with a view of making the child feel bad. In the same breath, a parent can also compare the child with one of their friends while letting them know that they think the friend is much better at something than the child is. Comparison seeks to let the child know that the people they are being compared with are better than them, which has the overall effect of undermining the child's self-esteem.

Emotional manipulation is something that many parents with the disorder prefer to use. Emotional manipulation entails letting the child know that the parent will not consider them their children unless they behave in a particular manner. In some cases, the parent can verbally disown their children to make them feel bad. The emotional manipulator is perhaps the worst kind of narcissistic parent since they can inflict severe emotional pain and distress to the child.

Children should be wary of such manipulative behavior on the part of their parents. Initially, narcissistic manipulation is designed to make the child feel bad about themselves. However, once you are aware of the rationale and way of thinking of a narcissistic parent, you will not be manipulated into behaving in a certain way. It is important to note that the end game of any manipulation is to make someone behave in a certain way. However, if you are aware that indeed you are being manipulated, you will not act in a particular manner to satisfy the needs of the manipulator. In narcissistic parents, manipulation is designed to make the child feel ill-equipped, sorry, and even indebted to the parent. But if the child knows that they are being manipulated, they will not exhibit such behavior, thus negating the objective of the manipulative parent.

HIGHLY REACTIVE

Some narcissistic parents exhibit extreme reactions to anything wrong that the child does. No child is perfect, and from time to time, children will do something wrong. For very young, children are meant to learn from their mistakes, since this is regarded as the most effective way to acquire life lessons. However, it is quite difficult for children with narcissistic parents. This is because the parents are wired to overact every time a child makes even the slightest mistake. Such children end up living in fear of their parent's reaction, which prevents them from trying out new things. Some parents might affect the children in their later lives since they will not attain their true potential.

You should not allow the fear of your parents to prevent you from fully experiencing the gift of life. Many teenagers out there and even young adults are still afraid of their parents. Because of this fear, they will allow their parents to have a profound impact on their lives, including making decisions about their careers, their potential husband or wife, and even going to the extent of allowing their parents to decide how they bring up their children. However, if such a parent has brought you up, it is high time you appreciate that you are not the one with a problem, but your parent is. You should try and conquer the fear you have for your parents since, in the end, fear can only keep you from experiencing your life to the full.

GENERAL LACK OF EMPATHY TOWARDS THE CHILD

Narcissistic parents will hardly ever empathize with their children. The parents will not try to see things from the child's perspective; instead, they will keep insisting that everything has to be done the way they want. It is important to note that children have feelings and opinions on various issues and that their opinion does indeed matter. Once children feel like their opinions do not matter, they are likely to distance themselves from their parents as they try to do things their way. Others may try to fight back to at least try to get their parents to see things from their perspective. Finally, and unfortunately, some children may end up pleasing their parents by adopting the parents' perspectives even when, deep down, they would instead pursue a different course of action. Such children end up being very good at putting on a show for their parents, which might eventually undermine their personalities.

At the end of it, the narcissistic personality of the parents is likely to have a profound impact on the child. Children growing up with narcissistic parents will likely develop into insecure or even narcissistic adults. This is because such children are programmed to believe that they are more critical than others and that it is suitable for the parents or adults always to have their way. Furthermore, a child who has been manipulated by their parents is also likely to be a master manipulator. It is important for the child to try to develop their perspectives and outlook in life, to appreciate that everyone is essential. Hence, as not end up being a victim of narcissistic parenting.

LANGUAGE AND COMMUNICATION OF A NARCISSISTIC PARENT

When a narcissist realizes that you are not willing to speak with them, they will have an ambassador in their place. This concept is known as sending out the Flying Monkeys. These people may or may not be aware of the situation or even that they are being used to help the narcissist get back into your life. You are in worse trouble if they are aware of their position, as they most likely are another narcissist that will work you on another angle.

The main reason narcissists end up chasing you is that they feel or think you have something they want. This can be the case in reality or a fantasy in their minds.

Narcissists are also reluctant to let go of a former victim before they have successfully controlled another. This is where you will find there are overlaps in relationships with a narcissist. It is a safety net for them to have someone they know they can get attention from a phone call away. Narcissists cannot stand being alone, and as such, are always on the prowl.

The amount of energy they will input to acquire the new victim depends on the level of use the narcissist has placed on their victim. If there is a low level of usefulness, they will put in little effort. However, if they feel the victim is invaluable, they will single-mindedly go after their goal with gusto.

When the victim finally takes the opportunity to leave the relationship, they may find that the narcissist cannot let them go. They will start with the manipulation process by beginning to love to bomb the ex or convince the victim that they are willing to change.

At this stage, the narcissist can promise the moon if they feel they are of any value any longer. Victims must be careful during this tricky step. It is easy to fall back into the same patterns that will land them right back to the situation they had left, but most likely, it will be worse this time. Remember that it never permanently gets better with a narcissist involved.

Even if the love bombing and honeymoon period lasted for months beforehand, do not think for one moment that this will happen again. It will likely be a month or less until the narcissist switches back to the manipulative and controlling partner.

Because of this, the times that the victim can escape from their hell need to be cherished and fully taken advantage of each time you leave and come back. The honeymoon period will get shorter and shorter. They quickly remember the reasons why they left and probably have another reason to add to the list.

When the victim decides to leave and implement no contact, this drives the narcissist into hyperactive mode. They scramble to do anything and everything in their power to bring you back to them and thus bring control back to the narcissist. Since the victim is the narcissist's attention supply, the narcissist is left completely powerless while feeling worthless and small.

The psychological power shift from the narcissist to the victim is instantaneous when no contact is implemented. The narcissist cannot function as they have lost the power they have worked so hard to possess and the emotional punching bag.

A common misconception of victims is when the narcissist changes their behavior to come back into their good graces to have a relationship again; they believe that the narcissist must love them. This is just repeating the cycle because this is how the narcissist could catch the victim in the first place.

This is a very difficult part of the process in which the victim needs to remain strong. They must remember the reasons why they left the narcissist and stick to their guns. It is because the victims are usually still very much in love with the narcissists despite it all, and it is quite easy to run back into the arms of the familiar. This would be the case if the narcissist had kept the victim isolated from the outside world for some time, as the victim will have difficulty adjusting to everyday life again.

Yes, the victims know that the relationship was negative for them and that they are walking straight back into the misery, but it is extremely easy to get drawn back in time and time again. Because they fell in love with the idea of a person that they could relate to, it is difficult to stop feeling those emotions when even a shimmer of the old partner shines through. It makes the victim believe that they were right about there being something good inside this monster of who their love has become.

The real reason behind the narcissist's return is that something they wanted in their life is not going as planned. It could be that they are having a difficult time securing another victim. It could be that their new catch is not as submissive and willing to give the attention that the old victim gave. It could also do with not having to learn a whole other person's weaknesses and going through the entire process again with someone else.

It could very well just be a power game to show the victim that the narcissist is still in control. They can manipulate the victim in any way they want to use them and then discard them again at their whim. They are in no way in love with the victim other than for what the victim can offer.

The narcissists will put on a complete act along with crocodile tears, if necessary, to display the level of emotion they feel for hurting the victim. They are so good at this act; many victims believe them in their fragile state and want to comfort the narcissist.

The narcissist knows the best way to get them back is through their emotions because it is the easiest way to manipulate a victim who is just coming out of this state of being. The victim has not yet been able to healthily deal with the emotions that were felt during the relationship and is not able to make rational decisions.

And of course, when the victim hears something they have been starved from for an extended amount of time, there is a psychological relief of finally getting recognition for the things they had experienced. When narcissists profess their love or say sorry when they have not said it for months, it is difficult for anyone not to pay attention and be drawn in.

These masters of falsehoods may even make up stories of how they need the help of the victim. It could be something simple that the victim knows better or an elaborate cry for help because something dramatic or embarrassing happened. The narcissist makes the victim feel special because they say that no one other than the victim would understand or help. In the end, it is the same story as a boy who cried wolf. This tactic can also be used as a way to drain the victim's time from their day.

Sometimes the narcissist will go to more extreme measures, especially if the love bombing and sorry phase do not make the victim come crawling back. They may start spreading nasty rumors about the victim to their friends, family members, coworkers, or even perfect strangers. This tactic is known as a smear campaign and can even go as far as to involve revenge porn.

The narcissist pulls out all the stops and lets their imagination run wild. The most bizarre stories will be invented to defame and slander the victim when they are forced to defend themselves. The narcissist will even go as far as calling the victim a narcissist, which brings the victim's supposed supporters to the narcissist's side. This is also the point that the narcissist will bring up the embarrassing acts that the victim shamefully did during the relationship and bring them to the public eye.

The smear campaigns effectively bring further shame to the victim and increase the isolation they most likely felt during the relationship. This often brings the victim back to the narcissist so that they can somehow prove to the narcissist that they are not that bad of a person and to clear their reputation.

However, the damage is already done. During the smut throwing, the victim finds out who their true friends and family members are as anyone who knows the real person, and they would not believe any of this manipulative shaming.

This is an extremely hurtful and vulnerable position for the victim, and the narcissist knows this. They are putting pressure on the victim to punish them for leaving, or they want them to feel like they cannot function properly without them.

The narcissist has been manipulating you the entire time, so why would they stop now? This is a good phrase to memorize and ponder during the times that the narcissist seemed to have changed back to the person that you always loved and knew was deep down inside of them somewhere.

The victim needs to block out the narcissist from their life if possible. Doing this will minimize the chance of them being drawn back in by the master manipulator. Know that even if the victim has not been in communication with their ex for a while, the moment they do, it can easily throw them back to the starting point.

When a victim is actively communicating with their ex, they are setting up their dissolution. They are tearing themselves down and all the healing that they have gained since going no contact. The manipulator makes the victim think they must stand up for themselves when the narcissist is gaining more power over the victim.

When a narcissist starts the cycle of wanting to return to a victim's life, this ensures that the victim still feels the pain caused during the relationship. It is a way to bring the victim back to ground zero and to the thick of it. This can even be done while stalking the victim or calling out of the blue after a long silence to instill the fear once again in the victim after they have hopefully moved on.

Just know that if the narcissist still sees you as something valuable, they will pull out any ropes you could not even imagine. Because they have no filter for proper behavior towards another human being, there is no limit to where they will stop if they want to be vindictive towards you or even to get you back.

You can tell if the person you are in a relationship with is a narcissist based on their behavior throughout your relationship. Ideally, you want to be able to figure out if your boyfriend, girlfriend, or even an acquaintance has narcissistic tendencies as soon as possible so that you can sever ties with them before you are too invested in that relationship.

LANGUAGE AND COMMUNICATION TO MANAGE/DEAL WITH A NARCISSISTIC PARTNER/PARENT

Depending on your circumstances and situation, the easiest way is to go no contact. Sometimes it's hard to believe that people behave that way and knowing the problem can be a great help. Recognize that their behavior is not "difficult," it's not normal, and rules do not apply. You may need to acknowledge and grieve the loss of a real, supportive parent or partner, the one you never had and will never have. This may be a bigger issue than you think at present, but not necessarily.

Accept that they will contact your friends or other family members to get them to put pressure on you to explain yourself, to feel guilty, or to get in touch. Your friends probably won't understand what's going on.

Don't try to reason or argue with your narcissistic parent or partner. Communicate quietly and factually in a contained and adult way, however much they try to make you feel like a naughty child. Don't try to argue; they will always believe that they are right.

Trust yourself to find your way of happy, independent living alongside having a narcissistic parent or partner. It will be your mix of approaches, and you will make it work for you. Trust yourself.

ASSERTING YOURSELF

Assertiveness is a technique for having difficult conversations. If you stick to the principles, it's surprisingly effective. You can use the DESC approach.

D = DESCRIBE	Describe what happened.
E = EXPRESS	Say how you feel about it
S = SPECIFY	Specify what you want
C = CONSEQUENCES	Say what happens if you don't get it.

Ways to make it work:

- Keep calm

- Don't argue

- Don't get angry or aggressive

- Keep it simple

- Repeat as necessary

- Do what you say you're going to do

USEFUL TIPS ON HOW TO TALK TO A NARCISSIST

KEEP SOME PERSPECTIVE

Narcissists are very wrapped up in their view of the world and ego needs. Try not to get drawn into their world because their view of the world and yours probably don't intersect. Keep calm. Try to see yourself as an observer of the interaction.

DON'T TAKE IT PERSONALLY

The nature of narcissism is that the world is seen through the narcissist's lens, and in their view, you will be seen as less important than them. Don't take this personally. That's how narcissists see everybody. Don't allow yourself to be put down.

STAY AWARE OF YOUR STRENGTHS

Remind yourself of your strengths before you interact with the narcissistic person. Remind yourself of your kindness, your intelligence, your flexibility, and your ability to be insightful. Your contact with the narcissist cannot take this away from you.

KEEP OUT OF DRAMA

Narcissists frequently find themselves in dramas with others. They will win over somebody in an argument, or they will be feeling hard done by. Don't let yourself be drawn in as a rescuer or a supporter.

LEARN FROM YOUR INTERACTIONS

It is good personal development to observe yourself and observe others. Your particular narcissistic person may be very difficult to deal with, but recovery from these kinds of relationships can provide learning opportunities. Nothing is wasted! Decide and trust your judgment, and you will find that you can reshape how you interact with your narcissistic parent or partner.

DON'T ASSUME THAT A NARCISSIST WILL CHANGE

It is natural to think that when you point out the error of their ways, then your narcissistic parent will immediately say, "Oh, wow, of course! I must start right away to treat you differently!" This is very unlikely because if they are that challenging to be around, they cannot moderate their behavior. They are more likely to blame you for raising the issue and make you look selfish or demanding. This method of deflecting responsibility onto other people is called projection. It is a common way to distance oneself from uncomfortable feelings by viewing someone else, or a whole group of people, as being the cause of them. Narcissists will often say what others want to hear. You may find that they say the right things to you and then behave in the same way.

DON'T ASSUME NARCISSISTS HAVE A CONSCIENCE

Most narcissists have a long history of offending others – it's part of how they are – and they are unlikely to show remorse. They are devoid of the faculty referred to as conscience, which causes us to feel guilty if we have gone against socially acceptable ways of treating others. Every narcissist is the center of their universe. It's not something to blame them for; it's how they are. They don't see it as a moral stance, it is a fixed structure of their thinking, and they cannot reflect on this.

It is very unlikely that a narcissist will feel bad about how they have treated you. They will have had very good reasons for behaving that way, and there is no possibility that they can take responsibility for any negative outcomes. They have always done things for the best, and that doesn't include getting anything wrong. Getting things wrong is someone else's fault.

SET FIRM BOUNDARIES

Personal boundaries are guidelines, rules, or limits that a person creates to identify reasonable, safe, and permissible ways other people behave towards them and respond when someone passes those limits.

- Physical boundaries refer to your personal space.

- Mental boundaries involve your thoughts.

- Emotional boundaries refer to your feelings.

- Spiritual boundaries refer to your spiritual preferences and beliefs.

Narcissists may intrude on any boundaries, especially telling you how to think and ignoring your feelings. Setting boundaries means deciding how far you will allow a narcissist to intrude on your personal space, time, or communication. Here are some examples of techniques that you might use:

- "If you keep making critical remarks about my partner (or job, or kids, or anything), I'm going to hang up." And do it.

- Determine how long you will spend with the narcissistic parent. One example I've used myself is, "I've just dropped by for ten minutes. I have to meet a client in half an hour." Or "I'm at the office all day today. I'll sort it out for you tomorrow."

- Learn to change the subject to your schedule. When your narcissist parent says, "How are you getting on with Linda? She's such a worrier", you answer, "Really well, thanks. Did I tell you I've got a new client at work; it might mean a promotion?"

- Don't share too much personal information; it will probably be used against you. If they criticize you, respond positively, for example: "I don't think that you know what you are doing!" You answer, "Thanks for your opinion, but I'm quite happy with the way I'm handling it."

- Mark out private time. "I'm going out for the day tomorrow. If you need anything, you'll need to call your career."

- Schedule time with your family, completely free from your parent. Minimize their influence on your children because they will often use your children against you. "I think you're too soft on him!" or, "She would have done better at a grammar school; you've ruined her chances!"

Why not compose a range of conversational techniques to suit your situation. Accept that your parent will find a variety of ways to sabotage your plans. Older parents will have medical emergencies while you are out for the day, even though the issue wasn't urgent. You need to be firm and to plan.

GREY ROCK

Don't argue with narcissists! The grey rock technique is useful if you are around a negative person, and narcissists are often negative about others. The key with grey rock is not to argue or engage with the criticism. The grey rock technique includes a whole range of "no comment" comments that you can use.

Once you realize that there is nothing to be gained by getting involved in your narcissistic parent or partner's conversational gambits, you can let out a gentle sigh of relief. It was never a conversation between two adults, and it was never going to work for you.

NO CONTACT

No contact or minimal contact is the ultimate boundary with a narcissistic parent. No contact means no contact of any kind, including birthdays and Christmas. The narcissist will take advantage of any opening. If your parent is malignant and control, this may be the only way ahead, and many children of narcissists take this approach.

However, it is not without its pitfalls. Many people feel very guilty and uncomfortable when they break off contact, and they may also miss out on contact with the other parent. Your siblings will have their views on it, and it takes a great deal of determination to deal with the comments of friends and family. However, if the hurt is too much, then no contact is the answer. How does it work?

First, decide how far you will go with no contact. Ask yourself:

- Will you see them at Christmas?

- Will you send them a birthday card?

- Will you cut off all contact?

- Will you remove them from your phone contacts?

- Will you block their number?

- Will you tell them that you are cutting off contact?

- Will you still talk to the other parent?

However you do it, expect friends and family to get in touch to say that they are worried about you or your parents. Your parent may get in touch with your children or friends to make contact that way. They may stalk you on social media. It takes many resolves, but sometimes it's the right thing, and only you can decide.

HOW YOU LIVE IN A FAMILY WITH A NARCISSISTIC PARTNER

There are many problems that can come up if you are in a relationship with someone who suffers from narcissistic personality disorder, particularly if it is a severe form. Learning more about what sort of problems typically arise when living with a narcissist will help you to better identify whether or not your partner is a narcissist.

Unequal investment in the relationship: if your partner is a narcissist, they will probably be unwilling or unable to invest as much in the relationship as you do. They will act ambivalent about the quality of the relationship and their role in maintaining it. This becomes problematic when you feel as if you are doing all the work to keep the relationship together while your partner carries on as if it is not their concern.

Unrealistic demands: a narcissistic partner will often expect a lot more from you than they expect of themselves when it comes to the relationship. He or she will require a lot of attention and constant validation, but fail to give you the same in return. It can take a huge emotional toll on you to constantly be supportive and caring for a person who acts as if they could not care less about your well-being. You might find yourself emotionally exhausted from trying to meet the unrealistic demands that your partner has set for you.

Distrust and jealousy: particularly with compensatory and fanatic narcissists, you may have to deal with an excessive amount of jealousy and distrust. The feelings of inferiority that lie at the core of a narcissist's psyche cause them to feel inadequate and even paranoid. This can lead to your partner becoming jealous over trivial things or distrusting you without any rational cause. Trust is a key element to a healthy relationship. When this is lacking (particularly when it is lacking without any rational cause), it leads to a lot of arguments and strife within the relationship. You may find yourself walking on eggshells just to make sure your partner can find no cause to distrust you.

Disloyalty: narcissists are especially prone to having affairs. This is even more the case with amorous narcissists as well as unprincipled and elitist narcissists. Often, this is because they require so much extra attention and validation that they seek it outside of the relationship as well as within it. A cheating partner has been the ruin of many relationships, but it is a particularly difficult issue to work through when your partner lacks the capacity to feel guilty about their actions.

Unsatisfied needs: because narcissists have difficulty with empathy, they are often inattentive to their partner's needs. You will find yourself unable to obtain the emotional support you should be getting out of the relationship. When you compound this with the unrealistic demands your partner has for you, the relationship will become emotionally draining rather than fulfilling and enjoyable.

Lack of respect: especially if your partner is an elitist narcissist, you may feel that he or she does not respect you. Your partner may be overly condescending or demeaning to you. He or she will also not recognize or praise your accomplishments. Instead, your partner will act superior and treat you as if you are inferior and owe him or her affection by virtue of this superiority. Like trust, respect helps form the foundation of a strong relationship. Without respect for each other as individuals, it is difficult to cultivate love and compassion.

Lack of intimacy: while you may be able to maintain a healthy sex life with your narcissistic partner, intimacy in other ways will be difficult to achieve. Narcissists do not open up emotionally, since doing so would risk exposing the vulnerability and inferiority that they refuse to acknowledge within themselves. Even if you take the initiative by opening up and making yourself vulnerable to your partner, this will not be reciprocated. The lack of reciprocation will leave you feeling exposed and isolated.

Emotional instability: narcissists often experience dramatic mood swings. When your partner wakes up in the morning, you can never be sure whether it will be a good day or a bad day. His or her mood could change dramatically over the course of the day without any rational cause. Living with such instability and unpredictability is difficult and can have a strong influence on your own emotional wellbeing.

Many of these problems can also occur in relationships where neither partner suffers from narcissistic personality disorder. The key difference is that a narcissist will have much more difficulty addressing these issues in a calm and rational way. In fact, a narcissistic partner will hardly be willing to acknowledge that these problems exist at all since he or she will feel entitled to all the benefits of the relationship without feeling any need to contribute.

Each of these problems can exist in varying levels of severity. If your partner is a narcissist, you are likely experiencing many — or even all — of them. When the problems are still relatively mild, it is possible to work through them if you do so carefully and if you feel that your partner and the relationship you have with him or her is worth saving. However, in their most extreme forms, these problems can become toxic and dangerous.

HOW YOUR CHILD LIVES IN A FAMILY WITH A NARCISSISTIC PARENT

What happens to a person who had a narcissist parent(s)? As far as the major statistics about the child is concerned, including their communication as a teen and the relationship problems experienced, one may ask: how does it affect their work-life? How does it affect their love life? The way narcissistic parents bring up their children has a lot of impact on the emotional, psychological, and social life of those children.

According to the American Psychological Association, people between the ages of 18 and 33 have the highest stress levels. This is a critical time in the life of any individual because it is the period where you chart your course for life and a time when society expects you to be at your best in terms of energy and vigor available to you. This kind of push is positive if, in a healthy amount, but it is usually to the extreme for children who grow up with narcissistic parents. The resultant effect of an extreme push is always on the negative side of the line.

These parents tend to feed their egos with their children's lives without giving careful thought or consideration to what the child wants. They force their will, ideologies, and desires on the child without paying attention to their individuality. In most cases, they subject the child to isolation or abandonment when they perceive they are trying to be their person.

They fail to understand that a child is a different entity and has a life of their own. The fact that you were the channel through which the child came does not necessarily make them one with you in reasoning and way of life. They are all concerned about their self-image and how they can constantly put pressure on their kids to help them polish their image. A child that grows up in that kind of environment sees the world from the perspective that their parents have presented.

Let's look at the effects of narcissistic parents on their children's communication, emotional, and working life.

LOW SELF-ESTEEM

Parents with narcissistic tendencies never see the good in their kids because they always expect them to do more. They tend to exert undue perfectionism, thereby putting extremely high pressure on these kids. Some of them will push themselves to the extent of using a reward-based system where a child earns love from their actions and achievement.

This kind of environment hurts a child's self-esteem; he gets to feel defeated in his mind even before he sets out on a mission. He constantly hears negative comments at home, and when these things register over time, the child will have a precise image of themselves. The child begins to blame himself for everything that happens and even for things yet to happen.

This kind of image usually depicts a lower than usual opinion of oneself. In life, you have got to win the battle in your mind before you get to the battlefield, and if you constantly dwell on the fact that you can only fail, it is very likely to happen. Growing up in a reward-based environment rather than a love-based one tends to foster low self-esteem in a child, and if proper care is not taken, it could affect that child through teenage years down to adulthood.

COMMUNICATION PROBLEMS

Most children brought up by narcissistic parents tend to be reserved and withdrawn from people. They are shy and are unable to communicate their feeling effectively. They grew up with the fear of making mistakes at anything they do, even with the words they utter. So, they are usually very careful and cautious about what they say.

Most of the time, they prefer not to talk for fear of saying something wrong because, while growing up, their parents could withhold love from them for speaking up or challenging their opinion in any way. They exhibit shyness instead of confidence. This robs these kids of living the kind of life they want to live and, if taken to adulthood, could even lead to loneliness and consequently depression. They are known to bottle up most of their emotions, which is usually not good for their emotional health.

INABILITY TO RECEIVE LOVE

People that grew up with narcissistic parents are accustomed to the feeling of not deserving love unless they have done something to earn it. After spending so much time with parents that make you work to earn their love, you get automatically bound to think you don't deserve to be loved. Most of these kids grow up unable to maintain love relationships with people because of their experiences in the past.

There is always a feeling of inadequacy attached to any gift or act of kindness they receive. I heard of a young man who had a narcissistic mom. His mom never saw anything good in him; in fact, he had to do something extraordinary to earn him a good meal. After he left the house to live on his own, of course, he found it difficult to maintain a relationship.

One day, his roommate's mom visited and wanted to make them a special meal, and the first thing he said was that he did not feel he did anything to deserve that kind of special meal. Something as simple as a meal. Huh? You wouldn't blame him because that was how he was brought up, and it will take an effort to break out of that thinking to enable him to receive love freely and give love to others.

The constant need for validation from others is one major effect of being brought up by narcissistic parents. You tend to crave approval from others, which is dangerous. It is dangerous because it makes you live the life that others expect of you instead of living the life of your dreams. You build your self-worth from what people think and say of you, making you a slave of another person's opinion.

It is not wrong to ask for people's opinions but making it a lifestyle and constantly craving to hear positive comments is a problem. Since these children didn't get these validations from their parents while growing up, they are usually hungry to receive them from other people.

Unhealthy competitive tendency: Growing up with narcissistic parents is a lot of work as they constantly keep you on your toes. They make you feel there is always something better to be done, someone out there for you to outdo, and the loop goes on. It never has an end with them. They do not celebrate the small victories of their kids; instead, they want them to do more.

Competition is good when it is healthy, when you strive for what you believe in, not primarily because you must outsmart somebody or be ahead of someone. When you have these kinds of parents, you are always on the go, trying to outdo someone, but the irony is that you will never live a happy life with that kind of mentality because there is always someone you will need to be ahead of. This makes it difficult for them to live happy lives because nothing is ever enough. When an individual grows into adulthood with this kind of mentality, it will be difficult for him to have good relationships with colleagues because he will always see them as his competitors. Narcissistic parenting leaves a bunch of effects on children, including guilt-tripping and emotional blackmail.

As the life of a victim of narcissistic parenting grows worse by the day due to low self-esteem, unhealthy competition, poor communication, and other factors such as the inability to receive love, the narcissist child channels this mindset and the level of negative energy acquired from this lifestyle into their work and in the life of other people, thus spreading the narcissist plague even further.

The unhealthy side for friends and relatives closes to the narcissist begins when they observe their lifestyle and then decide to distance themselves from the narcissist child. Narcissist children are mere victims of narcissist parents and may not even be narcissists themselves. Understandably, no one wants to be influenced by the life the narcissist lives or their ideology towards work, life, or relationships. However, no narcissist can recover from their mental disorder or behavior without care, love, and support from the people they interact with daily. The plague of narcissism can only be cured by love and good therapy. It can also be managed clinically by qualified psychologists who have been trained and have studied to help victims of narcissists.

When they have discovered that they are narcissists, that may be because people are distancing themselves away from them in order not to be influenced by their toxic behavior. A solution to this can be seeking clinical help and studying the best ways to overcome narcissist behavior. Allowing narcissistic parents to continue having a grip on you will only reduce your level of

self-worth and leave you feeling guilty and incapable of true
love and genuine acceptance by society.

UNDERSTANDING WHAT PARENTS FACE WITH A NARCISSISTIC OR BORDERLINE PARTNER

Relationship and narcissism do not fit together. Narcissism describes a person who is completely self-centered, selfish, and ruthless one-sided to fulfill his own needs. His fellow human beings of little interest and cannot move into the emotional world of the other. A narcissist lacks essential abilities, which are indispensable for a happy relationship.

Ideally, two people fall in love, respect, love and support each other. It is much more important for the narcissist to have a partner at his side, who admires him for his greatness, who takes away the annoying everyday care and spoils him according to all the rules of art. He does not want an independent, self-confident person by his side, with whom he can lead an equal relationship, but a marionette who dances to his pipe and renounces an authentic life of his own.

The typical partners of narcissists are modest people who do not have their requirements and have low self-esteem. They put their person in the background for the partner and sacrifice themselves for their needs. They see their fulfillment in fully adapting to another person and serving him. In this respect, the question is not whether these partners are in an equal relationship. They want to look at someone and admire him.

EVERYONE BENEFITS FROM THE RELATIONSHIP

In the end, they are doing this for a similar reason as the narcissist, namely, to experience the desired long-term attention and appreciation for their admiration. Their behavior also has narcissistic roots, so the typical partner of narcissists also speaks of the co-narcissist or complementary narcissist. Thus, relationship and narcissism essentially constitute a community for the mutual satisfaction of needs. One is useful to the other.

However, the fate in this relationship is that the co-partners can make as much effort as they want: it will never be enough. The never-ending need of the narcissist for admiration is not to be satisfied. If the partner does not adjust one hundred percent to the narcissist's wishes and does not deal with him every second as he imagines it, he has a problem. Narcissists have no understanding of lack of care. They are increasingly demanding and do not realize how much they are burdening their partner.

A narcissist does not have the human habit of thanking others for the contributions of the other partner in a relationship or even bringing the same appreciation to the partner. He considers the services of the partner self-evident, which need no express thanks. To be able to live together with such a great man seems to him to be gratifying.

A NARCISSIST UNDERSTANDS MASTERING HIS PARTNER

Everything feels so good at the start of a relationship. Absolutely nothing seems to indicate that this love could become a true nightmare. Narcissists are successful, charming persons with attractive charisma, with which they can draw everyone into their spell. A narcissist knows how to win the favor of a potential partner. He gives her the feeling of being very special. He appreciates her and flatters her. He knows how to build the partner's lack of self-esteem. Often, he promises her the fulfillment of her longing, desires and promises his partner to carry her on his hands for the rest of his life.

Who does not like to hear compliments, and who does not want to be seduced? It is not easy to resist a narcissist. Typical partners who don't know how to help themselves and have no vision don't cheat. They are well-educated persons of any age, social class, and financial or cultural background. Everyone can get a narcissist!

Therefore, anyone about to fall in love is advised to look for narcissistic characteristics before being blinded by them. The unique staging of the narcissist, the great and exaggerated advertising for the favor of the other, and his impressive and quite charming appearance alone should be reasons for caution. Once you are stuck in the clutches of the narcissist and are not aware of him, you may have to pay dearly for this mistake.

A NARCISSIST IS MAKING A DIFFERENCE IN THE RELATIONSHIP

In the course of the relationship, the narcissist will take more and more space. Everything has to turn around him. Once the generous gestures at the beginning of the relationship are no longer needed. He strangely took the partner and considered her as his property. The respect disappears to an intolerable minimum. Instead, he develops pleasure in dealing with his partner from above, harassing her and systematically deprecating her. The partner must not win power over him at all. Therefore, he does everything to shake her self-esteem, to disturb her, or to offend her.

The real conflict of perspectives lies in the extreme opposition of the two. The narcissist increases his sense of self-esteem through the permanent admiration of his partner. On the other hand, through the idealization of the narcissist and the fusion with him. This difference serves the other on its way. But, at the same time, each also depends on the other. The deceptive harmony can easily be disturbed.

As a rule, however, the narcissist will become suspicious with time and be afraid to depend on his partner. The narcissist will begin a quarrel and thus unbalance the steady relationship to which both have unconsciously ceased. It can also be that the partner withdraws from his admiration and begins to pursue his self-realization dreams. This is also a potential conflict because the narcissist cannot accept that the partner suddenly

314

becomes more independent and no longer puts him in the center. By all means, he will try to restore the old order.

If, as a result of the constant injuries of the narcissist, or simply because he is looking for a new adventure, the result is a separation, this usually proceeds dramatically. The narcissist in this situation by no means behaves as a cavalier, as at the beginning of the relationship. If he must break out of the relationship, he wants a quick end without much argument. If he leaves the partner, he feels this as a defeat and sees himself as a victim. The offense will trigger anger that can hardly be restrained, manifesting itself in a revenge campaign.

The narcissistic partner is incapable of really engaging with another person. It is only fixed on itself; they only need others as a kind of lackey at their service whenever they want. For children, they usually do not have much left. They set even higher goals and neglect the relationship.

The narcissist's partner is usually a completely subdued and humble person who is very concerned about their couple and who feels it as a special privilege to be with such a grandiose spouse. They are condemned to serve the other, read every wish from their lips, and keep themselves in the background. The right to independence is not recognized; independent action is not desired. They have to function according to the instructions of the dominant partner and can be found as a complementary narcissist at first.

THE NARCISSIST DOES NOT ALLOW THE PARTNER TO PARTICIPATE IN THEIR EMOTIONAL LIFE

They believe they have to cope with their feelings alone and do not even think of leaning against their partner's shoulder. Fearing that the other might interfere with their affairs or uncover their weaknesses, they will make a great circle around the spouse in emotional matters, even if the partner is trying to act with the best intentions. Too big is their fear of proximity, dependency, and injuries! At any cost, they want to maintain the image of the perfect woman or man who can help themselves in any living situation — or who has no problems at all.

THE NARCISSIST BELIEVES THE RELATIONSHIP IS COMPLETELY UNDER CONTROL

They give the outwards appearance of a perfect relationship in which everything works perfectly. They take care of the appropriate economic and social framework, have a good income, converse with interesting people, and cultivate a charming and varied life. Such a man or woman is always looking for new tasks; they cannot see a standstill. They always want to climb higher and higher. They do not notice that the partner can slip away. They secretly assume that whatever she or he pleases, also pleases the spouse.

THE NARCISSIST SHAPES THE RELATIONSHIP LIFE ALONE

They have a clear idea of how the relationship must work. They present peculiar game rules and expect a tacit acceptance. Independent actions of the partner that do not fit into their ideas are immediately combated and stifled in the bud. The partner is so surprised by a flood of insulting allegations that he or she will, in the future, abandon independent ventures and will no longer interfere with the design of the relationship.

A NARCISSIST IS VERY CAREFUL ABOUT THE BALANCE OF GIVING AND TAKING

When the narcissists have given a little bit of patience, they expect it to return immediately. If the relationship does not exist or the partner makes too many mind-bending maneuvers, they can exchange him or her with ease and without remorse. In the relationship, they behave highly parasitically.

IN ESSENCE, THE PARTNER IS OF NO GREAT IMPORTANCE TO THEM

They leave no real inner bond: they do not want to be dependent on anyone. They get people and send them away at will. The narcissist leads a single life within a relationship. They selfishly use the advantages of a relationship. The disadvantages blind them.

A RELATIONSHIP IS SOMETHING FOR THEM FROM WHICH THEY WANT TO BENEFIT

Narcissists often take relationships out of the pure calculation because they hope to benefit from the relationship with the partner. If this has stopped, the relationship becomes meaningless, and they move on. They behave exuberantly and quickly change the relationship when it loses its charm. Of course, they are convinced that the debt lies with the partner alone.

PROBLEMS OF FAMILIES IN WHICH THERE IS A NARCISSISTIC PARENT

Narcissistic parents don't treat their children as unique individuals but as extensions of their self-image. For a narcissist, the child's absolute trust and dependence on the caregiver make them the perfect source of narcissistic supply—that is, until the child begins to develop into an independent person. This is already a difficult task for the child of a narcissistic parent, who may never have experienced the combination of trust and healthy boundaries needed for healthy ego development. Still, most children will begin to develop a sense of self over time despite these barriers.

The narcissist cannot allow this, so the narcissistic parent interferes with the child's independent development to keep the child dependent on them. Through guilt-tripping, emotional blackmail, undermining, and all the other control and manipulation techniques, the narcissistic parent prevents the child from ever really growing up.

The narcissistic parent will often pressure the child to get good grades or excel in sports or impress others somehow. Affection and praise depend on high performance and are withheld as a punishment for any mistake. The narcissistic parent sees the child as an expression of his ideal self, but it can cause the child to see love and affection solely in terms of external validation. Without the experience of being loved for his own sake, the child of narcissistic parents can develop an unhealthy fixation on how other people perceive him.

Narcissistic parents insist on being the center of their children's lives. At the same time, they often belittle and undermine their children, especially for not living up to their unrealistic expectations. Over time, the child can learn that the only way to get praise and affection from others is to do just what they want at all times without question. They can just as easily learn that the most effective way to deal with others is through guilt-tripping, manipulation, and other head games.

In effect, the narcissistic parent trains the child to perceive the world and human relationships as dysfunctional. This doesn't always turn the child into another narcissist, but it is almost always profoundly damaging to the child's self-esteem.

NARCISSISTIC ENTITLEMENT

Henschel's research into permissive parenting might explain one of the most frustrating aspects of narcissistic behavior—the narcissist's seemingly endless sense of entitlement.

According to narcissistic abuse expert Melanie Tonia Evans, the narcissist feels entitled to get whatever he wants whenever he wants and perceives any refusal to give him what he wants as a horrible injustice. This can include anything from attention to affection to money to sex—there are no legitimate limits on what he has the right to expect from other people in the narcissist's eyes. Even though the narcissist treats others as if they have no rights, he expects others to respect his rights at all times.

Evans traces this colossal sense of entitlement to four separate causes, any one of which can produce a narcissist. The first is abuse and neglect, such as the experience of being raised by a narcissistic parent. The second is being raised by overly permissive parents who fail to establish boundaries and never say no. The third is being raised by excessively indulgent parents who try too hard to give the child everything he could ever want. The fourth is being raised by parents who put the child on a pedestal, creating an overblown but fragile sense of self-worth. The child ends up perceiving herself as being special and better than others, entitled to anything she wants, just like Violet Beauregard in Charlie and the Chocolate Factory.

As Evans pointed out, the act of putting your child on a pedestal like this is also narcissistic, as the child is treated as an extension of the parent's ego. This suggests that parental narcissism may be a factor even when the parent isn't abusive. The narcissistic parent uses the child to prop up his false self and influences the child to see the world in the same way.

OTHER FACTORS

Other factors may also contribute to the development of a narcissistic personality. Researchers have found some physical differences between the brains of people diagnosed with narcissistic personality disorder and other people.

The brain is connected with the ability to experience empathy for others, as well as the ability to regulate emotion. This implies that people with narcissistic personality disorder may have difficulty keeping their emotions from spiraling and find it hard to empathize with other people's feelings. Quick to feel anger or anxiety and slow to feel empathy, the narcissist may be at the mercy of her own emotions.

It's difficult to say whether these brain differences cause narcissistic personality disorder or whether they are just one factor among many. For example, having less gray matter in your left anterior insula might not make you narcissistic on its own. Still, it might make you more likely to become narcissistic with the right life experiences. As with many other mental health problems, a narcissistic personality disorder may be caused by a combination of environmental and genetic factors.

Narcissism tends to go along with other mental health problems and personality disorders. People diagnosed with NPD often suffer from depression. They can also be diagnosed with Bipolar Disorder, also known as manic depression. The person who has Bipolar Disorder will alternate between extremely depressed and manically energetic moods.

People with NPD have high rates of substance abuse issues and are especially likely to abuse cocaine. They have high rates of anorexia and may also have higher rates of other personality disorders, including Borderline, Anti-Social, and Paranoid disorders.

Narcissism is so strongly associated with other mental health issues that counselors usually diagnose NPD after the patient comes in for some other reason. For example, the narcissist may seek treatment for depression after a breakup caused by his narcissistic behavior, without any insight into his role in the breakdown of the relationship. Even though he can tell that something is wrong, he still believes the other person mistreated him rather than the other way around.

Although the narcissist is deeply unhappy and incapable of forming healthy relationships with others, most narcissists are unwilling and unable to see themselves as the problem. Seeking help for narcissism would mean admitting that the narcissist's ideal self is fake. Because the narcissist can't bear to do this, he blames everyone else for his problems instead.

The therapist who realizes her patient is narcissistic may diagnose NPD, but will have a hard time making any progress as long as the narcissist continues to cling to the false self. Narcissists in therapy are known for arguing with their therapists and being stubborn about treatment, impervious to any argument the counselor may present.

HOW TO PROTECT YOUR CHILD FROM YOUR NARCISSISTIC PARTNER

Maybe you've known for some time that your spouse is narcissistic, or maybe you're just now becoming aware of it. If this is your first encounter with narcissism, read everything you can about it to better understand what you're dealing with—seeing a therapist can be very beneficial in coping with your narcissistic partner, as long as you find someone knowledgeable about the topic. A therapist who is unfamiliar with narcissism's pathology may be invalidating and have dangerously bad advice.

It is important to recognize that the children face long-lasting emotional and physiological trauma when a narcissistic parent is present. The more you can do to assist them and mitigate potential damage, the better.

PUT AN END TO YOUR SELF-BLAME

To begin, release self-blame and regret. These are normal reactions that people have as they come to terms with their narcissist spouse's true existence.

You probably had no idea what you were getting yourself into when you became involved with your partner. For the most part, narcissists are adept at luring people in and concealing their true nature. Or maybe you believed you could cure the narcissist, unaware that they are generally "unfixable" due to the ingrained nature of their personality disorder and their unwillingness to change. Perhaps you were raised in a narcissistic home and are now repeating the pattern.

Whatever reason you became involved with a narcissist, wasting resources on regret and self-blame would only exacerbate the situation for you and your children.

HOW TO ASSIST YOUR CHILDREN

The most critical thing you can do as the family's stable adult is respected and protect your children as much as possible. You cannot alter their other parent's narcissism. That is something they must accept. However, you will make significant improvements to your children's condition and assist them in developing coping skills.

APPROPRIATELY VALIDATE THEIR FEELINGS

Validating the children's feelings is important. Since the narcissist parent regularly invalidates others by denial, guilt, mockery, and projection, your children are particularly in need of affirmation that their feelings are true, that they matter, and that they are legitimate. It is critical to validate that their feelings of hurt and rage are justified and do not deserve the treatment they are receiving, especially for the scapegoated child (constantly targeted by the narcissist parent).

You can be tempted to "cover" yourself and your children at home by denying the facts. However, ignoring a child's legitimate feelings benefits no one and undermines your child's confidence in you.

ASSIST THEM IN AVOIDING SELF-BLAME

Narcissists are experts at blaming others for their poor behavior, frequently for their own. If a narcissist has a temper tantrum, it is because you triggered it. "You compelled me to do it" is the narcissist's motto.

To cope with unbearable and deep-seated feelings of weakness and inferiority, narcissists must believe they are beyond reproach. Blaming others, especially a scapegoated kid, is as normal and essential as breathing for the narcissist personality.

Assisting your children in understanding that the narcissist's accusations are baseless, unjust, and not their fault is vital to their sense of an accurate truth instead of a highly twisted one engineered by your narcissist partner. Recognizing that they are not at fault would also relieve the children of a heavy burden that they do not have to bear.

INFORM THE TRUTH

The key about truth is that you must first see and understand it for yourself before assisting your children in doing so.

Truth-telling is a fraught territory in the narcissist household. The narcissist thrives on deception and concealment, and they are adamant about maintaining this state at home. Informing your children that their parent is a narcissist and providing information will backfire disastrously if they disclose your remarks to the other parent.

Children can deal with varying degrees of "fact" according to their age and maturity level. You must use your best judgment in determining when and how much honesty to share with your children about your narcissistic spouse and family life. You may wish to refrain from using the word narcissist with your child until they are older.

For younger children, you might demonstrate that their parent is extremely sensitive to criticism or perceived rejection (read: pathologically defensive) and overreacts (read: acts like a caged wolverine). Reiterate that your narcissistic spouse's anger (read: rage) is out of control and is not the fault or obligation of your kid.

Children are the greatest gauge of what they are ready to learn. Sometimes, the best way to incorporate knowledge is to wait until your child inquiries about something. Your communication style with your children will gradually change over time as they better understand family dynamics.

DEFEND THE NARCISSIST SPOUSE FROM DEMONIZATION

Avoid demonizing your spouse, as this may result in severe confusion and ambivalence in your children. Especially when they are young, they will love and seek approval from their other parent regardless of how badly he or she behaves. Managing your own emotions against an abusive partner can feel near-impossible.

However, resisting the urge to let go of your pain, frustration, and rage is critical for maintaining contact and confidence with your children, who are caught in the middle. When your children grow older, you will be able to discuss issues more freely and possibly share knowledge and tools about narcissistic personality disorder with them.

ASSIST YOUR CHILDREN IN DEVELOPING RESILIENCE

Our primary responsibility as parents is to instill courage in our children to face life's obstacles on their own two stable feet. This is particularly true for children raised in a narcissistic household. What you can do for them is to serve as a role model and cultivate their resilience through your actions.

Unconditional affection (which their other parent is incapable of providing); empathy for others; encouragement of hard work and achievement without false praise; support for an earned sense of competence; and affirmation of faith in and appreciation for their instincts.

TAKE YOUR CHILDREN'S ANGER IN STRIDE

It's unjust, but your children may sometimes vent their worst frustrations at you. This is because they cannot be open with their narcissistic parent and trust you enough to express their true feelings. They need to exorcise the pain and torment they are experiencing. Although you may already be bearing the brunt of the narcissist's rages and machinations, you will be called upon to stand far above the madness and be powerful for your baby. This does not imply, however, that you can tolerate child violence. Your unwavering loyalty and non-defensiveness are lifelines for your children, but you must also model self-respect and courage to the greatest extent possible.

HOW DO I SAFEGUARD MY CHILD?

In extreme situations with a narcissistic parent, you may need to take the case to court to request a court order suspending parental time before the other parent receives assistance.

When things do not go their way, narcissists may become frustrated or impatient. Since something is about them, it's difficult to cope when anything shows that it isn't. Screaming at the other parent, "This isn't about you; it's about our child's wants/needs," will accomplish nothing. Recognize that you cannot alter the behavior on your own.

You will soon notice this action, and your first thought will be to get angry. Take a deep breath when you remember the irritated or angry actions. There is no need to interact.

ALLOW SOME TIME

All has to be done immediately in today's world. When coping with a narcissistic parent, this can be detrimental and exacerbates the issue. Once you've become furious, come to a halt. Have a glass of wine and put your phone away. It's one thing when the behavior is directed at you, but what happens when the behavior is directed at my child?

Your child may not be resistant to this behavior, and one of the first steps you can take is to become aware of it so that you can include it in your parenting agreement. You should emphasize that no one is shouting or swearing at the boy. When you first learn about it, you should take action. Any agreement contains language prohibiting one parent from disparaging the other in front of the infant.

Take action the first time you hear it. When a narcissist lacks power, things spiral out of control. Do not allow their actions to prevent you from acting just because their anger makes you feel uneasy. The emotional and physical health of your child is at stake. You can order a petition with the court, and the court would almost certainly appoint a child's attorney.

This attorney will communicate with your kid. The attorney will examine the messages sent and received between you and your ex. It is essential that your messages are rational and calm. The council will witness the anger and will be able to assess the appropriateness of the responses. By remaining calm and in charge, you deprive the abusive parent of their ability to exert control over the situation. At that point, the narcissistic parent must seek support to manage their spectrum of emotions or risk losing parenting time.

SOLICIT THERAPEUTIC ASSISTANCE FOR YOUR CHILD

Your child has only two parents, and regardless of how good or poor they are, your child must learn how to interact with them. I'm not suggesting that your child must learn how to deal with a parent who belittles them to feel superior, but your child will have to learn how to deal with such parent. You and probably the child's attorney will be present. Still, your child will need the assistance of a psychologist to discuss their own emotions about the situation and gain a clearer understanding of it.

The most difficult aspect of raising a child with a narcissistic parent is imitating the parent's behavior. How do you deal with frustration? You do not want your child to behave like their narcissistic parent. If the child witnesses this behavior and there is no intervention, your child may begin to exhibit some of those characteristics. You will need to act quickly. Therapy is an excellent way to teach your child about positive behavior patterns and how to cope with undesirable actions.

Co-parenting with a narcissistic parent is difficult, but you have the power to change the situation. It is important for your child's health. There are ways to maintain parental involvement in your child's life without jeopardizing their welfare. Take care of the situation and, if necessary, seek counseling on your own to ensure that you are making sound decisions. When circumstances become untenable for your child, however, you must file the requisite court petition.

THE RISKS OF LOW SELF-ESTEEM, PROBLEMS WITH TRUST AND BELONGING, AND LACK OF SELF-COMPASSION IN CHILDREN WHO GROW UP WITH A NARCISSISTIC PARENT

Being the narcissist's kid is that you are programmed to feel like something is wrong with you from an early age. You may not think that this is the case initially, but your narcissistic parent will work hard to make you believe this. And believe it, you will, because you're naturally wired to trust your parents, and you have not yet gained the ability to objectively think about problems as a child. These tender formative years are the best for the narcissistic parent to work her voodoo on her mind.

Unrealistic Expectations of Yourself

Throughout your life with your narcissistic parent, he or she continued to feed you with a lie, covertly and overtly, through her actions and words. What was the lie? That you could earn their love if you did your very best. You grew up thinking you just had to be smart enough, or pretty enough, or strong enough, or whatever-enough, and you would have the love, approval, and attention that your parent has been withholding from you. They made you believe that you had to strive to be a perfect child, and once you were perfect, then he or she could love you.

CRUSHED SELF-ESTEEM

Narcissistic parents teach their children that they are worth nothing, right from birth. All your wants and needs mean nothing to the narc, which naturally makes you wonder why you're not getting them met. It must be because you're not worth it, you conclude.

The narcissistic parent finds so many different tactics to get you to believe you are nothing at all. Sadly, it worked. Even as an adult, you deal with feelings of inadequacy and low self-esteem. You do matter, though. You always have. That voice in mind says you don't mean anything. That's one more lie embedded in your noggin by your parent. That's one more lie you don't need to hold on to any longer.

ZERO CONFIDENCE

The fact is this is something that plagues every child who had a narcissistic parent raising them. You find you're not so confident, no matter where you find yourself. Even when you're alone, you're somehow judging yourself. Since you're always used to being judged by your parent, you do the same to yourself and expect others. Also, since they spent so much time and energy cutting you down, it's no wonder that you don't feel so sure about yourself or your skills.

LACK OF TRUST

You will find it hard to trust others as the child of a narcissistic parent. Not just any others, though. Women. In my case, it was any woman old enough to be my parent. It's like you expect every other woman to be just like your parent — unpredictable, manipulative, full of rage, toxic. Growing up with a narcissist for a mom means you always had to be on your toes. It could then lead you to project your parent's traits onto others. You find yourself unable and unwilling to trust them. It also doesn't help that you keep finding yourself with narcissists for friends and lovers. The tendency is to keep your heart shut for good. Don't do that! There are good people too.

CONCEALING EMOTIONS

As a kid, you learned that you should not express your emotions. You are not allowed to be mad; you are not permitted to be hurt. You'd better not show that you're either of these things while your narcissistic parent abuses you. Did you scrape your elbow? Is it bleeding terribly? Too bad. You would better not shout. Then you should better not cry. You'd better not pout. Your narcissistic parent is evil and selfish. The last thing she needs is you bothering her with your wailing. Unless, of course, there is some drama in it for her, meaning she has an audience and a chance to shine at being Super Mom.

You were also not allowed to express your positive emotions. If you did, she would feel like you were a threat, and she would do something about it. She also resents it when you're pleased. She resents when someone or something other than her is the reason for your smile. So, she sets out to make you miserable in any way she can. Did you get a toy from an uncle? She'll cease it once he's gone and only ever gives it to you once he's around. It happened to me. True story. Did you get an A in Math, but the A was 99 percent, not 100? Then she will dismiss you. Again, true story.

DISJOINTED THOUGHTS AND EMOTIONS

It is difficult for you to know your true feelings about the circumstances in your life. You don't even know what your thoughts are about a given situation. You're so used to believing that you cannot trust your point of view. You're so used to looking to your narcissistic parent to tell you what to think and how to feel. Where others can spontaneously express their thoughts and feelings, you need a lot of time to check in with yourself and figure you out.

When someone says something rude or horrible to you, you do not realize it at the moment. It hits you much, much sooner than they really should not have said what they said or treated you the way they did. It's almost as if the wires connecting your emotions to your mind have been chewed up and disconnected. But you can train yourself to combine both. In the process of healing, you will work this out. What you'll find is that you'll get better and better at expressing yourself at the moment as the days go by.

UNWILLINGNESS TO STAKE YOUR CLAIM

Growing up with your narcissistic parent means you were all about fulfilling their needs. You learned very quickly to ignore your own needs because if you didn't, you'd get into trouble for it. You were programmed to believe that getting your own needs met was incredibly selfish, and you should be ashamed of that.

Something to consider now you're an adult is what true selfishness is. When you're selfish, you make things that are not about you revolve around you. There are, however, times when something is actually about you. There's nothing wrong with that! In reality, your graduation is about you. Your birthday is about you. Your promotion at work is about you. Your newly born is about you and the baby, and that's that. You are not selfish for drawing a line and staking your claim on what is about you.

OVERACHIEVING AND UNDERACHIEVING

With the children of narcissistic parents, it usually pans out one of two ways. Either the child decides to do all they can to prove themselves and finally feel good enough. So, they become overachievers, or they are continually sabotaging themselves,

338

frequently having problems with finances, constantly failing because deep down, they do not feel deserving of good things.

It is because you were taught as a child that you're not good enough, smart enough, fast enough, pretty enough, and so on. You're not enough of those things for you to deserve approval, love, attention, validation, or empathy. You may have received money or other material things, but more often than not, it was envied by you after you had to grovel and beg. So, you grow up as an adult who has a problem accepting the good life has to offer.

CONSTANTLY FEELING LONELY

If you have somehow managed to keep in touch with your family as an adult, you somehow still feel lonely with them around. You've been unable to connect fully with them, no matter how hard you try. Why this happens is that they have no idea who the real you are. You can't even show them your authentic self because doing so would make you vulnerable. After all, the parent says that the real you is undesirable.

You might also find it incredibly difficult to establish connections with people outside of your family: lack of trust, or the anxiety you feel about whether you're worth knowing, or the lack of social skills because your parent kept you isolated.

SOCIAL ANXIETY

You most likely have to deal with crippling social anxiety. You don't know what's right and what isn't. You don't know the best way to behave when you're with others. You wonder if you're too quiet or too loud. You wonder if you were meant to go with red in place of blue. Where no one else can see, you carry a heavy load of shame deep down.

You're ashamed of yourself. You're ashamed of who you are. You are worried that nobody is going to love you. As a result, you find yourself creating a reality in which no one loves you, and that becomes a self-fulfilling prophecy. It's not because you're not the right person, or you're not sweet. It's because somehow others can tune into what we think of ourselves subconsciously, and they reflect you what you think.

NEVER SIMPLY ACCEPTING COMPLIMENTS

It is an unbelievably common effect of being raised by a narcissistic parent. Usually, it's because she never complimented you. It was followed by something to cut you down. When another person approves you, she would be quick with a cutting remark.

Since you don't believe you need to be complimented, you always throw them a compliment of your own. Now, this is tricky. There are times when it's excellent to give praise back, and times it isn't. How can you say the difference between both of them? Well, ask yourself why you're complimenting them. Are you doing so because you genuinely mean it, or are you doing so because you feel obligated to pay them back? There's your answer.

DEPRESSION

Children of narcissistic parents are often prone to depression. It's sad but true that there is no surprise that this happens. You would not be authorized to be your true self. You don't even know who your true self is. You feel like you don't fit in anywhere. You want to interact with others, but you're frightened, don't know how, or can't trust. Your self-esteem is almost nonexistent, thanks to your dear old mom or dad. You don't have the skills you need to move forward in life. You're constantly being criticized by your parent, despite your best efforts and intentions.

Even when you're not with them, their voices keep on going in your head, telling you how you're worthless, and you've got problems that can't be solved, telling you you're a horrible human being in general. You've believed all of that for years. You've watched other kids with well-adjusted parents and wondered why things were not that way for you. You've sacrificed all that you can to get even a little bit of love or attention from your parent.

POSSIBLE DIFFICULT RELATIONSHIPS AS AN ADULT

Children and family relationship management skills are often a work in progress. They learn how to manage their feelings, understanding, and behaviors through observation by acting out different scenarios on dolls or stuffed animals and talking with parents about the more difficult situations they may encounter. When children can use these skills earlier in their development (e.g., during preschool), the outcomes may be better for everyone involved — parents and children alike.

As children hit the teen years, they begin to test not only their parents but the adults in their lives. They feel more independent and want to do things independently for which they may or may not need permission. As a result, they may create many of the following scenarios in an attempt to test authority:

How does a parent handle these difficult situations? At first, parents must continue to supervise their teenagers closely. It is impossible to know when they are testing your boundaries. Continue to be clear with your teenagers about what you expect of them and why, and don't be afraid to set clear guidelines all the time.

Parents should model good values. Your teens can learn a great deal from watching how you interact with other adults that positively affect your family's happiness. If you have a conflict with another parent, do not take it out on your teen.

Adults often find that trying to maintain a close relationship with their parents is challenging at times. This is because the child may feel embarrassed or uncomfortable about their actions as adults and, instead of checking in with parents to make sure they're doing alright, the teen may try to keep away from that person as much as possible. This is often a result of a child wanting respect and the adult's ability to respect their needs. For this to work, both partners must find ways to better communicate with one another to voice desires and provide adequate support and encouragement effectively.

Parents will need to be sure to have good communication with their adult children. Communication is a vital part of having a lasting relationship. The main objectives of communication are sharing information, being aware of intentions, and reducing conflicts in situations that may lead to conflict.

Some people feel consistently distant from their biological parents because they never moved away from home or were always too busy for regular visits. This can cause the child or adult to grow up without knowing the love and care they need as they mature into adulthood.

If the parents cannot provide these needs for their children, they will most likely have a hard time feeling that their parents love them. To counteract this issue, it is essential to be involved in the life of your child. It is also helpful to try to develop a relationship with your child's friends even if they are older than you because children may feel more comfortable telling you things about themselves through their friends.

Relationships with siblings can be difficult at times as well. There are many times when there may be conflict or lack of understanding between siblings. There may also be a shortage of understanding between siblings and their parents.

Since many issues can go into relationships between siblings, it is important to communicate between everyone involved. To do this, both parents and children should establish a routine in which each individual knows what is expected. Also, both should be clear on when parents will see the children receive support and attention. This will allow each individual to feel more comfortable and less stressed.

When two siblings are involved in a relationship, they should understand what their boundaries are with one another. They should also recognize what to do if they need help while dealing with one another. For example, some families may rule that they won't fight or argue in front of others because it makes the parents uncomfortable. Other families may rule that they must go outside to do so when they are fighting or engaging in an argument.

If siblings choose to fight, both sides must respect the other one's feelings. If this doesn't occur, it could prolong the argument and make things more difficult for everyone. When it comes to managing family conflicts, it is important to know what the other person feels. If you don't know how you make them feel and don't know how they make you feel, there will be no way to resolve the issue.

Communication is very important when trying to communicate feelings and emotions with others. For siblings to communicate effectively, parents must set an example of good communication between themselves and their children. If siblings see their parents openly discussing feelings together, they will know how to do the same. Parents must also display good listening and understand that everyone is different and may process things differently.

Another way how they can help their children learn to communicate effectively is by assisting them to practice good communication skills at home and with friends. They have to encourage them to share their emotions and feelings lovingly with those around them. This will help the child learn that they can express themselves in a way that won't make others feel uncomfortable.

Children grow up hardwired to be afraid of strangers. Sadly, this often contributes to their reluctance to confide in adults.

When children are fearful, they usually do not like or trust adults, who are their caregivers and who have the power to protect them from physical harm and harm of any other kind.

HOW TO EFFECTIVELY INTERVENE TO BENEFIT CHILDREN

Children who struggle with schoolwork, disruptive behaviors, or foster care often need help. These needs can be around academics, behavior, or being in an unstable environment. Intervening is a service that includes many different aspects of helping the child. Interventions range from providing tutoring services to supervising a child's behavior at home and in school. The goal is to benefit the child and give value to the family.

There are many reasons why a child needs an intervention. Some of these reasons are:

Interventions can range from one-time events to ongoing ones; however, they all have certain features in common. Interventions have four main components: science, values, process, and outcomes. These components often blend, and each is important in its way, but understanding each individually enables an interventionist to be sure of the specific goals of service given any particular context or person.

This part of the intervention process focuses on the desired effect of the intervention. It includes considering what effect or

346

outcome a child is seeking in a specific situation. This might consist of academic achievement, behavior issues, coping skills (how do they cope with negative events), or changes in self-esteem. The desired effects could be short-term goals and long-term goals, such as improving behavior. This component may also include how an interventionist goes about measuring the effectiveness of their intervention(s).

This part of an intervention is defined as the action a person takes or plan they develop to accomplish the desired effect. These could be school plans, behavior plans, or emotional plans. The plan could have steps specific to what the child needs, such as tutoring services, social skill training, or cooking classes. The other way interventions can help children is by providing stable homes and environments for them. This could mean finding a stable place to stay or determining the best foster family for the child.

Another component of an intervention is the processes and skills involved in matching a child's needs to the right services or interventions. This includes identifying what is wrong (needs assessment), creating solutions, and establishing what to use to measure if these interventions are successful (evaluation). If needed, interventions can also include who will provide them, how long, and where they will occur.

This final point of the intervention process is the outcome. This includes the results that must be measured and documented to determine what was effective and what wasn't. These results can consist of changes in behavior, schoolwork or test scores, or changes in general attitude. The evaluation should also include how to measure these changes.

Interventions can be one-time events, or they can be ongoing. There are two main types of interventions. These two main types are direct and indirect interventions. Direct interventions are those where the interventionist is directly involved with a child or family. On the other hand, include indirect interventions directing families to resources they can use to help them with their issues instead of giving the specific instructions themselves.

Interventionists need to know who will be receiving their intervention as well as why they need it. This information will help determine the proper treatment to provide to a child. For example, if a child is failing in school, an interventionist may decide that tutoring is the best option. If the child has behavior problems in school but has no trouble at home or with homework and tests, direct instructions are probably not needed because it is not causing any issues in their life.

Interventions are most successful when they are personalized to the child's specific needs. This is because of the way interventions develop. The science, values, and processes contribute to the outcomes specific to a child and their needs.

Many problems can occur during the intervention process. The primary and most common problem is a failure. This happens when the desired outcomes are not met or there is no improvement in a child's situation. Sometimes failure occurs due to unrealistic expectations by the parents, school, or the child. Another problem that could happen during an intervention process is burnout. This happens when the treatments become too difficult for an interventionist to manage, and they get frustrated with their work or what they are doing. Another problem that could occur during the intervention process is when too much information is given too quickly. This could make an intervention ineffective and a waste of time.

HOW TO RAISE EMOTIONALLY HEALTHY CHILDREN, EVEN IN A NARCISSISTIC FAMILY SYSTEM

So, you may have just found out that your family might be operating in a narcissistic system. You can still raise emotionally healthy children in this kind of home and offer them the best life possible.

We will delve into how to raise emotionally healthy children when a narcissistic family system raises them — because it is possible. Whether they were raised by narcissists or not, these kids deserve unconditional love no matter what. Your job is to love them, whether they are ultra-hard-working children or kids who are spoiled and always getting what they want. You must earn their love, just like they will earn your trust and respect.

START RIGHT

You can't undo past mistakes, but you can make sure your kids don't have to suffer from them. This is going to be hard if your narcissistic family system has already caused emotional or physical damage. For instance, if your child was born addicted or premature because of a narcissistic relative who wanted a healthy baby but didn't want to wait for it in the womb, they may grow up with even more problems than the average person raised with narcissists.

If there were abuse in the family system or experiencing postpartum depression, this would take time to recover from. Remember that you can use this to help your children if they have suffered themselves because of a narcissistic parent or relative. You can show them how to get help and work through their issues. You may even want to seek counseling yourself for the sake of your kids — after all, you've been through what they have gone through and can help them work through it too.

Make sure that your kids are safe. If they have suffered physical abuse, it's essential that you call the child services agency in your area and work out what kind of support system is available to you. You will also have to learn how to advocate for your children to get the help they need. You can also contact local shelters for women and children if your narcissistic family is physically abusive.

YOU'VE GOT TO RESPECT YOURSELF

You cannot raise emotionally healthy children in a narcissistic family system if you don't respect yourself. This means setting boundaries for your well-being, which may or may not include divorce from your spouse. Also, take care of yourself and your needs while raising kids. The children need you to have a good relationship with yourself, whether you decide to marry again or not. They need you to be at peace with yourself and your life.

They need you to be able to handle yourself emotionally and protect your sense of self.

This will sound harsh, but you must learn to love yourself, even if your narcissistic family has never given you that chance. Love yourself for many things — not just for what you look like or how much money you make. Love yourself for your kindness and generosity. Love yourself for all the good things you do for others. You don't have to love everything about yourself, but you can learn to accept who you are and set boundaries that help you love the children in your life.

DON'T GIVE UP ON YOUR DREAMS

Know that you have a life outside of parenting. Whenever possible, make sure that your narcissistic family system isn't encroaching on those dreams — and vice versa. It's really easy to forget about what you wanted for yourself before you had children. The more you can keep these dreams alive, the better off your kids will be. Make that trip happen if you have always wanted to travel the world. If you always wanted to write a novel or play an instrument, don't give up on that dream just because of your family system.

If you have lost respect for yourself, set new goals and dreams for yourself (even if they are small).

YOU HAVE TO BE THERE FOR THE KIDS EMOTIONALLY NO MATTER WHAT

This is the most important thing about raising emotionally healthy children in a narcissistic family system. If you don't, they are going to suffer for it. You can't let them suffer alone — and they certainly won't if they know that everything possible is being done in their best interest. You have to be the beacon of hope in this kind of family, even if you are the parent who is getting blamed for everything.

You need to be there for your children emotionally, no matter what. Kids can tell when you're not happy, so don't think they won't notice if you are being torn down by a narcissist. They are going to notice — and they will suffer because of it. They can see right through your false smiles and love from afar. They will be able to tell that something isn't right, even if they don't know what it is.

You have to be the person who is there for your children, no matter what. You can't abandon them or let them suffer without showing up in their lives. They deserve better, and so do you. Don't lose yourself in this kind of family system — you'll need to be sure that you are set up to deal with the future of your child's emotional health and well-being.

The other thing is that you have to let go. You may have to be the parent who lets go of the grandiose dreams they have. You might have to help them learn how to be more realistic, something that is very hard if you are used to being the family member who goes after their dreams and works hard for them. Be aware of your own needs as a parent and make sure they are being met if you can.

DISCIPLINE WITH LOVE

You must use discipline with love in this kind of family system, no matter what. If you are stuck or have to use corporal punishment to discipline your children, understand that this will not work with emotionally healthy kids. Discipline needs to be accompanied by love and support — if the parent or guardian uses punishment, set up consequences and punishments that you can both agree with. This means developing a plan that works for everyone.

BE ACTIVE IN YOUR CHILDREN'S LIVES

If you are an involved and good parent, you will find that your children will look to you for direction. They will realize what to do and who to ask for help if they have problems. They will listen to their mother or father, which is a good thing for all of them. If somebody is too controlling or abusive, make sure that you set up boundaries that work for everyone and put the injured party in their place when necessary.

If you have a narcissistic family system, you are going to have a hard time with this. You will feel like everyone wants something from you, and you will have trouble helping your children with their emotional needs if they aren't happy and healthy. The good news is that most kids' emotional needs can be met with a little help from parents — but only if the parents set up some boundaries.

You must remember that you can do this! No matter what happens in your family system, remember that you can raise emotionally healthy children in a narcissistic family system. You can raise kids who do love you for the person that you are deep down inside. They will love and respect themselves and find their happiness with or without family support.

THE IMPORTANCE OF RESILIENCE

Resilience is the ability to bounce from adversity; it's a particular individual's ability to cope with difficult happenings in their life. Resilient people recover quickly and uneventfully from negative emotions and challenging situations.

Resiliency varies by age, gender, personality type, and culture. Knowing more about the people who have gone through difficult times can help us better understand how they manage and what we can learn to strengthen our resiliency.

The importance of resilience is something that comes up quite often. Some people will have different opinions about this concept, but one thing's for sure: resilience is a trait most people don't want to be without. However, those that are resilient will go through life much more easily. No matter what comes their way, they know that they will always be able to cope.

The reasons for this are clear: if you approach life knowing that difficulties will come up, you can better prepare yourself for those challenges.

Resilience is not something that you can force upon yourself. It is just a way of thinking that makes a person more confident in handling things.

Resilience comes with practice and diligent work. Resilient people believe that if they put their mind to it, they can do anything. It's an optimistic way of thinking that feeds off itself. Everyone must be resilient to succeed in life.

They are not the type that goes through life with a smile on their face no matter what happens. They know that there will be difficult times in life, but they also know how to deal with them effectively when it arrives, and they will understand what makes them angry or upset.

They know that it is necessary to be resilient in order to succeed in life. They know that they cannot let adversity hold them back and have learned to cope effectively with traumatic experiences so that they can close the door on those dark memories and move on with their lives.

The capability to adjust to difficult situations is something that should never be underestimated. They know that it is all part of life, and they learn from their mistakes and choose not to let them affect them anymore.

Resilience is the belief that can take you where you want to go, and it's a way of thinking that will ensure you succeed in life. It's not something that people are born with. It is something they must work hard to acquire. All it takes is determination.

If you can overcome even the most difficult situations and still come out on top, you have been resilient.

HOW TO BE RESILIENT

Resilient individuals are those who have had to face and overcome very difficult problems. Let's see what we can learn from some of these resilient people:

TAKE THINGS ONE STEP AT A TIME

We often rush to get things done without even taking a moment to think about their consequences. We want it all right now, and if we don't get it, we make a decision that will cause us more problems than anything else.

To be resilient, you need to take things one step instead of trying everything at once. It is impossible to do everything you have wanted to do, so it's best to take it one thing at a time.

Resilient people know that they don't need to rush. They know that there is plenty of time for everything, and they won't be letting anything hold them back from reaching their goals.

TAKE TIME TO LISTEN TO YOUR EMOTIONS

People need to learn how to control their emotions. This means that they must stop judging themselves for having a certain emotion and instead accept it. The only way they will be able to change things in their life is by understanding their feelings and why they are feeling the way they feel.

They don't let their emotions control them. Instead, they understand their feelings and try to find some logical reason behind them.

They know that no matter what it is that they are feeling, it will pass and that it won't be sticking around forever, even if it is something that has been bothering them for a long time.

NOTHING COMES EASY IN LIFE

It might seem as though things come easy all the time, but this isn't true. Resilient people understand that nothing comes without work, and they make sure that whatever they do requires a lot of hard work.

They can do everything to get what they want, but they know that even the smallest task can present many difficulties in their way. They put in hard work to make sure they can reach their goals.

It's just them taking things one step at a time and making sure that everything is done on time. They are determined and don't let anyone stop them from doing anything they have set out to do.

YOU CAN'T CONTROL OTHER PEOPLE, AND YOU CANNOT BLAME THEM FOR YOUR PROBLEMS

The events that happen to us and the way we feel are completely out of our control. We can't do anything about the people in our lives, and we shouldn't feel guilty about something they have done either. If they want to be a part of our lives, they will have to accept us for who we are, and we need to understand that there is nothing we can do about it.

They take responsibility for their actions and ensure that whatever they do is proud of.

THE IMPORTANCE OF SETTING SPECIFIC GOALS

Resilient people know what they want to achieve, and they know the best way to get there. They don't just wing it. They set goals in their lives and take time to sit down. These things will help them focus on what they need to do and make sure that everything comes together.

They know what they want and make sure to find a way around it no matter what obstacles they face. They are the type of people who set goals for themselves, think about their plans, and work towards accomplishing those things.

UNDERSTAND THE VALUE OF TAKING RISKS

Resilient people don't just stay in one place for too long. They like to keep things interesting and won't let anything or anyone hold them back from doing the things they want to do.

They don't take risks just for its fun, but they also know that some risks need to be taken to get what they want out of life. They also know what is worth taking a risk over and what isn't worth it.

LEARN HOW TO SACRIFICE

We often take the chance of being selfish and focusing on everything we want to get done but cannot. Some people think it's a good idea, but they can lose everything in the end because of it.

Resilient people do not to take the easy way out when it comes to what they desire and instead make sure that whatever they want is worth sacrificing for. They know that it will take a lot of work, but they also know that it will be worth it in the end.

KNOW WHEN TO TAKE A BREAK

We all deserve time off, and we should never feel bad about taking some time for ourselves. Taking breaks can help us in ways we never expected, but resilient people need some time to recover and rest from their hard work.

BE STRONG

Mentally strong people won't allow themselves to be pushed around by anyone. Regardless of the situation, they will stand their ground and find a way to get themselves out of whatever they have found themselves in.

They won't let anything stop them from achieving their goals and will do whatever it takes to get where they want to be in life. They understand that there will be people trying to bring them down all the time, but this only makes them stronger.

BE PERSISTENT

We decide based on incomplete information and then believe that everything will turn out the way we want. This is a bad idea because sometimes there will be things that we need to be persistent about, no matter how little we may think they are worth.

People who are mentally strong stay focused on what they want to do and don't let anything get in their way. They already know what they want to achieve and focus on ensuring they get there rather than worrying about how far off their goals are.

TAKE RESPONSIBILITY

Mentally strong people know that everything they have done, do and will do is their responsibility. They never accept the blame for other people's actions and realize that it's their fault if something goes wrong.

ADAPT TO THEIR ENVIRONMENT

There is no use in being in a place where you don't belong because you will only be miserable and resentful. Resilient people make sure that they learn about their surroundings and adapt to them to get what they want.

THE NEED FOR CHANGE

Resilient people aren't afraid of change. They look for it, but only if it's a positive change. They know that they can't just stay where they are doing the same thing repeatedly because this can cause a lot of problems in your life.

They think about how things could be, how they could change, and what they could do to make it happen.

HOW TO BUILD RESILIENCE WHEN YOU HAVE A NARCISSISTIC PARTNER

Befor you try to overcome any narcissist, you need to note that these individuals have no empathy. Their main objective is to make all the people close to the unhappy. It is difficult to change a narcissist, and most times, it is only possible with the help of a professional. The obvious solution to everything to do with narcissists is to leave as fast as possible.

DEFLECT

One way of dealing with a narcissist is avoiding engagement if you can. If this is not an option, a better alternative would be to learn to deflect.

Do not forget that the narcissist wants a constant supply of something you could offer. This could come in various forms, ranging from sex, money, attention, and so on. Narcissists feed on your sadness, anger, fear, among other feelings, simultaneously. To them, this is proof that they are affecting you. In addition to completely dominating you, a narcissist thrives on making you react from anger.

For a narcissist, it is impossible to have an open and genuine conversation. To get yourself ready for this, you need to anticipate the outcome of the conversation. Narcissists always want to be right, and regardless of how a conversation goes, you will end up taking all the blame.

Even if you can win the argument and make your stand with irrefutable facts, the narcissist will make you pay with various manipulation techniques. Considering all of this, utilizing deflection can help you ward off whatever the narcissist throws your way.

If a narcissist blames you for something, even if it is false, all you need to do is walk away. Do not argue, as this will only fuel the narcissist more and escalate things. If things escalate, the narcissist will try to get you provoked by dishing out insults. When this occurs, you can stay calm, and this is certain to throw off the narcissist.

SAY NO

For narcissists, other individuals are like a means to an end. They only need them to achieve some particular objectives. The moment they are done with them, they dump them. This is the reason they do not find it difficult to move on once a relationship has ended. They can quickly leave without thinking twice because they already have another individual who can provide a consistent supply of what they need.

This is the reason why saying no to them tends to break their spirits. Saying no when they want to use you once more, especially after a breakup, will let them understand they no longer have a hold over you.

If you are still in a relationship with a narcissist, he will want to kiss you or have you anytime he wants. He usually has no problem with this and easily gets away with victims, as their lives often revolve around him. To get around this, say no when he wants a kiss of love. Say no when he wants sex. Do it only when you desire, and gradually, you will take back your control from the narcissist you are in a relationship with. There is no worse feeling for narcissists than losing control over someone they believed they had under their control.

THEY MUST DESERVE ANYTHING YOU DO FOR THEM

Doing things for the one you love is not necessarily bad, especially when you are in a healthy relationship. However, when it comes to an emotionally abusive relationship with a narcissist, you need to tread more caution. When in a relationship, narcissists aim to dominate and control all areas of their partner's lives. They can easily coax them into doing anything they want, even when they do not deserve it. The victim does it without complaint because of the level of control the narcissist has over her.

Make a few adjustments if you aim to beat the narcissist at his game. Do not do things for him unless he deserves it. If they give you the silent treatment for a week and only speak to you because he needs your help, say NO! Let him only get favors when he has been genuinely deserving. In this way, he begins to become confused when he understands that his control over you has started to wane. In return, he might adapt and behave in a healthier way and treat you with the respect you deserve.

ORGANIZE OUTINGS WITH YOUR FRIENDS

Narcissists desire to control, especially in a relationship. They continuously want their victims walking on eggshells and off-balance, in a state where they can be controlled and manipulated. This way, the narcissist can expect you to wait around for them to make a plan or take you on outings. The goal is to ensure you stay guessing, not knowing their next move. This gives them the control they want over you in the relationship.

If you want to reverse the tables, you need to break the narcissist's control over you. If he refuses to organize an outing, plan one instead with your friends. Do not wait around for him to make a move. Now, he, too, won't know your next step, and it will begin to infuriate him that he is losing control over you. With time, he will start to understand that you have a life beyond him and will need to put in the effort if he wants to be a part of it.

CREATE AN ALTERNATIVE LIFE MADE OF HOBBIES, FRIENDS, GYM

Narcissists like it when your world revolves around them. They enjoy the control they get when you are unable to do anything without them being involved. They take advantage of this and refuse to include you in their activities until it suits them.

You need to let the narcissist understand that you have a life outside of him to counter this. To do this, make other plans with friends. You can also build your life around your hobbies. If you have none, this will be the time to pick up something. It could be painting, drawing, writing, or anything you enjoy that does not have to do with the narcissist.

If you want something less complicated, you could head to the gym. Make yourself look good while building a life that does not involve the narcissist. With time, when you have activities lined up, he will have to hold on to your schedule to clear up for him to spend time with you. When he starts to notice that your life is no longer revolving around him, he will begin to step up and do better. But in the end, you will have broken the shackles the narcissist has used in keeping you tied down.

PUT YOURSELF IN FIRST PLACE

When a narcissist is in a relationship, he consistently puts down his victim. He also makes his partner feel unappealing, leading to issues with self-esteem. All of these are done to break their spirit and ensure they do not outshine the narcissist. The implication of all this is a detriment to the mental and physical health of the victim.

You need to give yourself a priority to counter this. Take care of yourself and put more effort into your appearance. If you have added weight, head to the gym and engage in some extensive workout routines to help you build up muscle and confidence. Try out a new wardrobe and make yourself feel good once more. The instant you start to feel more beautiful, it will be harder for anything the narcissist says to get to you. This is one of the most natural means of destroying the narcissist in your life.

HOW TO BUILD RESILIENCE IN YOUR CHILD

Imagine a world free from peer pressure, bullying, diseases, poverty, or death. Imagine if we had the power to save our kids from all such nuisances and cruel realities of life. Wouldn't that make it a much happier world to live in?

Since we, unfortunately, can't, we have to ensure that they are ready to take care of themselves, their feelings, and emotions if the time comes. As parents, we want to keep them safe from everything bad, but for how long? How can we do that when they fly away from the nest and start their own families, careers, and separate lives? Our worries would still be the same. One of the biggest things anyone fears is change. And kids, well, they don't do well with it either. But change is inevitable. We have to work harder to prepare them for the unknown and life's uncertainties. We have to prepare them to face hardships and challenges and come out as victors and accept their failures and move on.

A resilient child is someone who knows how to bounce back from loss, grief, or failure. For them, it isn't just about surviving, but rather viewing the negative outcomes and finding something positive in them. It is the uniqueness of resilient kids that, unlike others, they can thrive and grow–no matter how big the setbacks.

Building resilience in kids is important for a number of reasons. For starters, it allows them to develop habits and coping mechanisms that will come in handy whenever they are faced with a challenging task or unexpected loss. It will prevent them from becoming overwhelmed by their emotions and let them determine the next course of action. Any step not taken with the right mind can have bitter consequences. Therefore, resilience helps kids find that balance between their emotions and actions and come out of stressful times tactfully.

Secondly, resilience also allows kids to take healthy and calculated risks. They can do so because failure no longer seems like a threat. They don't fear the unexpected and are accepting of their mistakes when they make them. They also feel more confident to move beyond their comfort zones and explore daring options. In general, they are brave, curious, and trust their instincts. All of these qualities aid them in achieving their goals and following their passions.

Resilient kids also face fewer mental health issues later in life. Although there is only some emerging evidence to imply a link, we still believe it possible. First, kids with mental health issues, such as chronic anxiety or depression, have a negative outlook on life. They hold on to their past, mistakes, and failures. A lack of resilience renders them helpless to overcome them. So, we can sense a pattern there. There are a few ideas worth sharing to help parents teach their children. These aim to help their children beat the crippling effects of anxiety and negativity on their minds and bodies.

OFFER THEM A HEALTHY ENVIRONMENT

Your foremost duty as a parent is to give them a healthy environment to survive in. They should engage in activities that help them stay calm and relaxed. They should be able to express themselves and be heard. They should be able to spend quality time with their parents and siblings fostering care, compassion, and affection. They should always feel supported and looked after.

FOCUS ON THEIR WELL-BEING

Any child who felt cared for and loved will be optimistic. Being loved by others offers us a sense of comfort. Your goal should be to build a strong emotional connection with them. This requires that you help them problem-solve, listen to their worries and concerns, and show empathy. When children feel loved, they feel empowered to take chances. They know that they have a strong support system backing them, and thus, they feel more confident to approach new things. It also builds their coping skills with negative emotions, like anger, frustration, angst, or sadness.

OFFER OPPORTUNITIES TO TAKE HEALTHY RISKS

Parents should also offer their children a chance to step out of their comfort zones and indulge in something that challenges them. In a world when we have made playgrounds safe by installing bouncy floors, it is very hard to find ways to encourage them to take healthy risks. Healthy risk is something that doesn't involve too much danger but still allows the child an opportunity to grow and learn. For instance, encouraging them to ride their bike without training wheels could be a start. This builds resilience in them over time, especially when they succeed.

REFRAME BAD EXPERIENCES

Help kids see bad experiences in a more positive light. Ask them what they learned from those events and what changes they are planning to make to counter any mistakes the next time—healthy conversation as such, open room for a new and improved perspective. Motivate them to look for the silver lining in all things—even failures and heartbreaks. If your teenage son just had a tough breakup, ask him to look at the reasons why it wasn't perfect in the first place and remind him not to repeat the errors the next time. Not only will it help with healing, but it will also build resilience.

TEACH THEM THE ART OF LETTING GO

Lastly, to beat negativity, children have to learn to focus on their present and future and let go of the things in the past. The best way to outdo negativity is to give today a chance to be better. Teach them to acknowledge, accept, and let go of what happened in the past and move on. When they start to focus on today and tomorrow, they will experience reduced stress and more anticipation of a happy future.

HOW TO BECOME A COMMONSENSE PARENT

Commonsense parenting means being a parent who makes good decisions based on knowledge of what most kids need. It doesn't mean that you instantly know how to do everything from changing a diaper to cooking a meal, but it means that you are courageous enough to make decisions when they're needed.

Ask yourself this: "What are the basic needs of children?" Next time your child is doing something new or different, ask yourself, "Is this worth celebrating?" If not, set boundaries and help them understand the difference between what's right and not right.

We will study some of the basics about how babies grow up, how they progress when they start to talk, and so on so that we can easily help our children while still having fun with them. This is not something that requires a huge amount of thought, just a little common sense.

It's easy to feel emotional when you have a new baby to care for, but deep down, we are all born with the capacity to be good parents if we let ourselves. That's where this comes in handy. It can help you understand what's going on inside your child and how you can support his development.

Babies don't come with an operating manual. They don't even come with a book of instructions. They are born from us, learn about the world from us, and depend on us to figure out how to stay healthy, happy, and alive. We are the experts about our kids because we know what they like and what works for them. As a parent, you have to use your best judgment based on children's knowledge in general and your child in particular.

At birth, our babies are born with a set of instincts that will help them to survive. They're hungry, cold, sleepy, have a sense of self or do-mine-ness, and they have a sense that everything is okay. To feel happy and secure, babies need to know what they can expect from their surroundings and their parents.

These are some useful tips that will help you become a commonsense parent:

KNOW WHAT YOUR CHILD NEEDS, LIKE IT OR NOT

A lot of parents don't realize that even newborns have strong likes and dislikes. You have to look around and find out what your baby will love as soon as possible so you can provide it for him. Don't give him the food he hates just because you think that's what he likes.

Hate eating baby food? Just give him solid foods. Don't like eating chicken with rice? Give him beef! Don't like taking a bath every day? Let your baby wear clothes and let him run around in the backyard or play outside.

In no time, you will have a baby who loves eating chicken and rice, sleeping with his clothes on, and being bathed daily. You will also have a baby who can be quite defiant at times and will not follow instructions that you've given up on.

CREATE A SAFE ENVIRONMENT FOR YOUR CHILD

Children need a safe environment to grow in. While we are there to protect them, they also have the capacity to protect themselves. Babies are hardwired to learn about the world around them and develop autonomy as their confidence grows.

A lot of parents think that babies can't possibly understand what they are being told. That's not true. Babies are capable of learning and understanding a lot more than you think.

DON'T OVERTHINK OR OVERCOMPLICATE SITUATIONS FOR YOUR BABY

Babies have a lot to deal with daily, especially when they're newborns, and start to learn how to communicate with their parents through crying (crying is like their language).

Don't worry if your child cries when you introduce him to something new. It's natural for babies to cry when they are afraid and don't understand what you are trying to teach them.

LET YOUR BABY EXPLORE HIS SURROUNDINGS

Babies are really curious creatures, and they're capable of learning a lot about the world around them if we let them explore on their own. Don't be afraid to let your baby touch the stove, take things out of the cabinets, or even put things back in.

GIVE YOUR CHILD CHOICES

Your child will learn to decide what they want to do when you give them a choice. They will also get used to making different decisions throughout their life because everyday situations require us to make quick decisions and take action.

BE FLEXIBLE

It's good for babies to have a structure in their lives to feel safe and comfortable, but don't be rigid when disciplining them. Let them know what's right and wrong, but also let them know that it's okay to make a mistake and you will forgive them if they do something wrong.

ALLOW YOUR BABY TO EXPRESS HIMSELF FREELY WITHOUT FEAR OF RETRIBUTION OR PUNISHMENT

Babies cry when they're hungry, tired, cold, sick, or in pain. Babies don't understand that sometimes they need to be quiet or make noise when trying to sleep. Babies want your attention and love, don't withhold it from them.

ENCOURAGE YOUR CHILD TO MAKE HEALTHY CHOICES BUT NEVER FORCE ANYTHING ON HIM THAT YOU KNOW IS WRONG

If you see something unhealthy for yourself or your child, speak up and let him know that you won't stand for it. Help your child make healthier choices.

RESPECT YOUR CHILD'S FEELINGS AND LET HIM KNOW THAT YOU CARE ABOUT HIM

Babies express when they are feeling sad, tired, sick, or scared. Show that you are concerned about making faces to mirror their expressions and asking them about their reaction when they feel any of these moods. Take your baby to the doctor if you think he is sick, and don't hesitate to get help if something doesn't feel right to you when something isn't right with your child.

LET YOUR CHILD HAVE FUN

Babies need to have fun so they can stay happy and positive about life. Play with them, laugh with them, and yes, even tickle them! Babies love things that make them giggle uncontrollably because they are just learning to control their emotions and learn how to express themselves.

BE SURE TO KEEP TRYING

When you first discover that you're a good mom, you will feel proud, but don't get complacent. Always try to find out what works best for your child and yourself as the parents. Often, the correct way to discipline your child is to play along with his bad behavior until he realizes what he's doing wrong or until he can't do it anymore.

It is a learning process for every parent, including the adults who have to watch their kids grow up. Make it a fun one! Learn what your baby likes and help him develop as a person.

VALUES TO PASS ON TO YOUR SON/DAUGHTER

We all want to raise kind and caring children. We desire to make them healthy, happy, and successful individuals. So, what should we do? A lot of parents focus on teaching their children values and morals. While this is a great idea, it is not the only way to go about it.

We all know how important love and acceptance are with children, but they also need limits. It's not easy being a parent, and they need to know you're in charge and you'll stand up for them when needed. You have to make clear several points to them and stick to it. These aren't easy things to do, but they're what your children need to learn.

It's easy to let them get away with things, but you need to establish boundaries for them because it will help them in the long run. When they're good, they'll be better, and when they're wrong, they'll know better next time.

UNCONDITIONAL LOVE

Their only job is to be there for them and accept them as they are. You're not perfect, and neither are they, so cut each other some slack. Never hold on to the mistakes you made in the past;

that will only hurt your relationship with your kids. Be proud of what they do right and try to build on it.

HONESTY

Trust is an essential thing in a child's life. If they can't trust you, who can they trust? They're going to need you like a rock for support. It's a challenging moment when you have to discipline your children for their misdeeds, but honesty is the best policy.

DISCIPLINE

They need to learn from mistakes, and there has to be a punishment for it. We like our kids always to be right, but it's not always possible that way. Sometimes they're going to cross lines and face the consequences for it. What you can do is get them back on the right track as soon as possible.

SELF-RESPECT

Your children need to be kind to themselves and respect their needs. They shouldn't put themselves down for their mistakes but rather try to learn from them. They shouldn't feel defeated by what they think is a weakness; instead, they should see it as a strength. The best way is through practicing self-love and self-respect.

BOUNDARIES

Parents need to set strong boundaries for their kids. The children, in turn, should respect those boundaries and not cross them. This is what will keep the stability going in the family and make sure things stay under control. Boundaries will keep your kids grounded and make them see how to treat others.

EMPATHY

They need to understand how it feels when someone else is suffering. If they can handle it themselves, they won't turn a blind eye to it when others are suffering, either. They need to learn to take care of others and put the needs of others first. When they hurt others, they'll feel the hurt as well.

COURTESY AND MANNERS

Children should learn how to be polite and courteous to their elders as well as their peers. Show them that treating people with respect is more important than what you want or expect from them. It's also important that they learn how to be a good friend before being a good son or daughter before being an adult.

ACCEPTANCE OF OTHERS

They should be accepting of people who are different from them. They should be kind to their peers and treat each other right. If they can be tolerant of differences, they'll feel better about themselves. Intolerant children don't feel good about themselves as individuals, and it shows in their relationship with others.

LIFE SKILLS

It's also important that children learn how to function in society. They need to know the correct actions to do in different situations. By teaching them about life, you're helping them move forward and have a positive outlook on life.

SELF-ESTEEM

They should never be quick to judge others, but rather give them the benefit of the doubt. Be sure to tell them how they should respect themselves in everything that they do. Encourage them to take pride in who they are and deserve it as well.

INDEPENDENCE

They have to understand how to be independent and work under their own steam; nobody owes them anything. They should know what's right and wrong from their experiences and not have others do it for them all the time.

Be firm with your children when they do something wrong or cross the line. Don't let them get away with it. If you're not in control of things, then who will be? They need to learn that they are not invincible, and they can stand up for themselves.

Make it clear that they are enrolled in your family. Show them that you're their protector and when they act up, you will stand up for them.

Understand that they need you right now and don't plan on leaving them alone. It's their fault, not yours, but their life to live. They need security and reassurance from time to time, so take care of them. They need to see that you're the one who has a good life for family and friends.

Don't let them get away with stuff without facing the consequences. Whether they realize it or not, the way you were raised will show in the way they are now living their life. If they aren't getting beaten up every day, why should they do so many illegal and immoral acts in life? You'll be setting a standard for them to live by.

Be clear about rules and consequences while being consistent. They need to see that you're taking the time to help them learn the ropes of how to function in society. They won't remember every single thing you did, but they'll remember the lessons you taught them.

When your kids are behaving properly, make sure you tell them to show your appreciation for it. It might be rare to see, but it's important to appreciate their efforts at behaving well. It's also nice to show them that you're proud of them and what they're doing.

The best way to teach your child values is by being a good role model yourself. You should be the one who sets the example for them. You can teach your kids all the rules in the world, but if you don't stick by them, then they won't take any notice. It's your job to stop them from being bad and to encourage them to be good.

Children tend to learn more from what you do than what you say. Be the person you want them to grow up into and show them how to live happily. You don't need to be perfect, and sometimes they'll need a correction, but don't give up trying.

COMPASSION AND SELF-COMPASSION

There are several ways to awaken self-compassion within yourself, and all of these require awareness of yourself as an individual. You should consistently be seeking forgiveness of yourself rather than condemnation on your road to recovery.

These steps will help guide you to becoming you again and understand that you can become better. After the experience you endured, you are close to the better half of an expert on narcissism. The following are the ways that will help you awaken self-compassion and trigger thoughts of forgiveness flowing.

DRINKING WATER WILL HELP YOU CLEAR YOUR MIND AND ALSO MAKE YOU FEEL BETTER PHYSICALLY

There is a reason why they recommend drinking water when you are feeling emotionally upset or are experiencing any kind of mental turmoil. Drinking water will help you flush toxins and help you get back on the right path to physical upkeep.

Feeling emotionally drained can often be because you have not focused on your physical needs for an amount of time.

Headaches, fatigue, and emotional stress can all be relieved through drinking water. Pick up that glass and start drinking! Suppose it helps you to drink throughout the day. In that case, they have some interesting and visually attractive water bottles on the market with varying levels drawn on the side of the bottle that indicate when you should drink throughout the day.

Make it fun if it is hard to remember to drink water regularly. Enjoy drinking fruit or vegetable and herb-infused water, such as cucumber with mint or lemon and basil. It is still healthy as it is just water and not flavored. If it helps to set the alarm on your phone telling you to drink, do it! Find what works for you, develop a new habit of drinking water, and know that it will make you feel better.

PHYSICAL ACTIVITY IS ONE BEST WAYS TO AWAKEN SELF-COMPASSION

Exercise not only makes you feel better physically through the release of endorphins, but it is a great way to release toxins. Exercising often and regularly helps keep your brain active and focused and can eliminate such conditions as anxiety. Running every day will help you tone down your generalized anxiety levels to a tolerable level.

Yoga is also an important way to help you combine your controlled breathing tactics and tone muscle. It also releases a relaxing chemical called GABA that makes it rather addicting once you start. Once you find a creative physical exercise outlet that you enjoy, stick to it. You owe it to yourself.

RESTING ENOUGH AND GETTING ENOUGH SLEEP IS VERY IMPORTANT

You must give yourself that opportunity to clear your brain and just relax. It can be difficult with anxiety and insomnia contributing to other daily stressors at work or home. If you find that it helps, rest during the day. Taking a quick nap can be life-changing and turn your day around if you are very tired, even for a few minutes! Create a schedule and aim to stick to it.

Tracking your sleep for a while can help you find the best sleeping schedule for you that will allow you the most rest possible. Sleep is conducive to help and recovery for the brain; do not cheat yourself of much-needed sleep and shuteye. Insomnia is all too common for those recovering from a narcissist, with overwhelming thoughts keeping you up, so find a schedule that works for you and get some rest.

YOUR LIVING SPACE AND SURROUNDINGS CAN DETERMINE HOW YOU FEEL AND BEHAVE

A clean and structured home environment will help you feel less cluttered and more in control of your life and behavior. If your home is in disarray, most likely you are as well. Taking the time to clean, making things fresh and pleasant to your taste in décor will help you find that you can relax and feel comfortable becoming you once more. Plants and nature or greenery are a great addition to any living space, and words of wisdom or quotes can be helpful when placed around the home.

POSITIVE MEDITATION CAN BE ONE OF THE MOST REWARDING WAYS TO FIND AND PRACTICE SELF-COMPASSION

Encouraging words and phrases combined with controlled breathing is one of the greatest ways to reconnect with yourself. Learning how to love yourself again is a large part of growth after a narcissistic relationship. Your significant other's manipulating lies no longer define you; you are you, and no one can take that from you. Rebuild your mental strength capacity and learn to love yourself once more. Forgive yourself, focus on your breathing, and just simply relax your mind and your body one muscle at a time. Even a few minutes of every day doing this can be effective in helping you learn how to relax.

SPEAKING WORDS OF GENUINE KINDNESS TO YOURSELF IS ONE OF THE BIGGEST ASPECTS OF SELF-COMPASSION

There is a push by society for perfection, but that is not attainable, nor is it healthy. You do not need to buy into that notion; you are enough, you are good, and you did not earn what happened to you. You were tricked by a wolf in sheep's clothing that sold you an illusion that you bought before second thoughts even had a chance to surface in your mind. Allow yourself to learn and to grow. Learn to love yourself once more.

Always remember that it is okay to make mistakes because you are learning. You are relearning many concepts throughout the recovery process from a narcissist that many others would not even begin to understand if you tried to explain. Love yourself and love others and know that everything will be okay. Growth is a process, and you must allow yourself that room to grow.

CONFIDENCE IN SELF AND OTHERS

If you had confidence before your relationship, the narcissist has likely taken that away from you. The most daunting task in your recovery process is building a new sense of confidence, different from before. This can only come as you make your self-esteem and perception of who you are and who you want to be. Maybe you didn't have much self-confidence either, so it's crucial that you start building it now so you can feel worthy and appreciative of yourself. By following the last two suggestions, forgiving yourself, and learning to listen to your intuition, you will also be building self-awareness, which promotes confidence. Through these three steps, your goals bring your awareness levels to a place where you can look at how the narcissist hurt you and which areas you need to work on the most. Learn your strengths and weaknesses, and in the process of working through your weaknesses, your confidence level will go up as well with everyone you overcome.

Building confidence cannot be done unless you investigate the traumatic experiences you endured before the narcissistic relationship. It could stem from childhood. Learn to break down and walk through these barriers to help you see just how strong you are, which will build a new level of confidence. You will learn to develop self-reflection by reaching out to support systems and teams like groups, classes, therapies, family, and friends. Self-reflection is crucial in learning more about yourself and seeing all the beautiful qualities the narcissist made you blind to. Take the pain that you feel, and use it to learn more about yourself, and you may find new attributes you had never seen about yourself before. By lighting up this whole new perception of yourself, you will find success and inner peace, which often leads to happiness.

Learning how to trust again is no easy task, but with patience and self-kindness and the help of others, it is possible. When you have successfully learned how to reach inside yourself and trust who matters, then you can start putting your trust in new people who come into your life. This is because with the trust you feel inside yourself, you can trust that you know best when you put your faith in someone else. This happens when you are perfectly in tune with your intuition. This is a moment when you will only follow your gut instinct if you have the confidence to believe that you are right. With forgiveness of your mistakes, you make along the way and patience to overcome whatever problems lie ahead for you, and you will finally learn the true meaning of trust in yourself and others.

When someone has low self-esteem, they are more vulnerable to narcissists and other people and situations that are primarily negative. Narcissists look for those with low self-esteem because they know that it will make it easier to get them into their web. When you have good self-esteem, you have a healthy level of self-respect and confidence in your abilities and worth. When self-esteem is low, someone is more likely to tolerate abusive situations, not live up to their potential, and become depressed.

Self-esteem is a part of everything that you do in life. It affects your performance at school, at work, and in your relationships. Low self-esteem can also stop you from living a full life since it is characterized by the fear of trying new things or test your limits.

Self-esteem ultimately comes from within. However, some factors can influence it. The people around you play a role in how you see yourself. This is especially true when it comes to those close to you and those you respect. For example, if a parent is always critical of a child, this can damage the child's self-esteem. On the other hand, when a parent is very supportive, it helps someone see their value, leading to healthy self-esteem.

Every person has that inner voice that essentially tells them what to think of themselves. For some, this inner voice can be highly negative and critical. When this happens, it is easy to believe the voice and feel as though you are inferior. It is common to have negative feelings, but you eventually start believing them when you allow them to dominate you. It is essential to listen to negative feelings but then put them into perspective. If your inner voice tells you that you are a failure, listen to it and do not question it, you will start to believe this, resulting in lower self-esteem.

Comparing yourself to other people is another influencer on your self-esteem. It is fine to evaluate those around you, but must not allow this to overshadow your strengths. Taking inventory of your weaknesses and strengths and focusing on what you are good at can help prevent the strengths of those around you from negatively impacting how you view yourself.

IMPROVING YOUR SELF-ESTEEM

Your low self-esteem does not have to remain. There are ways to boost and alleviate the negative thoughts and feelings from dominating your view of yourself. To get started, work on developing life skills that contribute to how you see yourself and the world around you. These include:

- Do not be afraid to identify and experience your feelings. When you push feelings down and try to ignore them, they will eventually come to the surface.

- Do not be terrified to walk away from negative situations and people.

- Be receptive to those around you and empathize with people.

- Think optionally and not in black and white. This allows you to solve problems better and learn new things.

- Be assertive when it is needed. Don't let others dominate the direction of your life.

- See the good things in your life and what you are good at. Low self-esteem can make it seem like you are not good enough at anything. However, it is easier to remember that it exists when you feel down than when you reflect on your good features.

- Make a learning opportunity out of every mistake. Every person fails and makes mistakes. This is a part of life. However, please do not dwell on these and the negative consequences that might come with them. Spend an hour being upset because it is important to experience your emotions. However, after an hour, go into action mode and consider why the mistake or failure occurred. You will always be able to find at least one lesson. This lesson reduces the risk of mistakes and failure in the future.

- Know that perfection is not possible. What is important is that you are putting in the effort and working on learning and getting better. No person is born being great at everything. Life is all about learning and working on developing the skills needed to achieve your goals.

- Remember that every person has their strengths. Imagine a world where every person is just good at everything. There would be no healthy competition, no learning, and no balance. Know your strengths and respect the strengths of others.

- Know what you cannot change. For example, if you are short, you are short. You cannot change this. Once you accept what cannot be changed, you can start focusing on your life areas that can be improved.

- Do not be afraid to try. You never know what you are good at until you test your limits. Have you always wanted to play soccer but were afraid you were not good enough? Get a game going with friends or join a local team. You may be great, or you may not. Either way, you tried it, and every new thing you try expands your horizons.

- Give yourself credit when you deserve it. When you do something great, be proud of yourself. It is easy to put more focus on flaws because this is just what humans do. However, when you switch your focus to the good stuff, your self-esteem will get a boost.

HOW TO HELP YOUR SON/DAUGHTER BECOME A CONFIDENT PERSON

Our mental health depends on our ability to be strong. It's a life skill that we carry into adulthood. Building resilience in youngsters makes it easier for them to overcome challenges and minimizes their risks of developing anxiety or other stress-related problems.

Children's mental health depends on their ability to be resilient. More resilient children are better equipped to cope with stress, which is a common reaction to adversity. If the degree of stress is extreme or chronic, it is a risk factor for mental health problems such as anxiety and depression.

Resilience is a crucial attribute for all of us to develop, and it is especially crucial for our children. We know that resilient children are happier and less stressed wherever they are, at home, in school, before and after school care, or at school vacation programs.

Building self-confidence requires resilience. When our child has self-confidence, they may take on new challenges and give it all.

Failing is not the same as making a mistake; it is the act of attempting something new. Many historical figures, such as

Abraham Lincoln, wrote about their failures in various areas before achieving success.

IT'S CRITICAL TO BE ABLE TO GET BACK UP AND TRY AGAIN

We are not born stars in any field, but with hard effort, perseverance, and self-confidence, as well as resilience, we can shine in our chosen sector.

Challenges are not just a part of life; they shape who we are. You must teach children resilience to cope with life as they grow older, to be better able to deal with life's ups and downs, disappointments, and setbacks that most of us experience. The sooner they figure out how to cope, the better.

Most people's lives will not go exactly as planned when they want them to. They will not be able to get all they desire at the time they desire it. Smoothing out every bump in the road, awarding awards for finishing first, and so on, will not help children grow into functioning individuals.

We need to educate youngsters on resilience to deal with the problems that will inevitably arise in their adult lives. There are so many circumstances beyond your control that raising a child exactly the way you want is impossible.

It's not like combining ingredients to make the desired concoction. We need to educate resilience because life rarely goes as planned, and we must learn to "roll with the punches."

Resilience emphasizes being tough, patient, and tolerant. We're talking about a trait that measures emotional health, and it helps to have a high level of resilience here because life is full of challenges at various stages.

A TOY SHRINKS AND BREAKS WHEN A CHILD IS SEVEN YEARS OLD

Parental reaction: Replace the toy or divert the child's attention to another toy or something more valuable.

This teaches children that rapid satisfaction is the best way to deal with a sudden disappointment or loss, and this behavior will lead them to use rapid pleasure in all situations. When a presentation at work goes badly wrong, they are likely to be blamed.

VERSUS

Another Parental Response: Allow the youngster to grieve and lament the loss with you and listen to their explanation of how it has affected them.

This teaches kids how to communicate their feelings to others, that it's normal to be vulnerable, and that disappointments and loss are inevitable parts of life. If the parent buys a toy a few days or weeks later, it has nothing to do with the episode. Enough time has passed before the youngster gets another toy, book, or anything else. It does soothe the pain of loss, but only when you're more emotional.

This is the concept of delayed gratification. The same heinous performance will be remembered, but it acts as a balm to that loss in a more emotionally intense phase. This is the concept of delayed gratification. They will lament the same dreadful presentation and the break-up, but they will have learned to let things pass and become more Resilient, which will allow for creative thinking and smart decision-making to emerge.

This second option instills resilience as a learned behavior that allows for sufficient emotional and mental maturity. After that, in addition to resilience, children must also be taught the virtue of compassion. Compassion and resiliency work together. Resilience breeds toughness and a sense of direction.

Resilience develops a harsh personality, while compassion develops a gentle and caring one. They not only fulfill emotional maturity, but they also form a harmonious individual when they work together.

Throughout their education, children are invariably confronted. But willingly and in a positive frame of mind. In the end, there is a sense of accomplishment.

Resilience is a natural part of the rearing process. Children learn by attempting again and again until they have mastered the scenario or the lesson. And they've mastered it to the point that they've outgrown the need for resiliency and can now bend the circumstances to their will.

Being self-sufficient, standing on our own two feet, or reclaiming authority are all examples of resilience.

It's significant because it can ameliorate some of the bullying's detrimental effects on children and teenagers. It is also a life skill that can benefit a child in many aspects of life; it will give them the confidence not just to speak up for themselves but also to champion the rights of others.

Resilience can help to raise a child's self-worth and restore self-esteem. It has the potential to prevent youngsters from adopting more serious measures such as self-harm or death and send a message to bullies that their tactics are ineffective. Resilient children will be able to cope with a variety of situations.

Resilient children are more self-sufficient in attending to their own needs.

They have to feel comfortable in their skin and are more willing to try new things.

Resilient children will be better at coping with issues, have better health, and be happier and more content when they become grown-ups.

They will also have a lower risk of developing mental issues such as despair or anxiety. Resilience is a skill that must be grown over time.

Some children may have a more positive character, which may make gaining resilience a little simpler for them; however, those who do not have such an 'easy' personality may require a bit more assistance in learning these skills to help them build resilience. Convey a message to bullies that what they're doing isn't working. Resilience helps teach children how to interact with people in a way that promotes their behavior and self-worth. Children should be taught how to solve problems and make decisions.

HOW TO INSTILL PEACE AND SERENITY IN YOUR CHILD DESPITE THE NARCISSISTIC PARTNER

As a parent, it's imperative to protect your children when dealing with a narcissistic co-parent. Constantly showing empathy can significantly help a child feel less trapped, especially when one parent is a narcissist and the other is just trying to keep the peace.

EMPATHY PARENTING

Children need empathy. They won't learn about it if their parents don't understand them or show them kindness. If they don't receive any empathy, they will begin to feel like their emotions don't matter.

Lots of parents often confuse sympathy and empathy. This is especially true for narcissists, who lack any form of empathy whatsoever. However, there is a significant difference between the two that makes a giant impact on your kids.

Sympathy is feeling sorry for someone else. Empathy is the capability to recognize and share the feelings of another person.

To illustrate, think of it like this:

Imagine and think of yourself sitting by the side of a swimming pool. Someone falls in and starts to drown. To sympathize, you would feel bad and tell the person a story of a time you were drowning. You make the problem about yourself, and nobody gets pulled from the water.

If you were to show empathy, think of yourself as throwing them a life raft. You understand their problem and accept that it causes the other person discomfort. Instead of making it about yourself, you stand outside of the issue as a means of support.

Sympathy, mainly when used by a narcissist, can become patronizing. It creates a separation between the narcissist and others, and any sympathetic advice may come across as condescending.

In parenting, if your partner or child is venting to you and you try to give them advice to "cure" the problem, this may seem like a good solution, but it's not always what the other person is seeking by confiding in you.

Instead of giving advice, you could try to show empathy by saying, "A lot of people struggle with this problem; you're not alone." It will give another person a sense of friendship, understanding, and hope to heal their pain.

In parenting, not showing empathy means we would never truly understand our kids and their motivations. We would ignore what makes our kids individuals and force our agendas on them.

We can still feel sorry for them, but that alone is not productive. It doesn't solve any problems. By showing empathy, we step into the child's shoes and help them feel understood and empowered to make their own decisions.

By constantly showing empathy, we increase our kids' likelihood of being more connected and open with us. Kids who are more comfortable around you will open more, feel safe to express their hardships and be more mentally healthy individuals.

To best show empathy to your children, try to mirror the tone and language they are using. Avoid using 'I' statements and truly listen to what the other person is saying.

Empathy requires detailed listening and compassion to understand the root of their issue truly. Navigating the waters of two co-parents that butt heads all the time can be incredibly stressful for a child; so, be sure to check in frequently to see how they are doing. Unfortunately, narcissists don't have empathy; you need to supply twice the normal amount.

EDUCATING THE CHILD ON HEALTHY VS. UNHEALTHY RELATIONSHIP DYNAMICS

Healthy communication requires recognizing, understanding, and then verbalizing the feelings you have. Children in narcissistic homes don't typically get a chance to verbalize their negative feelings. They are only allowed to display "happy" feelings because they are censored by the narcissist, taught to internalize, and hide all their negative feelings.

That's unhealthy emotional regulation. It doesn't allow your kids to speak out loud about their feelings, and instead, the children might feel shameful for how they think.

Teaching your child proper emotional regulation is a must. That's because chances are, they're not learning this at the other parent's household.

Unfortunately, co-parents often don't align on this issue. It's vital to teach your child that even though they might not get their feelings respected by your partner, it doesn't mean that their feelings aren't important.

This doesn't mean that a child will always get whatever they want. But it does emphasize the importance of communicating emotions as they arise. You can teach them that they won't always get their way, but you still respect how they feel.

LET THEM HAVE AN IDENTITY

A sense of identity is something a child develops. Children don't come into this world with a clear understanding of how they fit in. Support and help them establish a realistic and stabilized view of themselves.

Usually, their identity is something that they explore in different ways. The three primary ways we form our identities are:

- Exploration and experimentation

- The reactions of others

- Failure and success

Children don't want to build their identity around something they suck at, but instead what they like, what they're strong at, and how their abilities compare to others.

The key here is to let your kids decide and figure it out themselves without being overly pushy and critical.

Another way how kid forms their identity is through reactions from other people, especially adults and authority figures (i.e., parents, teachers, etc.). Affirmation is huge for kids, and giving kids compliments or rewards for their achievements helps foster confidence.

You may also affect your kid's identity indirectly by simply being yourself. For example, early in their childhood (and even into pre-puberty), my sons would pick up on my mannerisms and start using them in their daily communication. This type of mirroring is typical for kids developing their self-identities but can be a little more discreet to detect.

Finally, you've got successes and failures. As your kids explore and look at the reactions of others, they start to have both failures and successes in life. If a child sees that they're good at communicating with others and enjoys it, they might become talkative. They'll find that they are also not good at some things. And that's okay.

Narcissistic parents only want the child to do certain activities. To them, pursuing anything else is pointless, stupid, and wrong.

How do you compromise with your problem without compromising your child's identity? Well, you can try to encourage your children to at least explore a few of the things the narcissist approves of.

It is important to be supportive of your child's exploration into themselves. Let them work on trying new skills, and don't be afraid to have fun while doing it.

CHILDREN AND LOVE

Children need to realize and understand that they are loved. The problem, however, is that kids often don't get loved unconditionally by a narcissistic parent. They develop mental issues that prevent them from providing this kind of love. Narcissists don't know how to show consistent affection and typically only show it when they manipulate others. Narcissistic parents only care about positive emotions when it involves themselves. Otherwise, they don't care.

The main reason why narcissists can't show love is that they lack "object constancy." This is a term for people who can keep positive emotions, even when someone is hurt, frustrated, angry, or disappointed. Since people with NPD lack this trait, they cannot separate a single toxic issue from years of building trust with someone. They cannot feel any positive emotions during a conflict, which only causes a deeper spiral of toxicity. If they're angry or frustrated towards their child, narcissists cannot tap into loving feelings, creating this internal battle of emotions.

Narcissists also struggle with self-esteem. They think children are assets rather than individual people. They were used for personal gain.

This creates instability in children, especially since they feel they can't get love and affection. It also makes them feel like they're just pawns in the narcissist's game.

What can you do to help?

Try to create a safe space for your children. It means providing enduring love towards them. Even if you are upset, feel like you can give them the proper love and affection that they need. It stabilizes their identity and love towards you and makes you look loving in their eyes.

LET THEM FORM OPINIONS

As a parent, allow your child to explore and try new ideas so they can formulate their own belief, even if it's different from your opinion. Your child might not agree with you on everything, and that's okay. If it isn't hurting other people, it's not always a bad thing. Maybe your child is more concerned with society's problems and believes their efforts are better used for humanitarian programs. You might not think so, but let them investigate it and figure it out for themselves.

Spend time with your kids alone and give them a chance to explore different perspectives. Remember, your child might also take on the characteristics of the other parent, especially in how they think. It's best if you let them learn that it's okay to have different viewpoints. If they can explore those views with you, it helps create a stabilized environment.

CHILDREN AND SKILL TRAINING

Skill training is vital for children that deal with a narcissistic parent. It's essential for you to teach these skills because your child will not get this from the other parent. The narcissistic parent doesn't have these skills. Trying to get a narcissist to teach you empathy is NOT going to work.

However, you can be a better parent and teach your kids these valuable skills. That way, your kids do not lack essential, real-world skills.

Let me give you the best skills to teach your children and why these skills are essential for building better, stronger children.

HOW TO APOLOGIZE

Narcissistic parents don't know how to take responsibility, so they never apologize for bad behavior and often don't understand what they did wrong. A narcissist won't ever apologize since they view themselves as perfect, and apologizing is generally an admission of fault.

Sometimes children don't know how to apologize due to traumatic events in the past. When they're mistreated because of their mistakes, it can lead to criticism, sometimes almost too much. Whenever you make mistakes, admit that you created them. If you ever say something you don't mean, you must apologize. Don't apologize for everything, so to speak, but do own up to anything that you do incorrectly.

Even something as simple as a misunderstanding, respond by apologizing. Make apologizing for an easy and regular occurrence. Soon, apologizing won't be such a big deal.

This can take time since you're undoing the damage your narcissistic co-parent has already inflicted, but it does get easier.

Protecting your child is vital when dealing with a narcissistic co-parent. People with NPD are unconcerned with other people's feelings. Therefore, you can keep things from worsening in order to maintain your child's mental health and safety.

TIPS FOR EACH AGE OF YOUR CHILD IN CO-PARENTING

The changes associated with divorce or separation affect all family members. Just like you, your child's responses to these changes may vary from what is expected. Be aware of your child's individual needs to make it easier to come up with healthy and appropriate decisions while leading them to have a happy and successful life.

In general, children experience anger, fear, loneliness, insecurity, sadness, anxiety, and rejection associated with the divorce or separation. The responses of children vary depending on their age.

Throughout their lives, children will experience separation differently. While your child may be brilliant and seem to know and understand everything, their perception will grow deeper as they age. It is essential to share with your child great affirmation and love.

When you speak to your child, it would be best to encourage them to ask questions and express their feelings. Allow your child to assess how they feel and express them. This way, you are keeping open communication with your child while teaching them strategies for coping.

WHAT TO EXPECT FROM INFANTS AND TODDLERS

Infants become unhappy or distressed when there are major variations in their routine. They may demonstrate this through excessive crying. Infants may also show signs of sleeping or eating problems. The primary source of psychological stress of infants, in general, comes from hostility between parents, unpredictable daily routines, and exposure to emotional upset.

Toddlers, on the other hand, are more complicated than infants. Children between 18 and 24 months have some dependency needs, although they cultivate their developmental achievements. Toddlers, like infants, have security issues, specifically when they are away from their parents. As such, it can be very frightening for them to experience a partial or complete disappearance of a parent.

Toddlers may also demonstrate the same signs as infants; however, they may exhibit increased aggression, temper tantrums, lethargy, night terrors, and regression, including previously acquired skills such as toilet training. Toddlers also tend to show increased separation anxiety from one of the parents.

RESPONDING TO REACTIONS OF INFANTS AND TODDLERS

To assist an infant or toddler, it is best to create stability in every opportunity you get. This is because infants and toddlers depend on a stable environment as well as fixed routines or schedules. In general, it is advisable to provide constant contact with both parents.

It is advisable to support the idea of overnight stays with the non-resident parent except if there are unusual or exceptional circumstances that need to be addressed. Infants and toddlers love playing, cuddling, make-believes, and fantasy; thus, parents should provide them with a great deal of those activities.

WHAT TO EXPECT FROM PRESCHOOLERS

Children between ages 3 and 5 tend to blame themselves for their parent's separation because their ability to perceive a parental loss is limited. Children at these ages are inclined to believe that the anger or emotional distress is their fault. It is common for them to experience regression, specifically a loss of developmental accomplishments in various areas such as emotional independence, social relationships, toilet training, motor activity, eating, sleeping, and language. They also tend to manifest excessive crying or clinging, especially when a parent leaf. They also find it hard to adjust to two different households.

Preschoolers are inclined to exhibit increased temper tantrums and anger. As such, parents must identify these reactions and address them appropriately.

RESPONDING TO REACTIONS OF PRESCHOOLERS

Regardless of whether their parents are separated or not, most preschoolers have increased separation anxiety. This may intensify during or after divorce. Many children of this age level who are used to having both parents are inclined to anxiety when one parent moves out of the family home.

It is best to reassure them that the change entails having two homes to help them handle their anxiety. As much as possible, both parents should take the child to the new home and show where the father or the mother will be staying. This will make them feel comfortable with the change.

Preschoolers need reassurance that they are not to blame for the divorce. Parents should explain that relationships are often complex and may end even if the persons involved do not expect to. Preschoolers should also know that they have no obligation to keep their parents together; however, parents should remind their children that they will always remain as a family. At this age, preschoolers will only be able to understand ideas to a certain point.

WHAT TO EXPECT FROM EARLY ELEMENTARY-AGE SCHOOL CHILDREN

Children between the ages of 6 and 8 are in a stage of developing their competence and mastery of skills. As with other age groups already mentioned, children at this age also tend to regress and demonstrate less willingness or initiative to apply the skills they have acquired previously.

They may also show restlessness, anxiety, tantrums, heightened moodiness, stress, sadness, or depression. These can be manifested through the form of physical complaints, including stomach problems, tiredness, and headache. In some cases, children who undergo a divorce tend to withdraw from their friends and regular activities. They are also inclined to change their bedtime routine or refuse to go to school or do their homework. Sometimes, these are symptoms of their attempt to have more contact with both parents to obtain reassurance.

At this age, young children struggle to express their loyalty to both parents. For instance, they may express their loyalty by being perfect or trying to please their parents. Other children may express their loyalty negatively, such as being angry toward one or both of their parents. You can expect various reactions from children of this age. Often, it will be challenging for you to see their reactions; however, you should remind yourself that these are normal and, often, temporary.

RESPONDING TO REACTIONS OF EARLY ELEMENTARY-AGE SCHOOL CHILDREN

Minimizing parental conflict, especially in their presence, is the primary factor that protects young children. It is a protective factor for all children. When children are exposed openly and excessively to parental conflict, they have a poor psychological adjustment to transitions brought about by divorce.

Furthermore, parents should see to it that they always provide their children with emotional support, authoritative discipline, and adequate monitoring.

Early elementary-age school children equipped with these protective factors can adjust better to divorce than those whose parents are less supportive and use inappropriate discipline.

Based on several studies, children who have constant contact with both parents excel academically and have a more positive adjustment to transition brought about by divorce than those who do not maintain regular contact with their parents.

It is also important to keep specific practices, such as having consistent routines and keeping friendships and relationships with close relatives. Your child's teachers are also significant in adjusting your child to transitions; as such, it is advisable to make the teachers aware of the changes and ask them to speak to you promptly for any concerns regarding your child.

WHAT TO EXPECT FROM ELEMENTARY-SCHOOL CHILDREN

Children between ages 9 and 12 are inclined to feel extreme loss when they undergo divorce. Elementary-school children tend to have divided loyalty that can be painful and confusing if the parents try to take sides, specifically in an adversarial divorce process.

More often than not, children at this age convert their painful feelings of sadness, loss, and helplessness into anger. However, this is more endurable for them as compared to being vulnerable emotionally. These children are also inclined to having low self-esteem and diminished performance in school.

It is also common for children to direct their anger to one or both parents as they undergo divorce. They tend to believe that they are being mistreated, given that they have already established their belief system about family and parents. They are likely to take refuge from the parent whom they think is more hurt than the other. However, parents should discourage their children from taking sides or creating an alliance with one parent. Otherwise, as children grow older, they would foster the feeling of guilt.

At this age, it is expected for children to either spend a great deal of their time with friends or decrease their peer interactions considerably. While these may be normal reactions, parents should make room for them. In addition, parents should also be vigilant for extreme behaviors. Children at this age tend to make their fantasies and may include their parents patching things up and reconciling.

RESPONDING TO REACTIONS OF ELEMENTARY-SCHOOL CHILDREN

In general, when elementary-school children undergo a divorce, they tend to feel an extreme loss. However, it is still possible for parents to rebuild their children's sense of security by keeping the communication lines open. It is best to encourage children to express their feelings, although pressing it too much when they are not ready to speak can be damaging.

Parents should communicate to their children about consistent and precise expectations. It is essential to let the children know that their feelings about the divorce are valid. On the other hand, parents should emphasize that although their feelings are valid and normal, they should express them positively. For instance, if your child is angry, explain that it is normal; however, offer positive alternatives for expressing such anger. Make sure that your child is aware of the consequences of their inappropriate behavior.

WHAT TO EXPECT FROM ADOLESCENTS OR TEENAGERS

Adolescence is a stage wherein all developmental areas are caused to have significant changes. This is a period wherein teenagers become more aware of their sexuality and identity. It is also a period wherein they cope with peer pressure and strive to have increased liberty or self-reliance.

Adolescents who undergo their parents' divorce process should be able to deal with their developmental issues and, at the same time, adapt to transitions related to the divorce. Although most teenagers can adjust to the changes, some demonstrate emotional distress, either moderate or severe. Such distress is likely to manifest in all areas of a teenager's life.

Moreover, teenagers have their ways of expressing distress, and these are ways, which can be new and alarming. For instance, they can demonstrate intense anger and become involved in drug or alcohol abuse. They can also get involved in sexual activities, run away, get involved in juvenile delinquency, or hurt themselves physically. They also tend to associate their personality with the personality of one or both parents.

RESPONDING TO REACTIONS OF ADOLESCENTS OR TEENAGERS

A divorce entails increased emotional support, firm guidance, and abundant love for teenagers. As teenagers face the challenges related to divorce, parents should discern between normal responses and deeper or more severe reactions.

For instance, parents should distinguish if their teenagers are having regular mood swings or the depression and anger are both due to the stress brought about by the divorce. This can be quite tricky for parents because teenagers can manifest their depressed feelings as symptoms of depression. These symptoms include sleeping too much, low energy, depressed mood, trouble sleeping, poor concentration, and hopelessness.

To empower teenagers, many experts believe that children at this age should be involved in making decisions, specifically in living arrangements, visitation, and school. It will provide them with a sense of security and control while making them feel part of the process.

THE FIGURE AND THE IMPORTANCE OF A PSYCHOTHERAPIST

Apsychotherapist has specialized training and education and uses psychological knowledge to help individuals and groups understand, change, or cope with their difficulties. Psychotherapists can be trained in many fields, including psychology, social work, theology, sociology, and other professions.

The therapeutic relationship develops during this assessment process as the patient shares his problems and becomes more comfortable with the therapist. If it is found out that the patient does indeed have a psychological disorder or illness, then treatment therapies are initiated.

You will need help from some support system, as well as professionals who can help you move past the traumatic experience you've had over the years with your former narcissistic partner.

COGNITIVE BEHAVIORAL THERAPY

Cognitive-behavioral therapy is also known as CBT. It's a therapy that gets you talking about everything that you went through with the narcissist to help you better handle the problems you'll encounter as the aftermath of dealing with a narcissist for so long. The goal of CBT is to help you have a different, more beneficial perspective on reality and help you see how certain events about you could have made you vulnerable to being chosen as the narc's mark.

Therapists who practice CBT operate from the belief that there is a common thread between your actions, feelings, thoughts, and even bodily sensations. They believe that once you've got specific negative, disempowering thoughts and feelings on a loop in your mind, then it's easy for you to fall into the hands of yet another narcissist. So, the best way to heal is to address what's going on the inside.

The way CBT therapists go about this is to deconstruct all these issues which overwhelm you into smaller bits and then show you how you can easily redirect the pattern of negative thinking on the inside so that you get the results you desire on the outside.

The difference between other kinds of talking treatments and CBT is that with CBT, the spotlight is squarely on the problems facing you at the moment, rather than talking about issues from the past. It's all about giving you practical exercises you can do at the moment to help you achieve results each day, which snowball into a life you'll be proud to have.

PROLONGED EXPOSURE THERAPY

Prolonged Exposure Therapy (PET) is yet another method of psychotherapy commonly used for those who have post-traumatic stress disorder (PTSD). This is incredibly helpful for the narcissistic abuse victim who has PTSD or Complex PTSD.

PTSD happens when you've gone through a traumatic event. You get terrible nightmares, thoughts you don't want begin to swirl around in your head, you feel depressed, hopeless, and very suspicious of everyone and everything. Because of all the symptoms, sufferers naturally want to avoid anything that would remotely remind them of the terrors they had to live through during the traumatic period of their lives.

PET is geared towards helping you move past the trauma. It enables you to connect with life so that you're able to face things, which could potentially remind you of past trauma without breaking down and losing yourself. It helps you understand the difference between what's safe and what is not. As a result, you have fewer symptoms of PTSD to deal with.

COGNITIVE PROCESSING THERAPY

Known as CPT for short, Cognitive Processing Therapy is another kind of cognitive-behavioral therapy for treating PTSD. When you're plagued by so much anxiety, guilt, fear, and anger on account of all you went through at the hands of the narcissist, these emotions can make it impossible for you to recover and move on indeed.

CPT is an alternative healing method that gives you the skills you need to help you stare down the negative emotions and thoughts on the inside and then get a handle on them. This way, the impact of these emotions in your life is reduced to a minimum. If you do not have PTSD, then CPT is not the kind of therapy you need.

DIALECTICAL BEHAVIORAL THERAPY

The whole point behind dialectical behavioral therapy (DBT) is to help you out with new skills to help you deal with emotions that you find incredibly painful and assist you when you encounter conflict in your friendships and relationships.

With DBT, the focus is on giving you these skills in four major areas: Mindfulness, distress tolerance, emotion regulation, and interpersonal effectiveness. With mindfulness, the focus is on helping you be okay with the present and accept it the way it is. When it comes to distress tolerance, it's about helping you have a better threshold for negative emotions so that you can stop running away from those feelings. Emotion regulation is all about equipping you with the tools to properly handle all the supercharged emotions that come up and wreak havoc in your life. Interpersonal effectiveness shows you the best ways to communicate with the people around you while asserting your dominance, maintaining your self-respect, and empowering your relationships.

GROUP THERAPY

One of the best ways of addressing your problems is in a group. It's great to know that you are not the only one experiencing what you're going through and who is working on fixing the damage caused to their psyches by narcissistic abuse.

Group therapy often will involve a psychologist or even more and a group of patients numbering anywhere from five to 15. It might sound a bit weird or just downright intimidating, but the truth is that there are benefits you can get from group therapy that you wouldn't experience when it's just you and a therapist. Many of those benefits come from knowing that other people are going through the same thing you are, with diverse backgrounds and perspectives that will help you gain more clarity about everything that happened to you during your time with the narcissist.

SUPPORT GROUPS

Just like group therapy, you've got a group of people coming together who have similar experiences with narcissists as well. This gives you the space to share and learn coping mechanisms from one another.

A support group is usually led by an ordinary person, but could also be led by a professional therapist. You feel less alone and less judged with a support group, since others can relate to your experience. In a support group, you can be honest and open about how you feel. You also get the added benefit of feeling motivated and empowered by the others making progress in the group.

A few downsides to support groups is there might be a few members who are out to disrupt your meetings, as well as those who have no respect for confidentiality. You might also receive very unsound advice, so it's best if your support group has a professional to help oversee things as well.

It's essential to healing from trauma because this is how we get back to our fullest and truest sense of self. This is how we can connect with the person we were before the narcissist buried that person beneath the abuse they gave us. There are a few exciting and helpful alternative healing methods that you could try.

EYE MOVEMENT DESENSITIZATION AND REPROCESSING

Also known as EMDR, this treatment method is compelling when it comes to healing trauma from abuse, accidents, and relentless grief. Possessing multiple phases, EMDR works with psychotherapy as well as eye movements from the left to the right (or any other sort of repetitive movement) to help set you free from disturbing sensations in your body, horrific images in your mind, intense negative emotions, as well as regressive beliefs.

EMOTIONAL FREEDOM TECHNIQUE

Also called EFT, this technique is a combo of exposure therapy and cognitive therapy and acupressure. Some studies have shown that emotional problems and trauma are connected to relentless physical pain and debilitating disease.

The emotional freedom technique is an excellent treatment for anxiety, phobia, pain, and post-traumatic stress. It works by taking down the impact of the memories, which make you emotionally upset as you tap on the corresponding pressure points.

EFT can produce rapid and effective results, so definitely try this for yourself and understand how it can help you overcome the pain of a narcissistic injury.

YOGA

Yes, you read that right, not just any sort of yoga. We're talking about trauma-sensitive yoga, which is quite a new method of treatment that is incredibly effective when dealing with PTSD symptoms.

Trauma-sensitive yoga is excellent for helping you better handle your emotions and behavior when confronted with symptoms of PTSD. It's all about breathing techniques, meditation, and specific postures, as well as easy movements.

MIRROR WORK

Mirror work is all about teaching yourself to love yourself as you are and to think of the world as a safe, loving one. It incorporates affirmations, which are messages you give to your subconscious. They are your inner self-talk, and you have them all day, every day.

The key with mirror work is to say these affirmations in front of a mirror, which encourages you to create new ways of thinking and acting. It helps you release the past, embrace the now, and consequently expect and attract only the best in the future.

While you may have heard of affirmations before now, they are the strongest and the best when they are said as you look at yourself in the mirror. This is because the mirror reflects you and shows you where you might be resisting goodness and abundance in your life and where you are letting it flow.

ART THERAPY

Art therapy is all about treating the narcissistic injury you've suffered using artistic methods. The whole idea behind art therapy is that expressing yourself through art is a great way to encourage healing and give you a better, healthier state of mental health.

Whether you're viewing art or creating it, it's an excellent outlet for you to express your emotions and discover the meaning behind it all. Art therapy can help you get in touch with your true self, deal with stress, give you healthy self-esteem, and teach you better social skills as well.

Art therapy is a fusion of the creative process along with the standard psychotherapeutic healing modalities to help you gain insight into all you've been through, as well as better coping skills.

SHEDDING LIGHT ON TRAUMA

For the most part, people think about trauma as just random stuff that happens, like when there's a hurricane or flooding or an earthquake or a plane crash. The fact is that trauma has many different forms.

The trauma that you experience from being abused by the narcissist is one of the worst kinds. It's a slow burn, slowly seeping into your very soul, crushing the essence of you. It can affect you for years and years on end.

When it comes to narcissistic injury, the healing process needs a different approach than healing from other traumatic events, which are isolated. Over time, it occurs to you that while everyone else is living it up, for some reason, you're the only one who's got this dark cloud over you, constantly stopping you from fully experiencing the best life has to offer.

You always have the power. You can make a choice. It might not be easy to do in the heat of the moment when you're overwhelmed by all sorts of emotions. But even during an emotional storm, there's always a few seconds where that voice speaks up a bit louder, telling you that you need to end this now, while you can.

HOW TO MANAGE DISPUTES WITH THE NARCISSISTIC PARTNER IN FRONT OF YOUR CHILD

N arcissistic parents often struggle with how to manage disputes in front of their children. Some narcissists need their children to believe that they are the "good" parent to avoid arguments in front of their children. Other narcissists feel that it is essential for their children to see them as strong people and not succumb to another's demands and allow arguments in front of kids.

Difficult disputes are most likely to arise when you feel that the other parent has wronged you. It is essential to develop a strategy to deal with these types of situations and help prepare you for other difficult confrontations in the future.

ALLOW YOUR CHILD TO SEE THAT YOU ARE ANGRY

If you show your child that arguments are not a "big deal" and will likely get the issue resolved, then they will be less likely to internalize problems between the two of you. Children need to verbalize their feelings around the family breakup and seeing that you can express your anger with the other parent is important for them.

DO NOT TAKE THINGS TOO PERSONALLY

Narcissists are usually not direct about the issues they have with the other parent. If you become overly irritated, that would be seen as an illustration of how you feel. Instead, let them know how your child is feeling. It is also important to articulate your feelings around being angry and upset so your child can see that these emotions are normal and normal things happen when parents are upset.

REMIND YOUR CHILD OF WHAT A GOOD PARENT LOOKS LIKE

Narcissists are often the type of parents who will have their child do chores while being upset with the other parent or go to the doctor and even yell at other kids' parents for not taking care of them in a manner that is consistent with how they would want a friend to take care of their child. They may also buy their children things as an act of love.

TEACH YOUR CHILD ABOUT COPING SKILLS

Narcissists are often not very good at accepting that they could not overcome a problem, and your child will need to be able to see that they can be strong if they need to. This will allow them to have the coping skills they need in order for them to be successful in life.

ENCOURAGE YOUR CHILD'S AUTONOMY AND INDEPENDENCE

Narcissists are often controlling parents who want their children to do exactly what they say and otherwise have little understanding of how their children develop as individuals. This often results in children developing behaviors which are inconsistent with who they are and their best interests.

TEACH YOUR CHILD TO ASSERT THEMSELVES WHEN APPROPRIATE

This can be challenging for some children to learn, mainly when they are very young and cannot understand why the rules may be different from other people's rules or why the restrictions they learned in the past may not apply in all situations today. Mindfulness is a tactic often used by therapists in helping children learn this skill.

ASK YOUR CHILD IF THEY FEEL SAFE IN THE OTHER PARENT'S HOME

The rule of thumb is no harm, no foul, and if your child is not comfortable with the home environment, it does not matter what else happens. If there is an issue of safety, it needs to be addressed.

DO NOT FIGHT IN FRONT OF YOUR CHILDREN

If you cannot achieve any resolution with the other parent, it is best not to argue in front of your children and tell them that you will resolve the issue when they are not present. That approach may work better for some parents than others.

If you need help to solve the issue, ask for it.

Narcissists are often very good at being their own therapist, and it is crucial that your child not feel like they have to rely on the narcissist in this situation.

DEVELOP A PROCESS FOR RESOLVING THE ISSUE

Narcissists will often minimize the problem and make it seem like it is not that big of a deal. Still, if you can develop a process to address the concern, your child can see that you are working through difficult issues together, and they can have hope that working through issues with you will result in them feeling better.

It can be beneficial to create a list of plan B for managing disputes and deciding where you will talk about these issues if the other parent is not willing or available. Let them feel and know you love them, even when upset with the other parent.

WHAT TO SAY AND WHAT NOT TO SAY TO YOUR SON/DAUGHTER ABOUT THE NARCISSISTIC PARENT

You may have found it difficult to raise your children with a narcissistic parent around. Narcissistic parents can be demanding, intrusive, and exploitative of their child's success. They will take credit for the child's accomplishments and often put others down to make themselves seem better. But even though it is difficult to raise children with a narcissist around, you should not talk about your feelings to your child. It will increase the chances of them becoming narcissistic themselves.

WHAT TO SAY

Don't tell your child how much the narcissist has hurt you. Your child will take this as an opportunity to hurt the parent back and won't understand why that is not okay. You do not want them to take revenge on the parent, so keep all you feel hidden from them.

Don't ask your child to defend you from their narcissistic parent. Narcissists will use anything they can to make themselves feel better and blame their victims whenever possible. If you ask your child to defend you from the narcissist, they will be used against you.

Don't mention the narcissist's behavior around your kids, as negative attention gets them more involved. Let it go unless it is affecting them directly.

There is no reason to be upset about the narcissist around a child. Attend to your children and keep them happy and healthy. Don't worry if the narcissist gets involved in these things, as long as it doesn't affect their wellbeing. You don't have anything to worry about.

Don't be too worried about the behavior of the narcissist around your child. They will notice it and will think it is not normal behavior. Your goal is to keep them safe from this person, and you don't want to be teaching them it's okay to treat others like this.

Don't show that you are upset by the narcissist's behavior toward you, or they will think it is okay for their parent to treat others that way. But don't avoid them. Efforts should be made to talk over the situation, even if it is not going well.

WHEN TO SAY

If your child has been told by a parent that they have hurt them or are inappropriate, make sure you let them know that they were wrong and explain why. If the narcissist talks about their intentions, you can let your child know that they are dishonest about their behavior. You do not want them to believe in something they shouldn't.

Don't talk about your feelings with your children. They will take it as a reason to hate the narcissist, which is not healthy for them. You have to let them know that hating someone doesn't solve anything and will only make it worse.

If you want your child to understand why something is inappropriate or hurtful, tell them about it. They won't learn anything by not saying anything at all. Once you have explained the situation to them, make sure they understand why things were wrong.

Don't let the narcissist put you down in front of your children, as it will make them feel like it is okay to treat people like that. If the narcissist puts you down, keep your response calm and don't react to their hurtful words or actions. Don't let them get your child involved in the situation so they can use them against you as well. Don't allow your child to get hurt by the narcissist, either. Once they are older, you can explain to them why it is not appropriate.

Make sure you explain the situation correctly when there is an issue with the narcissist, and you want your child to know what happened. If they mix up their feelings about a situation, you have to let them know that it was not appropriate for someone else to do that and explain why.

If there are situations they don't understand about family dynamics and relationships, let them know. It doesn't matter how young they are. They can understand simple words and feelings. They can learn by being taught, so use the opportunity to explain things correctly.

WHAT NOT TO SAY

Don't tell your child that they don't listen or understand things because they are not grown up enough for this. Their parent is not responsible for whether or not they are intelligent enough to hear the truth.

Don't discuss how you feel about the narcissist with your child. It will lessen their feelings of involvement with you.

Don't remind your children all the time that they are not bad and have no negative traits. Narcissists do this to make themselves seem better, so you don't want to do it too if you aren't narcissistic yourself.

Don't blame the narcissist for your feelings or things going poorly in your life. Your kids will believe that it is their fault if you do this.

Don't make your children take the blame for the narcissist's wrongdoings or make them feel responsible for fixing things between you and the narcissist. If they try to take responsibility, let them know that they are not the only ones who can fix things or try to fix things. Narcissists usually try to make their children believe it is all up to them, so you don't want to reinforce that idea.

WHEN NOT TO SAY

If you have asked your child for help and speak to them as if they were a small child, do not expect them to act like an adult.

If you are an adult child of a narcissist, it is not easy to deal with their behavior without being bitter or angry. This has to be done on your own and not by involving your children.

Don't tell your child that you can't cope because you do not have enough support from them or other people in the situation. It is always possible to get help, even if it isn't easy, so don't let yourself down like this.

Don't criticize yourself for things you can't control. It is not your fault to help someone who does not really want any help but wants you to be there.

If you have been thinking about how to explain things to your children, do it! They will be very interested in learning about who they are and where they come from. Make sure you understand what happened and why the situation was a bad one before you talk. You should do everything you can to help them understand why things were bad and that they don't have to be so bad for them. Do not project your own feelings on the situation, as this will only confuse them.

If you need help with your own feelings, make sure you get it before bringing it up with your children. This can make it worse for them if they don't want to talk about what happened.

If you cannot deal with your feelings, wait until you can before discussing the situation with your children. You owe them the emotional support they need and deserve from you.

It is normal to be sad or angry when dealing with a situation like this, but make sure to take care of yourself first before taking care of your children as well.

Don't try to explain too much to your children at once. It may upset them and make them think it is their fault when they may not be able to understand it all. This can also confuse if there was a lot of manipulation involved. First, explain simple points such as what the narcissist did and why it wasn't okay or necessary to do that stuff. If there is a lot for you to explain, make sure you do this in stages. You can also show them how to say or write things that say that sort of situations when they are older.

If the narcissist has been abusive, it is important that you explain how this has affected your children and how they will have to deal with it as well. The NPD does not like boundaries, and if there aren't any set ones between you and the narcissist, your child will have a hard time understanding this as well. It will make it hard for your child to deal with other people who try to violate their boundaries. If the narcissist is in their life, they need to know how this affects them and why it is important not to let them break any boundaries.

Do whatever you have to do, but try not to let the situation get any worse for your children than it already is. Consider how they feel about the narcissist and what kinds of feelings they have towards them.

HOW TO PROTECT YOUR CHILD FROM ALIENATION AND LOYALTY CONFLICTS

T he goal of co-parenting is simple. It is to protect your child from the relationship issues between you and your ex. Even if the marriage fell apart and there was no chance of salvaging it, you have to remember that your child need not be affected significantly.

This is where smart co-parenting comes into the picture. Suppose you truly want the arrangement to work. In that case, you need to understand, first and foremost, that co-parenting is all about helping your child feel loved through positive relationships and encouraging good behavior.

How do you make children feel loved? By giving them what they needed before, including structure, stability, security, emotional support, protection, and care from a loving parent.

Detailed Plan

Going to battle unarmed is setting yourself up to lose, not to mention that it's plain foolish. For co-parenting to work, you need a detailed plan.

COMMUNICATION

Keeping the communication lines open between parents is of utmost importance. It doesn't have to be face-to-face. You can use emails, texts, or phone calls to update each other. The key is to eliminate conflict and biases for the communication to be as effective as it can be.

When speaking with your ex, will keep in mind the following:

Use a businesslike tone: Consider the new relationship as a business where your child is the main concern. A businesslike tone will set the right mood where both parties can arrange without being clouded with personal inhibitions.

Make requests instead of demands: When talking or making a decision with your ex, making a request instead of commands and orders is a far better option.

Listen carefully: If you have opinions, so does your ex-spouse. Allow the other parent to voice out opinions, suggestions, and changes.

Commit to regular updates: Communicating regularly with your ex will be hard, but it is necessary to convey a united front for your child.

TEAMWORK

Whether you like it or not, your kid has the right to two parents. And the only way for co-parenting to be successful is if you and your ex-work as a team. Even if the thought nearly kills you, it has to be done to make it easier for the kids.

For the team to thrive, aiming for consistency helps. You have to set proper ground rules and discipline guidelines and a consistent schedule comfortable for the child.

As part of a team, compromises play a key role in keeping the arrangement conflict-free as much as possible. Even if you don't agree with your ex's parenting style, you have to allow flexibility to avoid bickering and rehashing the past.

KID-FOCUSED

The most essential aspect of co-parenting is the child. It makes sense to keep the focus on your primary business — your child's well-being— all the time. When you feel like the anger is simmering and becoming too overwhelming, make sure to step back and remember who you are doing this for.

All conversations with your ex after the divorce should only talk about the children. Never allow it to rehash the past or bring up your needs.

SMART AND PRACTICAL TIPS TO EFFECTIVE CO-PARENTING

To ensure the success of the co-parenting arrangement, make sure to incorporate a detailed plan, kid-focused conversations, communication, and teamwork. The process of helping your child adapt to the new changes will be much easier by keeping in mind the following smart tips to effective co-parenting:

SEE THE SITUATION IN YOUR CHILD'S EYES

Moving as far away from your ex as possible may be your best option but not your child's. In addition to the separation, what will worsen the situation is adjusting to living in two households. If possible, parents should live near each other just until the child fully understands the circumstances.

NO BAD-MOUTHING YOUR EX

You may be tempted, especially if you're the wronged party, but never badmouth your ex to your child. When they ask questions, answer them in the most non-judgmental way possible. Give them appropriate answers and stop there to avoid putting your ex down.

SEPARATE ANGER AND HURT FEELINGS

To co-parent effectively, you need to set aside your feelings. Vent it out somewhere else, maybe with a therapist or your support group, but not with your child.

NEVER BLAME THE KIDS

Blaming the kids does no good. Avoid putting them in the middle by making them feel like it's their fault the divorce happened. They are guilty enough as it is and blaming will not help.

NEVER MAKE THE KIDS CHOOSE

Even if you're joking, never make the kids choose between you and your ex. It's not their fault the relationship has to end. The least you can do is allow the child to enjoy both parents without pressure.

CONTAIN CONFLICT

Disagreeing with your ex will happen, that's for sure. But for the sake of the kids, contain it. There is a proper venue for you to deal with that.

ESTABLISH A ROUTINE

To provide stability after the traumatic divorce, make sure to establish routine and similar rules in both households. Rules such as no video games and TV after 9 PM should apply in both houses.

BE PRESENT DURING SPECIAL OCCASIONS

This is always not convenient, but you have to remember that co-parenting is about your child's best interests in mind. If kids see their divorced parents present during special occasions, school milestones, and important events, they'd feel more loved knowing that you can set aside differences for their sake.

DON'T BE TOO FRIENDLY

Be civil and businesslike when dealing with your ex, but never too friendly. Too much friendliness will only confuse the kids to the point that they may even wish for reconciliation. Do not give them a chance to latch on false hopes.

BALANCE OUT FINANCIAL DIFFERENCES

The wealthier parent should try to be more generous and ensure that living arrangements are similar in two households. Significant differences in lifestyles result in bad setups. If you are the one with more money, keep in mind that you are giving for the children, not your ex.

TREAT EACH OTHER AS BUSINESS PARTNERS

Even if you hate your ex immensely, the marriage has been over when the divorce was finalized. In the spirit of effective co-parenting, let go of the grudge and treat your ex as a business partner.

PICK YOUR BATTLES

Even business partners disagree on some points; and so do you and your ex. When these disagreements are too much to handle, pick and prioritize the most important concerns that affect your child's welfare.

GET HELP WHEN NEEDED

If you reach an impasse at some point while co-parenting your kids, it's probably high time to get some help. A professional or expert in co-parenting should be able to help resolve conflicts and act as a mediator if necessary.

WHEN IT IS APPROPRIATE TO STEP AWAY FROM THE RELATIONSHIP

U p to now, we've concentrated on the background of narcissism. We've done this to make a solid and healthy decision, and you need to have all the facts.

By this point, you should be pretty clear on the picture of narcissism and why there isn't much hope for your relationship. It sounds harsh to say such things, but we want you to decide that is right you; it will allow you to flourish and break free from damaging patterns and emotional abuse. You might still be on the fence.

You want to go, you want to feel better and look forward to a brighter future, but you're not 100% sure. You love this person, you are married to them, and it could be that you share things, such as a house and material items, and you might even have children.

In that case, you have to be very certain in your decision to divorce your narcissist and move forward in your life. This will give you five final reasons why you are making the right decision by doing this.

After that, when you choose to move forward, we're going to get practical. We're going to talk you through, step by step, what you need to know and what you need to do to get the divorce ball rolling and the differences that you might encounter when a narcissist is involved in the whole process.

With that in mind, let's run through five reasons why leaving a narcissist is the best idea.

YOU DESERVE HAPPINESS

Why do you feel like you deserve to be beaten down every day of your life? Why do you deserve to be living through a rollercoaster of emotions every single day? Do you believe that you deserve to be controlled and manipulated?

It is highly unlikely that you can, hand on heart, say that you are happy in your relationship. You might have convinced yourself that you are, and when your narcissist is happy and showing you the attention that you crave, you probably are, but it doesn't last, right? The highs are high, and the lows are very low. Do not live with this constant up and down pattern. You can be happy on an even level. Sure, nobody is happy all the time, but it's not normal to be so up and down through the space of a day.

Taking the brave decision to break away from your narcissistic marriage and seek a final divorce will allow you to seek closure. You will be able to seek out the support you need to overcome the lasting effects of the emotional abuse you've been subjected to, and you can look forward to a brighter future as a result.

CHILDREN WITHIN A NARCISSISTIC MARRIAGE ARE AFFECTED

You need to be very aware of their effect if you have children. Children will assume that this is a normal pattern of behavior and will copy it in their future relationships. It's also possible that they're being subjected to emotional abuse on a different level simply because your narcissistic partner doesn't have the empathy to show them love they deserve and need.

If you want a real push in the right direction or a good reason to leave, do it for your children if you have them. You cannot raise healthy children in a marriage that is one part narcissist. There will be lasting effects, and whether they're mild or not, they're still effects that your children don't deserve to be subjected to.

You might think your children are happy, and they probably are, but they're not being shown a healthy relationship with their parents. This will move into their future and cause them to act in unfair and unnecessary ways to their future partners. Do it for your children and their future.

YOUR MENTAL HEALTH IS SUFFERING

Being subjected to emotional abuse on any level affects your self-esteem and self-worth, and affects your mental health. This leads you down a very dark and dangerous path which could put your overall well-being at risk.

It's quite common for the survivors of narcissistic abuse to have mental health damage when they break free. Those who stay in these types of unions are running the risk of serious problems, with depression and anxiety, stress, and even PTSD after the event becoming a reality.

Of course, we all have mental health, just as we all have physical health, but we don't tend to do things that endanger our physical health. With that in mind, why would you do something which would endanger your mental health?

It's time to place more importance on mental health overall and recognize the very damaging effects that problems such as being subjected to emotional abuse over some time can do.

THE RELATIONSHIP HAS NO FUTURE

In our first chapter, giving you the basics of narcissism, we talked about a narcissist's treatment options. The available treatment options might as well be zero simply because narcissists extremely rarely take them up, and even then, there's no guarantee that it will work.

With that in mind, your relationship is never going to change. They are not going to be cured, and they're not going to change. They're not suddenly going to stop treating you badly or making you feel like everything is your fault, and it's going to stay this way for the rest of your lives together.

Do you want that?

Be honest. Of course, you don't.

This relationship does not have a future. Sure, it has some future, but it won't be a happy or healthy one. Again, going back to our first reason, you deserve better, and whether you love this person or not (and we're assuming you do), sometimes you have to hold your hands up and give up, say you gave it your best shot, and walk away. It's the best option in the end.

RELATIONSHIPS AREN'T ABOUT CONTROL

The final reason is to know what a real relationship is and what it feels like and looks like. A truly healthy and happy relationship doesn't have a requirement to control the other person within it. A narcissist needs to control, and they have to be the one holding the reins to everything because that way, they can steer everything to make themselves look better than everyone else.

Healthy relationships allow each partner the space to grow and develop themselves while being part of a partnership that allows them to flourish as people. This isn't possible in a narcissistic relationship because everything is one-sided. You will never feel able to follow your dreams and be supported. You will always be dragged down. This means your life will never be fulfilling, and you'll come to regret the time you wasted.

Break free from the Control and look forward to a better life. The only way you can do that is by leaving the relationship and ending it for good. Yes, divorce is hard, and you might not know where to start the whole process. But remember that there is a lot of help and support out there. There are even legal professionals who have experience dealing with divorces with narcissistic partners.

HOW TO WALK AWAY FROM A NARCISSIST

As you have read through the information on narcissism and how to handle a narcissist, perhaps you decided you are ready to walk away from the narcissist in your life. If you are at liberty to do so and have no reason to interact with this person, this is a tough but wise decision.

You will learn what you need to do when you walk away. Ending a relationship with a narcissist is different than ending other relationships, and you need to plan and mentally prepare for what you will likely encounter.

It is not easy to walk away from a narcissist. Typically, the love-bombing phases are wonderful, and the attachment you feel is real and intense. Narcissists are very good at what they do, and you will most likely struggle with guilt and fear, wondering if you are making the right decision. You may wonder if you are over-reacting, and you may start to consider the things the narcissist has told you in the past that have kept you under their control. However, if you have the opportunity to walk away, do it. It will be tough. It will possibly take some time.

Let me state once again that if you feel that you are in immediate danger or that your loved ones are in immediate danger, get out now. Get to safety, call the police, and get whatever help you need to be safe. Although it is ideal to have a plan in place and have everything settled, a plan is not more important than your safety. Listen to your instincts, and if they tell you that you need to go, then go. Don't rationalize, compromise, or minimize what your instincts are telling you. If you need to get to safety now, get to safety. Everything else can be worked out later.

DEVELOP A SUPPORT NETWORK

As you have learned and seen, narcissists want to control and manipulate their victims and often do whatever they can to isolate them. You must have a support network in place before you leave. Your network can include such individuals as friends, family, a therapist, a lawyer, a victim advocate, or a recovery group.

The goal is to surround yourself with several different encouraging voices who will support you when you start to waiver and give you strong, solid advice when you feel confused or uncertain of what to do next. You will make one of the biggest and most difficult choices in your life, and you should not try and do it alone. It is better now to lean into your friends, not pull away.

CREATE A PLAN

This is the time to sit down and develop a concrete, specific plan. Get away from your home, head to a coffee shop or the library, and use a pen and notebook to write down your plan.

Be as detailed as possible in your plan, and once it is in writing, give the notebook to a trusted friend or family member for safekeeping.

If the narcissist in your life begins to suspect that something is changing or that you are pulling away a bit, they may start to go through your personal belongings or search on your computer to try and find out what is going on. Having your friend or family member keep the notebook for you will help you keep your intentions quiet until it is time to act.

As you create your plan, start at the beginning of the journey and walk through every step of the way. Don't worry if you don't have all the answers right now. This will help you see where you need to learn more and what you need to get into place before you act.

First, write down when you want to walk away. You do not need to choose a specific time and date, although you certainly can narrow it down to at least a timeframe. How long will it be to set aside some financial resources? Is there a life event coming up that will bring additional stress to you?

For example, if you know that you have a major work project coming up in the next few weeks and will need to be at your very best mentally and emotionally, you may want to wait until that is finished before you walk away. Or, if you have a loved one who is very sick or in crisis, you may want to wait until the stress and emotions of that situation have settled a bit.

This is not to say that everything needs to be perfect and smooth before you leave. As you are well aware, life with a narcissist is never completely perfect or smooth. Consider if there are any additional, foreseeable events that will require your full time and attention, and plan accordingly.

After you have determined when you will leave, decide where you will go. If you share a home with a narcissist, you will most likely need to leave home for good, or at least be prepared to leave. Even if you don't share a home with the narcissist, if it is at all possible, you may want to consider going out of town for a week or two. You could take a mini-vacation or visit friends or family.

Once you know when and where you are going, determine how much it will cost. How much money will you need to live on? If you have not been in control of your finances, meet with someone who can give you a realistic picture of your financial needs. What will you do as you work to get the finances you need? What is your transitional plan?

Determine what you will do to keep yourself from getting pulled back into the narcissist's web.

What will you do when the narcissist tries to call you and apologize, promising that they really will change this time?

How will you handle it when the narcissist goes around and tries to discredit you, telling lies to everyone you know?

What will be your response when the narcissist suddenly has a major emergency and tells you that you are the only one who can help them through it?

What will you say when the narcissist threatens to commit suicide?

These are not meant to prevent you from taking action or walking away, but they are questions you need to consider. These are all very real scenarios and being prepared for them will help keep you on your path to freedom.

Once you have finished creating your plan to walk away, take time to consider what you will do if the narcissist decides to leave you first. They may start to suspect something is changing in you. They may realize they have lost control over you or may sense that you are pulling away.

When this happens, they will want to save face and may decide that they will walk away from you before you have the chance to leave them. When this happens, what will you do? Consider many of the same questions you answered when formulating your original plan but be aware that you may have to jump into action much sooner and more abruptly than you originally thought.

DO NOT ANNOUNCE YOUR PLANS

Share your plan with a few trusted people, but do not let the narcissist know what you are doing. If they get ideas on your plans, they will do whatever they can to try to stop you. They will try every technique they know to try to change your mind. Once they realize they cannot change your mind, they will try to sabotage you. Keep your plan a secret, and do not say anything until it is time to act.

SECURE YOUR PERSONAL INFORMATION

Before you leave, take time to secure all of your personal information. Make sure your birth certificate, social security card, passport, and all other important papers are in a safe location. Once the narcissist realizes that they are losing control of you, they will get desperate and do anything they can to reel you back in. This can include destroying important documents. Remember, the narcissist does not care about you. The narcissist wants control over you and wants to manipulate you.

If the narcissist cannot maintain control over you, they will have no qualms about making your life more difficult, to feel a bit better about themself. Securing your personal information will help keep your mind at ease and give you one less thing you need to worry about.

SECURE YOUR FINANCIAL SITUATION

If you are financially tied to the narcissist in your life, set up your own separate accounts. Get your own bank account and get your own credit card if you can. Set aside as much cash as you can, and keep it in a secure location, preferably in a place where the narcissist will not go. Know that the narcissist will not think twice about taking your money, hiding money from you, or restricting your access to credit cards.

The narcissist wants to control you, and if that means leaving you completely broke, they will do it. They will believe that if you are financially dependent on them, you won't go anywhere, so they will do as much financial damage as possible. Do not let this knowledge frighten you out of acting. Know what you are facing and make your plans.

As you secure your financial situation, you may need to ask for help from friends and family. This may be difficult to do, and you will most likely feel some guilt or shame about being in this position. Do not let them take root in your mind.

You have nothing to be ashamed of and nothing to feel guilty about. You have realized you were in a terrible situation, and now you are doing whatever you need to do to get out of it. You are taking strong, brave steps forward, and you are asking for help to get where you need to go. Remember that your family and friends will always love you. They also want you to be safe, secure, and happy. Let them help you.

Do not feel ashamed, but instead, feel brave that you are taking the difficult journey to freedom.

Do not let your guard down once you have gotten free and the narcissist has stopped trying to contact you. They will very likely try to lure you back in again after some time has passed. It may take weeks or months, but be prepared for attempted contact. The narcissist will likely have a story that they have changed or grown or declare that they already learned their lesson and will never mistreat you again. As promising as this may sound, and as much as you may want to believe it, do not believe them. Do not give in.

Narcissists are manipulators, and they know what they can say and do to try and convince you that things are better. Keep ahold of all that you have learned and experienced, and do not waiver in your resolve.

HOW TO AVOID A NARCISSIST

Interacting with narcissistic personality disorder can be tedious, draining, and at times, downright painful, particularly if you are gaining nothing from it. You can begin by seeing if there are any areas that you can change your perspective on. You might not like the plan of changing yourself, particularly when the one with narcissism should change, but it might be a good place to start.

ACCEPT THAT YOU CAN'T CHANGE THEM

The hard reality here is that it's impossible to change someone else and trying will only hurt you. What you can start with is changing the way you see the situation. For example, you can view your interactions with the narcissistic personality as a way to train your mind in areas of self-control, patience, and general focus. Since listening to a narcissist at work can be so draining, this is a great chance to improve yourself.

ASSESS THE SITUATION REALISTICALLY

The next step is to assess this situation realistically. How unacceptable is this person's behavior? Are they exhibiting mild symptoms of this disorder or severe symptoms? How are they affecting you? What were you like before? Depend on your answers to these questions. It might be necessary, for your good, to cut off all contact with this person. Let's assume that this isn't possible for you.

IF YOU MUST INTERACT WITH A NARCISSISTIC PERSON

If you don't have a choice but to be around this person, there are a few ways you can protect yourself from their ways and come out relatively unscathed. Here are some examples:

Lower your Expectations: When dealing with someone like this, having high expectations is only setting yourself up for disappointment. Part of realistically assessing the situation realizes that they will care about themselves first and foremost and others second.

Resist Challenging them: Unless you are in a situation where they can cause you harm, resist confrontation with a narcissist. In some cases, such as a person invading your personal space, you will have to put your foot down, but in conversation, it's easier, at times, to simply let them run the show.

These steps are not the best way to approach a narcissist in every situation, but they can be helpful when you feel like avoiding a lot of drama. These work best if the narcissist in question is someone you have to work with or to date.

TIPS ON ENDING A TALK WITH A NARCISSIST QUICKLY

However, if you find yourself stuck talking to a narcissist and simply want the conversation to end, use these techniques:

Stick to Boring Topics: If you are stuck in a talk with a narcissist, it helps to talk about boring subjects, repeating your ideas over and overusing different words.

Give Yourself a Limit: When you know you must be engaged with someone like this, plan ahead of time to only talk with them for 20 minutes or a half-hour, then leave.

Here is a helpful secret for you that will help you navigate a narcissist; people with this disorder do not gravitate toward losers, but pick the brightest and best to victimize. A narcissistic person wins their confidence by choosing a successful, attractive, and confident person and lowering their self-esteem over a long time period. Needy people do not present enough of a challenge for a narcissist, and looking at it this way, the fact that a narcissist is drawn to you shows that you are capable and above average. This is a positive thing.

Regain your Sense of Confidence: Now is the best time to regain your sense of self-confidence, which the narcissist may have either stolen from you or attempted to steal from you. This begins with getting confident again. If you plan to stay involved with the narcissistic person, you have to wear this sense of confidence to ward off the digs, manipulation, and insults they attempt to hand to you. This is simply the way narcissists function, and it's unlikely to end. When you are confident, you can realistically assess what they are saying and see that it isn't true.

Take Time to Yourself: Spending plenty of time alone to recharge will help you build your confidence back up. Find out what makes you feel good about yourself and pursue those activities. This could be taking walks by yourself at least once or twice a day, picking up a new activity, or even volunteering to work with animals nearby.

Surround Yourself with Positive Friends: Replace the energy drained by being around the narcissistic person in your life by making time with positive influences and friends who lift you. Being around positive people goes a long way, especially if you're used to only being around someone who tears you down or is full of negativity and self-serving talk.

Don't Engage in their Tantrums: You need to recognize how to say "no" to the tantrums this person throws at you. Enduring anger is never a fun activity, regardless of who the angry person is, but it's a different level when a narcissist gets mad.

Unspoken Negativity: Keep in mind that this anger doesn't necessarily have to be something spoken aloud. Even a simple disgusted look can affect you negatively. Someone narcissistic has a special ability to hurt others simply by entering a room while in a bad mood.

Resist the Temptation to "Fix" it: This anger, and the way it affects you, can lead to you wanting to fix that to avoid the negativity, but you have to teach yourself how to stop engaging and walk away instead. Someone with a narcissistic personality disorder will get mad if you correct them, disagree with them, or simply because the wind blows by. This is how they control other people, and you have to end this by walking away.

Stop Arguing with Them: As soon as the narcissistic personality starts arguing, their sense of wrong and right goes straight out the window. They will accuse, make outlandish or crazy claims, or twist your words to fit the point they are trying to make. Their arguments will be incomprehensible and confusing, but don't get intimidated by what they are saying. See it, instead, for what it is. As soon as you can do this at will, it becomes a lot easier not to let it get to you.

Get Your Independence Back: The very first thing a person with a narcissistic personality disorder will attempt to take from you is your independence. It's crucial for you to either get this back if you lost it or maintain it if you still have it. Start a business from home, begin studying a new subject, or get a day job if you usually stay home and live with the person. If you don't, start seeing them less.

Quit Blaming Yourself: You need to realize that this is about them, not you. It is never your fault when a narcissist attempts to manipulate or belittle you. At times, people can get into a bad habit of self-blame for whatever the narcissist has been doing.

This is a tempting trap that can be hard to resist, but don't do it. It could be alluring to think that you would never be treated like this again if only you acted correctly. But accept that this is their personality, their problem, and has nothing to do with you.

Narcissists thrive on drama, blaming other people for their actions and convincing everyone around them that they were never in the wrong. A narcissist might even accept a portion of the blame, only to turn around and put it on someone else more easily. This is easy to see through as soon as you recognize the behavior.

Never Trust Them: A narcissistic person has gotten so good at and comfortable with being deceitful that they will lie even when there's no solid reason to do so. Deception and lying are the main way they know how to communicate. This type of person will look you straight in the eye and say that the sky is green, even when it's blue. If you wish to survive this type of person, you have to start looking out for yourself, never allowing yourself to fall into the latest deception they have cooked up.

It's Possible to Survive a Narcissist: You can survive interactions with a narcissistic person as long as you know what you're dealing with. If you recognized a few of these signs, you should be on guard. If possible, disengage from the person altogether, and if not, accept that a relationship with a narcissist is bound to be toxic and unhealthy. Most of the time, they are simply incapable of caring for others genuinely or healthily, and if you look closely, you'll always see a selfish or insecure motive behind their words or actions. Hopefully, the ideas and concepts here made you feel empowered and ready to take on your situation with confidence and a poised state of mind.

You aren't crazy, and you are not alone. It's hard not to feel drain and exhausted when living with or dealing with a person with a narcissistic personality disorder. But once you start recognizing these patterns of behavior and their negative effects on you, you can begin standing up for yourself and what's right. You are always in control of what you allow to bother you and bring you down and fostering a healthy relationship with yourself is the first step to beating this struggle. Once you decide to do it, it's only a matter of staying true to yourself and being committed to receiving respect.

HOW TO END MANIPULATION BY A NARCISSIST

W hy the great concern about stopping manipulation by a narcissist? After all, people are always doing things to influence others. Whereas that is a valid question, it is important to note that a narcissist's manipulation is of an extreme degree. Narcissists are so engrossed in influencing things towards their end that they do not seem to realize it even when other people discover the manipulation for what it is. They do not even show any shame for their behavior, unlike someone caught trying to unduly influence a one-off deal.

Many people with narcissists who are close family relations or close friends often find themselves succumbing to their manipulation, not because they have not discovered this negative tendency, but because it seems much easier to give in than argue about it. Manipulation is part of a narcissist's behavior, so they do not find themselves expending unnecessary energy – to them, that's life. However, the antagonistic atmosphere created by a narcissist's attempt at manipulation can be draining to other people. And the unfortunate bit is that the narcissist learns fast what buttons to press to get you unduly influenced. They capitalize on your fears and concerns or even your passions. The truth is, they can capitalize on any part of your personality to make things suit them.

What is the natural reaction when narcissistic behavior becomes overwhelming? Well, two contrasting reactions come to mind:

FALLING INTO A RAGE

Does it help – you getting annoyed at your narcissist partner or colleague and probably getting into a verbal argument?

FEELING SORRY FOR THE NARCISSIST

Does this help? It surely doesn't. Narcissists just view that as an opportunity for them to advance further their manipulation.

IMPROVING YOUR JOURNEY WITH A NARCISSIST

From what you have gathered so far, would it be surprising that anyone would seek skills to cope with the behavior of a narcissist? If you don't do that and you continue living with your narcissist partner or someone else with this disorder and who is close to you, you risk having a meltdown yourself. What's the use of accommodating the behavior of others to the extent that you go bonkers yourself?

SOME TIPS TO HELP YOU THROUGH YOUR JOURNEY IN LIFE WITH A NARCISSIST

YOU WOULD NOT BE A LOSER IF THE NARCISSIST CHOSE TO BE WITH YOU

Oh yes! Narcissists do not go for losers. You are so successful they want you to illuminate their lives. With your brilliance and your charming nature, the narcissist wanted you as a trophy when they chose you – some piece of possession to show off with.

TURNING YOU INTO OCEAN SLUDGE

But open your eyes and see what the narcissist has been doing to you – tearing you down slowly to establish that feeling of power and superiority. Do you feel confident and attractive or even successful for the period you have spent with your narcissist? A narcissist could not have picked on a loser because then they would not have the satisfaction they hunger for. Losers do not provide anything high to bring down, nothing complex to dismantle, and nothing shiny to blur – and that is the twisted behavior of a narcissist.

YOU NEED TO EMBARK ON REGAINING YOUR CONFIDENCE

Regaining what you have lost from your relationship with a narcissist can begin with regaining your self-confidence. Much as a break from the narcissist would do you some good whilst the narcissist gets professional help, and you may find yourself still living or associating with the person. It is important that you feel confident because it helps you deflect those toxic arrows that the narcissist inevitably continues to throw at you. With self-confidence, you are able to:

Keep your cool even when the narcissist tries to provoke you into an argument.

RECOGNIZE THE NARCISSIST'S LIES

ALLOW YOURSELF TO GET THE BEST

After a life of letting your narcissistic partner enjoy the cream as you wait to consume the crumbs, it is time for you to allow yourself enjoyment because you deserve it. It is fine to sacrifice here and there for the common good, but that does not mean you let yourself be someone else's servant. And that is actually what a narcissist makes you. You need to reclaim your worth by demanding a quality life as opposed to one of subservience. Demand to have your needs addressed first, for once – and that includes places you like, people you would like to associate with, and personal goals you would like to work on.

PRACTICE WALKING AWAY FROM TEMPER DRIVEN TANTRUMS

How horrible it is to encounter someone seething with rage! But then, when it comes to narcissists, partner victims have said it is more intimidating to see a narcissist annoyed than any other look you could encounter. For one, enraged narcissists wear a face of disgust. Then their eyes are full of evil. That whole picture just makes your stomach churn. And how do you react to that? Well, ordinarily, you pray you can quickly identify what the narcissist wants you to do, whether you enjoy doing it or not. You are fodder for their rage.

Sometimes your narcissist partner gets annoyed just because you corrected them. You disagreed with a certain point they made or because of something that had nothing to do with you – like stumbling on a door frame. You need to stop trying to fill the narcissist in your life by making explanations or doing their bidding – simply walk away. If situations do not allow you to walk away, just rolling your eyes in a manner that says, what the heck, and totally ignoring them might help. Here you are essentially avoiding a situation where you get to respond and give them the courage to continue drawing your attention.

AVOID ENGAGING IN AN ARGUMENT WITH A NARCISSIST

Do you recall an earlier mention that the narcissist chose you because you had admirable qualities, with a mark of success? So, definitely, he or she knows there is no way they can win an argument with you logically. Whenever they engage you in an argument, expect incomprehensible stuff being dropped randomly. And, of course, that's after you have repulsed an attempt at intimidation in a situation where the narcissists often throw you wild accusations, statements you can only term as crazy, and words made out of context.

And remember, as a person who is mentally whole and stable, some behavior exhibited by the narcissist can be embarrassing to you in addition to draining your energy. Here is another instance where you just need to walk away instead of wasting your time with someone you pretty well know is not interested in listening and reasoning logically.

WORK ON RE-ESTABLISHING YOURSELF

You will notice how much independence you have lost once you are true to yourself. Has your narcissist partner lost independence because of your relationship? Think hard, and you will see that your narcissist partner gets to do what he or she wants at the end of the day. You need to begin doing something that you love as well, like a hobby, a class, something that makes you feel free. You need to stop living like someone in a yoke.

AVOID FALLING INTO THE TRAP OF VICTIM-BLAMING

Victim blaming is a tendency observed over the years. You begin telling people you know what you have been doing wrong when that is actually something to give you false psychological satisfaction. You have room to improve and bring your relationship with the narcissist back to normal. Well, that calculation can only be realized if the normal you are talking about is a repeat of the previous life – drama and more drama from your narcissistic partner. You are always giving way and doing your partner's bidding.

To get you back into their snare without them changing an ounce, you may find them also purporting to take part of the blame. But pay good attention; sooner or later, that blame will be twisted to fall on your footstep. Since when did a narcissist take the blame for anything? If you know that is not normal, can you not then see that your narcissist partner is simply manipulating you?

YOU NEED TO STOP TAKING THEIR WORD SERIOUSLY

Lying is the narcissist's middle name. You do not need to give a narcissist reason to lie – it is just part of them, kind of engrained in their biological fabric. This may sound insane, but believe me, a narcissist can tell you they have been sitting on Chair A when they have actually been sitting on Chair B, yet both of those chairs are replicas of each other, and no location is better than the other.

And learn not to report anything a narcissist tells you to someone else without counterchecking first; otherwise, you may end up making a fool of yourself and risk being labeled a liar.

In case you decide you stick it out with the narcissist, just be realistic about whom you are living with – a liar who is prone to drama, deceit, and conceit, and someone who is prone to antagonizing other people. Pretending you are living with a normal person and trying to cover for your narcissistic partner would be one great mistake on your part. This is because you would only be making yourself vulnerable to the narcissist's toxic ways. Besides, you may end up becoming the subject of pity to observers who can see your vulnerabilities for what they are.

PARENTING AND HEALING FOR YOUR WOUNDED CHILDREN

After you have divorced a narcissist, you are still going to be facing many challenges. When children are involved, those challenges become even more difficult. Your children will need help learning how to cope with divorce and dealing with the damage their narcissistic parent has caused. Things with a narcissist are never easy, and it causes a detrimental impact on your children. Learning different strategies to help them heal and cope will be necessary for ensuring they lead healthy and fulfilling lives.

There is a lot of common advice given to parents who have gone through a divorce and have children involved; unfortunately, this advice is not going to work or apply to those of you who divorced a narcissist. Trying to co-parent with a narcissist is almost impossible. You will, more often than not, be working on reducing conflict. At this point, you realize that narcissists love drama and will do anything they can to provoke you and even your children so that they can keep playing their games of control and manipulation.

You want to protect your children from the abuse that narcissists dish out. One of the best ways is to refuse to engage

•

with them, especially when their behavior is inappropriate. The narcissist will try for any attention, and whether it is negative or positive, it does not matter. Shutting down the opportunity by disengaging will work well in favor of both you and your children.

Disengaging with a narcissist can be a scary thing. In theory, it should be easy, but as you well know, there is nothing easy when you have a narcissist to deal with. When they realize what you are doing, it could escalate. They may become volatile. The best thing you can do is stand your ground. Eventually, the narcissist will realize that they cannot provoke you into a battle, and they will move on to another target. You must be patient and strong through the process because this can take a great amount of time.

When you are trying to disengage and keep the peace between you and the narcissistic parent, you need to remember that conversations with them need to be minimal. You will need to talk to them about matters concerning the kids, but that does not mean that you need to talk about anything else. You must also remember that communicating with your ex does not mean you need to talk to them.

In today's world, there are various ways to contact someone without ever speaking a word. Between text messaging, email, and social media, there are plenty of ways to communicate about the children without talking. When you talk to a narcissist, they will do their best to manipulate you through their words. This is why avoiding actual conversations is going to be advantageous. It helps to protect you and allows you time to work through your emotions instead of flying off the handle when they say something awful or outrageous.

The narcissistic parent will need to have at least one phone number that can be used to reach out to the children. That is pretty much the only phone number they need. Save yourself some extra trouble and keep your personal number to yourself. You can even set up an alternate email address so that they are only contacting you in one specific spot. This can cut down on the drama that the narcissist is always trying to cause.

Using email as the main source of contact between you and your ex is good for various reasons. If the narcissist decides to get nasty in an email, you can process the information before reacting to it. Additionally, it gives you hard evidence of what your ex is saying, and this could be helpful if you end up back in court for any reason.

On top of all that, it also provides you with a record of any agreements, changes to schedules, or other information that a court may need if your ex tries to start major problems.

Limiting communication between you and the narcissistic parent is going to be advantageous for your children. They will not be privy to the non-sense that your ex, and it won't hurt them hear you fight. So, keeping them at a distance as much as possible is good for everyone involved.

When you need to parent wounded children and help them heal, one of your main focuses is your health. If you have survived the abuse that a narcissist causes in a relationship, you will certainly need to work on healing. The healthier you are internal, the stronger you will be able to be for your children.

Support groups and counselors should be used. When looking for a support group, you must find one that specifically talks about the abuse that narcissists delve out. Support groups can help you understand how to set boundaries and stick to them. This can help you keep the focus on your healing and the healing of your children.

AS A PARENT, KEEPING CONFLICT AT A MINIMUM SHOULD BE THE MAIN FOCUS

A close second is going to be making sure your children are empowered and validated. Narcissists will treat their children just as they treat everyone else. You will not be able to stop this unless the court decides that the environment is not safe for the children.

It is almost impossible to safeguard your children from the toxic behaviors of their narcissistic parents.

You may think that keeping them away from the other parent is the best course of action, but realistically kids need both of their parents. Your children love both of you even if one doesn't give it back to them in healthy ways. They need to see their other parent and make decisions regarding them for themselves.

Watching your children go through the trauma that a narcissist can cause is very difficult, but you have to take a step back. If you interfere, you will likely do more harm than good. You may even end up with children that resent you because they can't understand why you would put a stop to their relationship with their other parent. As hard as it is, you must sit back and allow them to figure out their narcissistic parent on their own.

Even though you don't have a lot of power when it comes to your children and their other parent, you do hold power for you and your children's relationship.

When you want to do something, choose to be their biggest fan and supporter. Allow them to talk to you about anything and validate the things that they are saying and facing. Their narcissistic parent will tell them lies and manipulate them, it distorts their reality, and you need to be the one that helps keep them grounded.

When you listen to your children and learn about their experiences, you need to be careful not to talk badly about their other parents. Instead, try to use neutral statements like, "I'm sure it doesn't feel good to hear that" or "I'm sorry you experienced that." You can keep things neutral and simple but still support your children in the way they need to be supported and validated. You should also note that none of the behaviors the other parent shows have anything to do with them. They are not to blame.

The structure will also be very helpful for children who are trying to heal from divorce and the abuse that the narcissistic parent hands down. When you structure their lives, it can help keep them to stay in this reality.

The emotions they will go through while dealing with their narcissistic parent will be like riding a roller coaster. So, the more structure they have with you, the better off they will be. You can provide them with a sense of safety and balance, which they will need to continue to lead healthy lives.

You also should be careful about handling your children, and you should do your best not to feel sorry for them. Sure, growing up with a narcissistic parent will not be easy, but there are worse situations they could find themselves in. When we pity our children, it helps them take on a victim complex, which can be detrimental to them as they grow. When you have the mentality that you are a victim, it tends to stop you in your tracks, making moving past the problem insanely difficult. Additionally, they are more apt to end up in toxic relationships rather than searching for healthy ones.

Your narcissistic ex will likely become emotionally intense from time to time. They will try and goad you into getting on this ride with them, but you must refrain and take into consideration the impact all of this has on their children. Instead of playing the narcissist's game, you need to stay calm, non-emotional, and pleasant. This will be an extremely difficult thing to do, but you have to do your best. Practicing mindfulness, deep breathing, and meditation can help you find balance and calmness more easily.

When you are trying to make sure your children can traverse this tumultuous past, you will have to let go a little bit. This means you should limit the amount of texting and contact you have with your kids while they are with their other parents, and your ex should do the same when they are with you. If there is an emergency, you should both feel free to reach out, but other than that, you should both allow uninterrupted time with the children.

If your children are contacting you about every little thing your ex is doing, it can cause a lot of stress and make the situation even more difficult.

When you allow your children to assert themselves to their narcissistic parents, it helps them to cope with the situation and learn how to deal with difficult people throughout their entire lives.

You will be benefiting your kids in a great way if you teach them about emotional intelligence. Additionally, you should practice what you preach to help them understand and learn it even more. Give them examples of some successful single-family households that they can use to understand how they are currently and how they should be. Helping your kids understand how to regulate their emotions and cope with the difficult things in life early is a good thing.

The only way you will help your children heal successfully is to find ways and allow yourself to heal. You need to be their strength and encouragement in life. Focusing on your children and recognizing their wants, needs, and desires will go a long way.

Over time, your children may start to ask questions that are difficult for you to answer. You should not avoid these questions. Don't be afraid to be truthful and tell them that you don't have all of the answers that they seek. It is a good time to encourage them to reach out to their therapist or support groups geared toward adolescence.

CONCLUSION

There is no doubt that narcissistic parents have their children feeling emasculated, angry, and sad. But they also take on an important role in raising resilient children. They teach their kids critical life skills, like how to stand up for themselves, to follow rules and regulations, and not to let others walk all over them. To successfully raise a child who doesn't become the victim of abuse from these parents requires self-awareness and discipline on the part of those who may be uncomfortable being responsible for another person's life. It requires a great degree of self-sacrifice and the courage to do what is necessary to raise a healthy, happy, productive individual.

But there is hope. You cannot change the very fundamental nature of your parent, but you can make choices that will help put you to happiness and fulfillment.

That's why it's helpful for children to practice self-care. Inspire them to do things that make them happy, like exercising or reading a book. They should also get enough sleep, go to social events they enjoy and have hobbies that give them a sense of accomplishment. Exercise can also help children feel empowered because it increases their physical strength.

It's also essential for them to learn how to identify their emotions and communicate them effectively. This can help them know how they feel in a given situation and take care of it. More than that, it can help them express themselves clearly, even when they're feeling upset, anxious, or fearful.

Above all, it's helpful for children to learn how to cope with their emotions. Many do this by turning to food, alcohol, or drugs because these are easy substitutes for trauma.

Focus on being good to yourself in all situations. Do not allow others to take advantage of you emotionally or financially. Pay attention to your children and how they are responding to their narcissistic parents. You may be enabling them or helping them develop the tools they need to have a good relationship with that parent.

With the right wisdom and commitment, you can make yourself a good parent and give your children the tools to have even better relationships than you do. They are not doomed to suffer the same fate you have and be trapped in a cycle of abuse from a parent who doesn't know any better.

You, yourself, do know better, and whether you realize it or not, you are teaching your children very valuable lessons on how to handle difficult situations when they arise. If they have a healthy parent practicing what he preaches, they will learn to stand up for themselves and be there for others. They will learn how to recognize the importance of healthy boundaries. They will learn the value of looking out for themselves in a healthy way.

Get involved in an organization like Narcissistic Abuse Recovery (NAR), find a therapist or spiritual advisor who has experience with narcissistic abuse, and give them some feedback when you are able. You are not alone in this battle against evil. Others have been there and can offer ideas on how to improve your situation and the lives of your children.

Made in the USA
Monee, IL
01 September 2022

12997566R00269